THE WALTER LYNWOOD FLEMING LECTURES IN SOUTHERN HISTORY

Louisiana State University

BERTRAM WYATT-BROWN

hearts of darkness

WELLSPRINGS OF A SOUTHERN LITERARY TRADITION

🌼 LOUISIANA STATE UNIVERSITY PRESS BATON ROUGE

Manufactured in the United States of America
First printing
cloth
12 11 10 09 08 07 06 05 04 03
5 4 3 2 1
paper
12 11 10 09 08 07 06 05 04 03
5 4 3 2 1

Designer: Amanda McDonald Scallan
Typeface: Sabon
Typesetter: Coghill Composition Co. Inc.
Printer and binder: Thomson-Shore, Inc.

Library of Congress Cataloging-in-Publication Data:

Wyatt-Brown, Bertram, 1932–
   Hearts of darkness : wellsprings of a southern literary tradition /
Bertram Wyatt-Brown.
      p. cm. — (Walter Lynwood Fleming lectures in southern history)
Includes bibliographical references and index.
   ISBN 0-8071-2822-8 (alk. paper) — ISBN 0-8071-2844-9 (pbk. : alk. paper)
1. American literature—Southern States—History and criticism. 2. Southern States—In literature.
3. Imagination in literature. 4. Melancholy in literature. 5. Honor in literature. I. Title. II. Series.
   PS261 .W93 2003
   810.9′975—dc21   2002009144

Some of the photographs in this book were published with the assistance of the Richard J. Milbauer
Endowment of the University of Florida Foundation.

Anne Marbury Wyatt-Brown
My steadfast and loving companion in everyday life and in the life of the mind
&
Natalie Wyatt-Brown, Christopher Stall
&
their son, Anders Hunter Stall

Contents

Illustrations

Preface

Melancholy is at the bottom of everything, just as at the end of all rivers is the sea.
. . . Can it be otherwise in a world where nothing lasts, where all we have loved or
shall love must die? Is death, then, the secret of life? The gloom of an eternal mourning enwraps every serious and thoughtful soul, as night enwraps the universe.
      —Henri-Frederick Amiel

The intensest light of reason and revelation, combined, can not shed such blazonings
upon the deeper truths in man, as will sometimes proceed from his own profoundest
gloom. Utter darkness is then his light.
      —Herman Melville

THE three themes that inform the following pages, which are based on
the Fleming Lectures that I delivered at Louisiana State University in 1995,
have occupied much of my intellectual concerns for the last twenty years.
They are the ethic of honor, the tragedy of melancholy, and the personal
origins of artistic imagination. As a southern historian, I have thought it
crucial to understand the close interconnection of these elements in the region's cultural life. The sequence by which I arrived at the interpretation to
inform these pages may clarify my meaning. During the late 1970s, I was
preparing what I thought would be a study of the southern family and kinship relations in the Old South. By sheer luck in wandering through the
stacks of a library, I found a short sketch by an obscure writer. Published in

1860, it dealt with an incident that had occurred long before. Colonel James Creecy, the author, described in sensational detail the aborted trial and subsequent ghastly fate of one James Foster Jr., who belonged to a wealthy Natchez, Mississippi, planter family. His father, the patriarch, had died leaving his undereducated children floundering. In March 1833 James Foster had killed his young wife in a fit of drunken rage. Foster's attorney, Felix Huston, later a general in Sam Houston's revolutionary Texas army, managed to have the case dismissed on a common-law technicality. The irate citizens waiting outside the Adams County courthouse, however, were in no forgiving mood. With the assent of his defense attorney as well as the high-toned prosecutor, the mob rushed their captive to another part of town and whipped him into near insensibility with 150 lashes well laid on. Then they tarred and feathered the victim, tethered him to the back of a cart, and marched him back, stumbling, weeping, and totally humiliated, to the jailhouse. There he was reincarcerated, only this time for his own protection. Kinsmen rescued him later that night. A soon as the disgraced killer had recovered from his injuries in the late spring, he fled to Texas, never to marry again.[1]

Clearly the Fosters' family life and the inevitability of its disintegration were essential to the story of how patriarchy, so prominent a feature of southern life, in this instance had miserably failed. Yet the account prompted me to inquire more deeply into why so primitive a form of extra-legal justice could take place in as civilized a location as Adams County, the wealthiest community in the South and perhaps the nation. What did tar and feathers signify to those performing the ritual? Why was it so necessary to deny the prisoner any element of his humanness? They had turned him into the replica of a chicken with the feathers all turned inside out, as Creecy had marveled.

A recourse to anthropology proved invaluable to help unravel the mystery. In the work of social scientists who had explored at a conference in the 1960s the ethics of Mediterranean peoples, I found a clue. Honor and its opposite, shame, anthropologists Julian Pitt-Rivers, Pierre Bourdieu, and others explained, were primordial modes of conduct and evaluation that were more highly complex than historians like me had ever been aware. From these scholars' fascinating studies, I learned that honor did not mean

---

1. Colonel James Creecy, *Scenes in the South, and Other Miscellaneous Pieces* (Washington: Thomas McGill, 1860), 54; Bertram Wyatt-Brown, *Southern Honor: Ethics and Behavior in the Old South* (New York: Oxford University Press, 1982), 462–93.

upright behavior, moral worth, and refinement of manners. Rather, it was, they argued, an ancient, preliterate mode of thinking about individual identity and the outer world by apprehending the self and society through the lens of those belonging to a watchful, close-knit community. As a code primarily privileging male behavior, honor required a behavioral approximation of ideal manhood. By that means the claimant assessed his standing and his moral worth according to the reputation he held or gained among his betters, his fellows, and those beneath him. To lose that position of honorableness through some observed offense or flaw of character—cowardice, deceit, perversion, disloyalty—could provoke the kind of penalty that the mob exacted from Foster. He had been judged a failed protector of his wife (a husband's first duty), a murderer of a child-bride, and, as I later discovered, a professional gambler who brazenly cheated at games of chance.[2]

This inquiry into an obscure but dramatic incident resulted in my writing a lengthy analysis titled *Southern Honor*. But more insight into southern life was to come. In the course of writing the book, I discovered an interesting and unexpected emotional effect of the conventions that the ethic of honor demanded. It was most evident in the duel, often deemed the epitome of honorable conduct. The consequence of encounters on the dueling field was not the joyful vindication of personal esteem that the winner anticipated. Instead, the duelist who killed his opponent sometimes fell, it seemed obvious to me, into a deep depression. We might call such reactions by the awkward terminology of post-traumatic stress disorder or what used to be labeled shell-shock. Yet the origin of the duelist's distress might not lie in the bitter exchange of hot words—liar, poltroon, coward. Those were some of the epithets flung to bring on challenges. Instead, the psychology—the demands—of honor allowed the duelist temporarily to suppress despair at his own unworthiness and to project those feelings upon an unsuspecting and justifiably outraged rival or enemy. In other words, honor scarcely encourages introspection—rather, quite the opposite.[3]

2. Julian Pitt-Rivers, "Honor," in *International Encyclopedia of the Social Sciences,* 17 vols., ed. David L. Sills (New York: Macmillan, 1968), 6:503–11. Also see Mervyn E. James, "English Politics and the Concept of Honour, 1485–1642," *Past and Present* suppl. no. 3 (1978): 27. Among other essays in the following volume, I mention in particular Julian Pitt-Rivers, "The Stranger, the Guest, and the Hostile Host: Introduction to the Study of the Laws of Hospitality," in *Contributions to Mediterranean Sociology: Mediterranean Rural Communities and Social Change,* ed. J. G. Peristiany (Paris: Mouton, 1967), 13–30. In contrast, see an older understanding of honor in Clement Eaton, "The Role of Honor in Southern Society," *Southern Humanities Review* 10 (suppl. 1976): 47–58.
3. Wyatt-Brown, *Southern Honor,* 350–61.

The stifling of inner knowledge could lead to serious emotional reactions: violence, emotional outbursts, over-drinking, and deteriorating personality. According to two highly respected specialists in manic-depression, patients they examined in East Asia usually blamed outside forces or individuals for their prolonged unhappiness and seldom any disarrangement in their own minds.[4] In societies where loss of face is a social disaster, there is no room for self-examination. So it was, too, in the nineteenth-century South.

In seeking examples of other forms of depression in the psyches of southerners, I became aware of John Kennedy Toole, author of the hilarious satire *The Confederacy of Dunces,* who had committed suicide a few years after writing his masterpiece.[5] For the first time in my thinking, depression, honor, and literary art were linked together and given some brief play in an article I published in the *Georgia Review.*[6] Then, yet another chance discovery led to a more elaborate project on the subject. The foreword for Toole's posthumously published novel had been written by Walker Percy. I had recently read one of Walker Percy's novels, *Love in the Ruins,* and was intrigued with his style, imaginative gifts, and broad sense of humor.[7] With thoughts of writing something about him or his family, I visited the Mississippi state archives in Jackson. In the Percy family papers, which are housed there, I found a note written sometime in the spring of 1929. It was in the hand of the novelist's mother, Martha Susan Phinizy Percy, and addressed to her husband's uncle, former Senator LeRoy Percy of Greenville, Mississippi. She thanked him for a recent visit to Roy, her ailing partner, and mentioned that he had so improved that "he has had no tenseness at all, in spite of 'the Crouching Beast.'" Intrigued by the reference to Henry James's short story "The Beast in the Jungle," I later asked Walker Percy if the "crouching

4. Arthur Kleinman and Byron Good, eds., *Culture and Depression: Studies in the Anthropology and Cross-Cultural Psychiatry of Affect and Disorder* (Berkeley: University of California Press, 1985), 1–33.

5. John Kennedy Toole, *Confederacy of Dunces* (Baton Rouge: Louisiana State University Press, 1980). The title itself comes from Jonathan Swift, who said, "When a true genius appears in the world, you shall know him by this sign, that the dunces are all in confederacy against him." See Phelps Gay, review of *Confederacy of Dunces,* in *New Republic,* July 19, 1980, p. 34.

6. Bertram Wyatt-Brown, "The Evolution of Heroes' Honor in the Southern Literary Tradition," *Georgia Review* 40 (Winter 1986): 990–1007.

7. Walker Percy, *Love in the Ruins: The Adventures of a Bad Catholic at a Time Near the End of the World* (New York: Farrar, Straus & Giroux, 1971); Bertram Wyatt-Brown, *The House of Percy: Honor, Melancholy, and Imagination in a Southern Family* (New York: Oxford University Press, 1994), 294, 295, 305, 306.

beast" was his father's term for the agony of depression. With a reluctant but definite nod of his head, he replied that it was. Walker's father, I knew by then, had died at his own hand within weeks or even days of the hopeful note that his wife had written.[8]

Further investigation revealed the succession of suicides and mentally depressed members of the Percy family, stretching back to the late eighteenth century. There, at the main stem of the genealogical tree, lay tragedy. Charles Percy, the founder of the American clan, had killed himself in January 1794. All his life he insisted that he belonged to the Northumberland household. These princes of the North possessed the greatest wealth in all England, apart from the monarchy's. They ranked at the very top of British nobility. The Percy succession of earls and later dukes was situated at Alnwick Castle on the Scottish border and also at the enormous palace, Northumberland House, in London. But as a bigamist, Charles alienated his family, nearly wiping out all traces of his British ancestry. I spent seven years tracing the adventuresome Percy's origins. In an attic in western Massachusetts, I eventually found documents that proved them. He had not served as an officer in the royal army as he had claimed. Instead, Charles Percy was a young foot soldier in a short-lived, undistinguished Irish regiment hastily drawn up at the close of the Seven Years War. But the larger task was to investigate the role of depression in shaping the suicidal Charles Percy's descendants. Only one of the six generations that followed revealed no suicides.[9]

At the same time that I was following the thread of depression running through the Percys' august lineage, a link between other elements came forcibly into view: the relationship of artistic creativity to the concept and practice of honorable behavior and the fearful dread of shame. No family in American life better exemplified the positive aspects of honorable principles than did the Percys. At the same time, no other, to my knowledge, has had so fascinating a record of artistic energy. In the nineteenth century, I discovered, the clan had produced four female novelists, poets, and short story writers—Eleanor Percy Lee, her sister Catherine Ann Warfield, their first cousin Sarah Dorsey, and Eleanor's daughter Kate Ferguson. None is a

8. Martha Susan Phinizy Percy to LeRoy Percy, "Thursday night," n.d., Percy Family Papers, Mississippi Department of Archives and History, Jackson; interview with Walker Percy, 13 June 1987. See Leon Edel, *Henry James* (1960: New York, Penguin, 1972), 1:603–11, 793; Henry James, "The Beast in the Jungle," in *The Novels and Tales of Henry James* (New York: Scribner, 1909).

9. See Wyatt-Brown, *House of Percy,* 334–55.

household name. Yet, two of them—Warfield and Dorsey—were quite popular practitioners of the somber, gothic mode of fiction and helped to advance the role of women in the realm of letters.[10] In the twentieth century, William Alexander Percy and Walker Percy were much more significant as writers of note. Both of them masterfully handled the themes of melancholy and honor in their own unique modes of expression.[11]

Thus the question arose: Were the Percys unique in embodying the qualities of depression, honor, and imagination, or did something in southern culture itself promote such a conjoining of emotional and cultural forces? In dealing with this larger issue, personal factors clearly entered. Although born and first reared in Pennsylvania, I was sent to live with my grandmother in 1940 in Sewanee, Tennessee, at the age of eight. The transition from the relatively urban environment of Harrisburg to the rural enclave on the Cumberland plateau was not easy. The requirements of southern customs, especially the duty to yes'm and no'm, yes sir and no sir, struck me as a freakish peculiarity. A gauntlet of switches, organized by fellow pupils in the small school I attended, soon set me straight. Thereafter I dutifully complied, but a southern drawl never developed, perhaps in unconscious resistance. Surrounded on all sides with memorabilia of the Confederacy, the mountain residents could hardly escape an atmosphere of Old South glory. The names of the streets, the monuments, the battle flags in the Episcopal sanctuary, all bespoke the region's ancien regime.[12] Our family physician, who helped me through chronic nasal hemorrhages, was old "Dr. Henry," son of Edmund Kirby Smith, last Confederate general to surrender in 1865.

10. See Bertram Wyatt-Brown, *The Literary Percys: Family History, Gender, and Legend* (Athens: University of Georgia Press, 1994); idem, "A Family Tradition of Letters: The Female Percys and the Brontëan Mode," in *In Joy and in Sorrow: Women, Family, and Marriage in the Victorian South*, ed. Carol Bleser (New York: Oxford University Press, 1991), 176–95, notes 309–14; idem, "Walker Percy's Female Literary Forebears," in *Faith, Fiction, and Philosophy: The Works of Walker Percy*, ed. Jan Nordby Gretlund (Jackson: University Press of Mississippi, 1991), 55–64; idem, "Melancholy's Daughters: Mania and Depression in Southern Women Writers," Twelfth International Conference in Literature and Psychoanalysis, 1995, Freiburg, Germany, June 22.

11. Bertram Wyatt-Brown, "Will, Walker, and Honor Dying: The Percys and Literary Creativity," in *Looking South: Chapters in the Story of an American Region*, ed. Winfred B. Moore Jr. and Joseph F. Tripp (Westport, Conn.: Greenwood Press, 1989), 229–58; idem, "Walker Percy: Autobiographical Fiction and the Aging Process," *Journal of Gerontological Studies* 3 (January 1989): 81–9.

12. See Bertram Wyatt-Brown, "Sewanee: How to Make a Yankee Southern: Memories of the 1940s," in *American Places: Encounters with History: A Celebration of Sheldon Meyer*, ed. William Leuchtenberg (New York: Oxford University Press, 2000), 365–88.

Honor was everywhere resplendent, undying. But what did it mean? I like to think that even at an early age, I had charted a voyage to discover who I was, what the South had been and still might be.

Sewanee, seat of the University of the South, had its own highly creative side. Allen Tate, Caroline Gordon, Peter Taylor, Father Flye (James Agee's mentor), Robert Penn Warren (whom I once watched playing croquet with John Palmer, editor of the *Sewanee Review*), William Alexander Percy, and his adopted son Walker Percy—these writers inhabited or frequently visited the college domain at one time or another. In elementary school and later in college at Sewanee, I met some of them. Although my first interest remained history, my nearly equal devotion to English literature, especially southern fiction, was no doubt enhanced by a proximity to such an array of literary talents.

But the last, more painful subject is the origin of my intimate concern for melancholy. While my engrossment in the subject is mostly intellectual, personal experiences have, of course, introduced me, as it has to so many others, the afflictions of grief. Happily, in contrast with most of the writers herein, whose parents died before they reached their teens, I suffered no such deprivation. My father died when I was already a college sophomore. That was still a blow. But by far a more difficult and grievous loss was the death of our first child from brain cancer at age seven in 1971, some twenty years later. For two years thereafter I remained in the classroom but was unable to write even a book review. My colleagues at Case Western Reserve University were most supportive. Gradually grief of that kind has a way of receding, though it is never, be assured, absent altogether. Unpredictably the demon returns to stab the soul.

In 1986, for reasons both intellectual and personal, I was quite struck by a lecture that Linda Wagner-Martin gave at a convention of the Modern Language Association. Her discussion was basically a preview of her forthcoming book, *Sylvia Plath: A Biography*. Unlike other biographies that soon followed, Wagner-Martin showed a ready sympathy for Plath and her mental breakdowns as well as an appreciation for her extraordinary poetic gifts.[13] I had known Sylvia at Cambridge and had a small part in her meeting up with her future husband, the poet Ted Hughes. The year before, Ted had stayed in St. Botolph's Rectory, or rather in the rented garden shed out back, but had since gone down to read scripts for J. Arthur Rank Studios. As a

13. Linda Wagner-Martin, *Sylvia Plath: A Biography* (New York: Simon and Schuster, 1987).

Kingsman living outside the college gates, I was then ensconced in the rented dining room, under the roof of Helen Hitchcock, the penurious widow of the former rector of St. Botolph's Church in town. Sylvia lived around the corner at Whitstead Cottage on the Selwyn College grounds. I ran into her periodically since I was dating her housemate, Jane Baltzell, another brilliant and charming American. The poetic crowd that swarmed around Ted on his frequent visits to Cambridge graciously made allowances for a non-poet like me, a slave to facts, as they no doubt saw it. I was happy to join their circle at the Anchor, where occasionally another American, the young Harold Bloom, downed pints of bitter with us. It was an exhilarating time in the history of English poetry. What a surprise it was, however, when in 1963 I learned that Sylvia had committed suicide not long after she and Ted had separated. Years later, Linda Wagner-Martin's speech brought back a flood of half-forgotten memories. Her reconstruction of Sylvia's life, particularly her last days, induced me to investigate the causes for her suicide, but also, more broadly, to probe the reasons why artists appeared to be so prone to depression and sometimes to its termination in death itself.[14]

These experiences have helped to shape the pages that follow. Yet we enter a murky realm when dealing with such elusive concepts and slippery emotional particulars. Only partial answers are really available. It is impossible to fathom with complete assurance the inner workings of the literary mind, southern and otherwise. Nonetheless, relating an artist's temperament to the work created deepens an appreciation of both authors and the fruits of their pens. In the words of the psychiatrist Barry Panter, thinkers struggle with their psychological devils and then "use the conflicts and torments as elements of the creative process. In this way, the artist discovers a transcendent path through the great universal emotional issues that confront all of us." It can be inspirational when its less paralyzing forms arise. Kay Redfield Jamison, the psychiatrist and author, declares, "Melancholy itself often acts as a bittersweet potion and muse, adding a tincture of sadness and wistfulness to the creative process. 'Yet naught did my despair / But sweeten the strange sweetness,' wrote the English poet Edward Thomas."[15]

14. Bertram Wyatt-Brown, "Reuben Davis, Sylvia Plath, and Emotional Struggle," in *An Emotional History of the United States,* ed. Peter Stearns and Jan Lewis (New York: New York University Press, 1998), 431–59; idem, "Sylvia Plath, Depression, and Suicide: A New Interpretation," in *Eleventh International Conference on Literature and Psychoanalysis,* ed. Frederico Pereira (Lisbon: Instituto Superior de Psicologia Aplicada, 1997), 177–97.

15. Barry M. Panter, "Preface," in *Creativity and Madness: Psychological Studies of Art and Artists,* ed. Barry Panter, Mary Lou Panter, Evelyn Virshup, and Bernard Virshup (Bur-

At the same time, alienation of mind and heart involves a "positive and active anguish, a sort of psychical neuralgia wholly unknown to normal life," according to William James, himself a lifelong sufferer. In quoting James's words from *The Varieties of Religious Experience,* the southern novelist William Styron emphatically agrees. His own chronicle of despair, *Darkness Visible,* traces his bouts with severe depression. Yet, paradoxically, as Styron's fiction demonstrates, imagination is somehow enhanced by the experience of unbearable gloom. Melville makes the same point quite well in the opening epigraph. By no means do I suggest that an incontestable formulation explains all the sources of artistic ingeniousness. Yet some psychological experts and knowledgeable literary specialists have offered helpful propositions. Among the factors identified is the effect of early trauma in childhood, which stirs sensitive offspring to withdraw into an inner world of fantasy. Many of the literary artists and aspirants discussed throughout this book suffered early and devastating losses of parents or of others important to him or her as a child. A profound mournfulness, owing to a lengthy estrangement of parents or the death of the father, the mother—or both—may isolate or even terrorize a child. To compensate for the blow, the child's imagination fills the void and momentarily buries injuries to the heart. Spilling out words on a page may become a way to clasp the missing emotional elements that adults ordinarily provide the vulnerable youngster. Based on extensive interviews with artists and writers, two analysts have generalized that their subjects had long been almost belligerently autonomous—to the point of eccentricity. At the same time on the whole they were "at once introverted and bold," confident of their powers but also troubled.[16]

In addition to parental loss or abusive inattention, genetic factors can

---

bank, Calif.: Aimed Press, 1994), xi; Kay Redfield Jamison, *Touched with Fire: Manic-Depressive Illness and the Artistic Temperament* (New York: Free Press, 1993), 119.

16. Quotation, William Styron, *Darkness Visible: A Memoir of Madness* (New York: Random House, 1990), 17. See Sigmund Freud, "Mourning and Melancholia," in *Collected Papers of Sigmund Freud,* trans. Joan Riviere, 25 vols. (London: Hogarth Press, 1924–25), 4:152–70; Felix Brown, "Bereavement and Lack of a Parent in Childhood," in *Foundations of Child Psychiatry,* ed. Elizabeth Miller (London: Pergamon, 1968), 435–55; Jay Martin, *Who Am I This Time: Uncovering the Fictive Personality* (New York: W. W. Norton, 1988), 172–86; Joseph Sandler and W. G. Joffe, "Notes on Childhood Depression," *International Journal of Psycho-Analysis* 46 (Part 1, 1965): 88–95; quotation in John E. Drevdahl and Raymond B. Cattell, "Personality and Creativity in Artists and Writers," *Journal of Clinical Psychology* 14 (1958): 107–17. On the effect of parental breaches of love and trust, see Kay Redfield Jamison, *An Unquiet Mind* (New York: Knopf, 1995), 34–5.

play a considerable role in shaping the growing child's solitariness. Over
the last thirty years genetic research has demonstrated such a relationship.
Lord Byron and Alfred Lord Tennyson in the nineteenth century, Tennessee
Williams and Walker Percy in the twentieth—to name just four familiar
figures—all had certifiably distracted ancestors. They all inherited a predisposition to suicide or chronic melancholy that could be traced back through
several generations. The productivity of these and other literary artists, of
course, never permanently banished brooding, chaotic, or even suicidal
moods. Nonetheless the act of composing furnished them an emotional outlet by means of self-expression and literary experiment. Another possible
element connecting feelings of alienation and artistic development is a
child's physical disability—slight frame, excess weight, athletic incompe-
tence, general clumsiness, a stutter, blindness, near-sightedness, deafness, or
chronic ill-health. This issue, however, has not been so prominently studied
as the genetic link, nor does it apply to as many authors.[17]

Whatever the myriad factors animating the artist might be, works of fiction or poetry tend to be at least partially autobiographical. "Writers will
deny it, but it is so," southern novelist Harry Crews has observed. "They
will claim that we shouldn't confuse the artist's life with his characters, but
all the characters come out of the writer's head and reflect experiences

17. On inherited depressive natures, see Jamison, *Touched with Fire,* 61–2, 69, 149–90,
196–201; Wyatt-Brown, *The House of Percy;* S. Kety, "Genetic Factors in Suicide," in *Suicide,*
ed. A. Roy (Baltimore: Williams and Wilkins, 1986), 41–5; Donald Spoto, *The Kindness of
Strangers: The Life of Tennessee Williams* (New York: Ballantine, 1985); Tennessee Williams,
Five O'Clock Angel: Letters of Tennessee Williams to Maria St. Just, 1948–1982 (New York:
Knopf, 1990). On childhood physical disabilities, see Arnold M. Ludwig, *The Price of Greatness: Resolving the Creativity and Madness Controversy* (New York: Guilford Press, 1995),
40–4, 187–9. Geneticists have been very active in locating the sources of bipolar affective disorders, Elliot S. Gershon of the National Institute of Health being a prominent figure in such
work. See David L. Dunner, Elliot S. Gershon, and Frederick K. Goodwin, "Heritable Factors
in the Severity of Affective Illness," *Biological Psychiatry* 11 (No. 1, 1976): 31–42; E. S. Gershon, J. H. Hamovitz, J. J. Guroff, and J. I. Nurnberger Jr., "Birth Cohort Changes in Manic
and Depressive Disorders in Relatives of Bipolar and Schizoaffective Patients," *Archives of
General Psychiatry* 44 (No. 4, 1987): 314–9; Wade H. Berrettini, Lynn R. Goldin, John I. Nurnberger Jr., and Elliot S. Gershon, "Genetic Factors in Affective Illness," *Journal of Psychiatric
Research* 18 (No. 4: 1984): 329–50; George H. Pollock, "The Mourning Process, the Creative
Process, and the Creation," in *The Problems of Loss and Mourning: Psychoanalytic Perspectives,* ed. David Dietrich and Peter Shabad (Madison, Conn.: International Universities Press,
1989): 27–59; George H. Pollock, "On Mourning, Immortality, and Utopia," *Journal of American Psychoanalytic Association* 23 (1975): 334–62; George H. Pollock, "The Mourning Process," *Chicago Theological Seminary Register* 57 (December, 1966): 15–23.

known first-hand."[18] Of course, those in the depths of inanition cannot function, much less write with conviction and power. When lucidity returns, however, the wellsprings of creativity again rise up. Two major women writers, Kaye Gibbons and Gail Godwin, have been most outspoken about the trials of manic-depression, the sudden and tragic losses of their parents in childhood and early adult years, and their urge to write as a way out of hell. In an interview, Gibbons remarked that her mother suffered from major depression in the days before the discovery of lithium and Prozac. She had inherited the problem. "If you look at manic-depression on a scale of zero to ten, with zero being the doldrums and ten being uncontrolled mania, when I am working at about six and a half [the hypomanic stage], I'm very productive," she says. Like Gibbons, Godwin lost both her mother and father, the latter to suicide. She has confessed that when she was in "a fit of despair," she found solace in *The Sorrow of the World* by the English bishop Francis Paget. He had written, "Through humbly and simply doing what we can, we retrieve the power of doing what we would." That, Godwin told an interviewer, was how she wrote: "It comes from the unconscious, if you humbly and simply do what you can, you sometimes get the power of insight." Southern fiction writer Fred Chappell argues that the literary experience is itself so intense that behind it there must be "disciplined suffering" or even a "careful-self-destruction." His comments remind us that a fragmentation of the artist's personality contributes to the imaginative process. The famous psychoanalyst D. W. Winnicott pointed out as early as 1951 that the universal impulse for wish-fulfilling illusion that artists transform into lasting creations "may be the essential basis for all true objectivity."[19] In sum, the literary artist may feel the wretchedness of isolation but converts that mood into something that may be recognized as distinctive, insightful, and extraordinarily original. That is about as far as one needs to go along this line of inquiry.

One further issue yet remains: the pertinence of a study limited to south-

18. Harry Crews, remarks before an undergraduate honors seminar, "Growing Up Southern: History and Literature 1800–1965," November 5, 1987, University of Florida, Gainesville.

19. Kaye Gibbons and Gail Godwin quoted in *Parting the Curtains: Interviews with Southern Writers,* ed. Dannye Romine Powell (Winston, N.C.: John F. Blair, 1994), 123, 152; Fred Chappell interview in *Parting the Curtains,* 38; D. W. Winnicott, "Marion Milner: Critical Notice of *On Not Being Able to Paint,*" in *Psychoanalytic Explorations: D. W. Winnicott,* ed. Clare Winnicott, Ray Shepherd, and Madeline Davis (Cambridge, Mass.: Harvard University Press, 1989), 391.

ern literary culture. Again we are on muddy terrain because a high percentage of intellectuals in any country and any time—ancient, medieval, early modern, or contemporary—bears the special burden of alienation and loss. Nonetheless, some nations or regions may be more intensely affected by a pervasive sense of fatalism, nostalgia, and dread of change than others. According to Robert Burton, the great seventeenth-century expert, melancholia afflicts "certain kingdoms, provinces, and Political Bodies." Not just individuals are affected. So it can be said that historical and cultural factors may influence the mentalité of a country, to greater or lesser degree.[20] Admittedly the stereotyping of a whole people entails high risks. Yet we all succumb to the temptation—and probably with some justification. After his visit to America, Alexis de Tocqueville was certainly undeterred from pronouncing broad generalizations. He found, for instance, that Americans were so eager for advancement, so fixated on establishing an "equality of condition," that they subjected themselves to a "strange melancholy," one that "haunts the inhabitants of a democratic countries in the midst of abundance."[21]

As Amiel observes in the other epigraph, the depressive condition of mind is universal in the human psyche. Therefore one must ask was the nineteenth-century South and its intelligentsia more prone to collective and individual dejection than the rest of the nation? I contend that it was, and not merely because of the cataclysmic defeat of 1865 and the desperate struggle to restore the South's former prosperity. Even in the prewar years death was prevalent. Semitropical diseases frequently carried off small children, lovers, wives, husbands, and fathers before their expected time and at a much greater rate than elsewhere on the continent. Also slavery, outside criticism of it, and periodic anxieties about white safety and black resistance engendered a particular note of dread. We have already touched on the effects of an honor code. It required a stifling of introspectiveness, an unyielding demand for reticence to avoid vulnerability. Confession of wrongdoing or of evil thoughts might suit the pious but only so long as the sins were common failings in the community, quickly forgiven.

Solitude was the subtle enemy of honor, which required public self-pre-

20. Robert Burton quoted in Wolf Lepenies, *Melancholy and Society,* trans. Jeremy Gaines and Doris Jones, 2 vols. (Cambridge, Mass.: Harvard University Press, 1992), 15. See Andrew Delbanco, *The Real American Dream: A Meditation on Hope* (Cambridge, Mass.: Harvard University Press, 1999), 2.

21. Alexis de Tocqueville, *Democracy in America,* trans. Phillips Bradley, 2 vols. (New York: Vintage, 1990), 2:138–9.

PREFACE

sentation, and made southerners accordingly fear it. As I explained in *Southern Honor,* "The comings and goings of relatives and friends, the thin excuses to go up to the courthouse . . . the personal contests of arms and fists attested not only to Southerners' desperate need to conquer *ennui* but also their compulsion to find social place in the midst of gatherings. That was the great charm of the South, the willingness to create good times with others, but behind that trait was dread of being left alone, bored, and depressed."[22]

With these thoughts in mind, I treat here the development of a southern literary tradition in which honor, melancholy, and imagination produced a unique configuration. The account begins with Edgar Allan Poe, the early-nineteenth-century South's most troubled and most ingenious practitioner of the literary craft. It closes with a study of late-nineteenth-century female writers, the first, I argue, to publish modern, introspective fiction.

22. Wyatt-Brown, *Southern Honor,* 328–30 (quotation 329), 349–61.

Acknowledgments

Great Wits are sure to Madness near ally'd;
And thin Partitions do their Bounds divide.
—John Dryden

I wish to thank the graduate school and the department of history of Louisiana State University for inviting me to give the 1995 Walter Lynwood Fleming Lectures in southern history. The germ of this book on melancholy, creativity, and southern letters grew from the three lectures presented under the title "The Desperate Imagination and the Evolution of Southern Literature." I also express my gratefulness to William J. Cooper, Dean of Graduate Studies; Charles Royster; and Anne C. Loveland—all members of the history department, Louisiana State University, who assisted in my appointment to address the graduate school audience. I thank Les Phillabaum, Maureen Hewitt, and above all, Sylvia Frank Rodrigue of the Louisiana State University Press. They are editors and publishers of unusual distinction and helpfulness, whose encouragement and almost inexhaustible patience in awaiting receipt of the text were much needed. I am obliged not just to them but also to other members of their staff for invaluable assistance. It is a pleasure to acknowledge Ph.D. candidate Randall Stephens, a tireless researcher and copy editor who has served as my assistant in the final editing of the text and notes. Also Ph.D. candidates Susan Lewis and

Pat Campbell, secretarial assistants, have been indispensable in the production and editing of the work.

In addition, a happy sojourn at the National Humanities Center, Research Triangle Park, North Carolina, in 1998–1999, deserves special recognition. The Henry Luce Foundation of New York supplied the fellowship that I held there. I specifically name W. Robert Connor, Director; Kent Mullikin, Deputy Director; Linda Morgan, computer expert; and Alan Tuttle, Eliza Robertson, and Jean Houston of the library staff for their splendid management of the best place on earth to write in congenial surroundings. Those offering useful advice about the first chapter on Poe were members of a stimulating biographical seminar at the Center: R. W. B. Lewis, Anthony LaVopa, Rochelle Gurstein, Suzanne Raitt, Edward Friedman, Elizabeth McHenry, Marilynn Richtarik, Wilfred Prest, Anne Wyatt-Brown, and Ashraf Rushdy. Joseph P. Parsons published portions of this chapter in *Ideas* 6, no. 1 (1999):16–27, a publication of the National Humanities Center. Susan Donaldson of William and Mary, Charles Joyner of Coastal Carolina University, and an anonymous reader for LSU Press provided much useful criticism of the text. Jessie Poesch, Professor of Art, Tulane University, answered my call for help in locating and retrieving the engraving used for the cover of this book.

As always in my scholarly pursuits, Anne Wyatt-Brown has been a guiding presence and inspiration. Her quick and observant mind soon uncovers factual error, incomplete exposition, weak grammar, and poor construction of sentence, paragraph, and chapter. As always, she offered astonishing insights about the text too often for me to acknowledge them in the references. I apologize to those whom I may have left out of this all too brief statement of gratitude.

I

THE ORIGINS OF SOUTHERN LITERARY MELANCHOLY

Alienation and Art

Poe's Raven

It is not in the power of any mere *worldly* considerations, to depress me. . . . No, my sadness is *unaccountable,* and this makes me more sad. I am full of dark forebodings.
                    —Edgar Allan Poe

Poe as God sits silent in darkness. Here the movement of tragedy is reversed: there is no action. Man as angel becomes a demon who cannot initiate the first motion of love, and we can feel only compassion with his suffering, for it is potentially ours.
                    —Allen Tate

NOT surprisingly, a study of southern literary alienation and self-reflection must begin with the romantic poet, fiction writer, and literary critic Edgar Allan Poe. This tragic and mysterious artist of Richmond, Virginia, provides one of the earliest, most salient, and most famous examples of the interconnection of creativity and melancholy in the literary culture of the South. Poe's life and works also demonstrate how his agony reached, through fiction, the same wellsprings of depression and art that other writers had known or were to experience from their own similar sufferings. Friedrich Nietzsche, for instance, linked Poe with Lord Byron, Charles Baudelaire, and Alfred de Musset as poets with "souls in which they usually try to conceal some fracture; often taking revenge with their works for some inner contamination, often seeking with their high flights to escape into forgetfulness from an all-too-faithful memory; often lost in the mud, and almost in love with it."[1] Nietzsche's own battles with mental demons permitted him so poignant an insight.

Throughout his life Poe remained the quintessential outsider. He faced and even invited problems of failed honor and insanity—issues that paradoxically help to account for a literary authority that established precedents and patterns of literature in his home region and beyond. As J. Gerald Kennedy observes, Poe's alienation was the result of "the excesses and cruelties in his work," which displayed "the radical oppositional temperament that complicated and indeed sabotaged his personal life and professional career." Poe's burning interest in the mathematical sciences and the human powers of ratiocination and logic was incorporated into his morbid tales and poems. Affirmation and subversion, theatrical fantasy and down-to-earth truth-telling, were thoroughly interwoven in his work.[2] Whether fully conscious of his aims, Poe found ways to deal imaginatively with the inexpressible, the horrors that the mind can conjure, the darkest boundaries of experience. Yet he did so without revealing any more of the inner torture he experienced himself than he wished to convey to his readership.

Poe's stories often exhibit a preoccupation with pride and its opposites, shame and self-hatred. A Poe narrator belligerently asserts the self-concern of who-I-am but encounters a senior or peer who mocks his narcissism and pretensions to authenticity. Out of dread that the accusing tongue may speak the truth, the protagonist seeks vengeance. That purpose, no matter how inhuman, seems honorable and fully justified to him. Yet after he commits the murderous act, remorse and self-condemnation immediately bring home an ignominy that warrants the accuser's charge. The narrator confesses to the reader his own degradation.

Such a sequence punctuated Poe's literary career. He translated his maddened cycle of triumph and pain in his art. In "The Black Cat," for instance, the victim of the alcoholic narrator's self-despisement is a beast whom he seizes. Terrified, the animal fights back. In fury, he cuts out the cat's eye with his penknife. Later, in another drunken and hysterical moment, he tries to

1. Quoted in Jeffrey Meyers, *Edgar Allan Poe: His Life and Legacy* (London: John Murray, 1992), 270.

2. See J. Gerald Kennedy, "The Violence of Melancholy: Poe against Himself," *American Literary History* 8 (Fall 1996): 533–51, quotation, 534. See also Leon Chai, *The Romantic Foundations of the American Renaissance* (Ithaca: Cornell University Press, 1987), 103–41 and Evan Carton, *The Rhetoric of American Romance: Dialectic and Identity in Emerson, Dickinson, Poe, and Hawthorne* (Baltimore: Johns Hopkins University Press, 1985), 132–3.

decapitate the creature, but his wife prevents him. In a further escalation of madness, he strikes her down and buries the body in a wall of the house. When the police come, he plays the role of complete innocence. To demonstrate his guilelessness, he strikes the wall with his cane, and it crumbles away to reveal the body. Upon the top of the cadaver's skull "sat the hideous beast whose craft had seduced me into murder. . . . I had walled the monster up within the tomb."[3]

Is it credible that Poe failed to recognize himself in the account? In that romantic, pre-Freudian era, however, the eruption of irrational passions required no further exploration, as it would at the end of the century. Poe used his creative impulse as the means to expose the enormity of his own offenses, not as they were, but as he often exaggerated them to be. He did so without actually facing up to his "debaucheries," a vague term he often utilized. Poe felt the full blast of humiliation that usually strikes down his narrators and renders them helpless, impotent, forlorn. He wanted that kind of resolution, as if he gained an affirming gratification from wretchedness. To understand his art the character of his life and the ways in which he translated wretchedness into fiction and poetry become useful.

The sources of Poe's alienation are generally understood to lie in the personal traumas that affected his early life. Some scholars, however, have proposed instead an alleged disenchantment with his honor-conscious culture.[4] To be sure, as a white and privileged southerner he was naturally reared in the atmosphere of gentility and under the rubrics of the cavalier mode. The customs of the country required that southern aspirants to high status possess a strong sense of manhood. But also the rules of gentlefolk entailed a dread of shame for failing to match heroic expectations. To exhibit an appearance of cowardice would not only ruin personal reputation but a family's standing as well. Poe embraced these principles of southern life. He had no affinity for northern reform movements, especially abolitionism. At the same time he recognized his social and moral inadequacy by the existing standards of respectability.

The reasons for that self-loathing, as it came to be, arose from the poet's sad, unlucky childhood. Poe not only lost both parents but was reared by a

3. "The Black Cat," in *The Complete Tales and Poems of Edgar Allan Poe* (New York: Random House, 1975), 223–30, quotation, 230.

4. See, for instance, Lewis P. Simpson, *The Dispossessed Garden: Pastoral and History in Southern Literature* (1975; reprint, Baton Rouge: Louisiana State University Press, 1983), 66–71.

foster father who entirely misunderstood his charge and his urgent needs for reassurance and affection. Edgar's natural father, David Poe Jr., had given up a law career in his native Baltimore to marry Elizabeth Arnold, a popular actress. He joined her profession—a decision that itself was a social declension in that rank-conscious world. Still worse, David Poe was not even good in his new vocation. As one contemporary theater critic put it, his talents should have limited him to play footmen and nothing grander. Whatever his dramatic deficiencies were, he scarcely made up for them in his domestic conduct. David Poe was usually in debt, probably faithless, and often "indisposed," as theater folk preferred to label the drive for drink. His irascibility matched his other failings. In a surviving note to a cousin, from whom he demanded but failed to receive a loan, David Poe asked whether he was "to be despised by (as I understand) a rich relation because when a *wild boy* I join'd a profession which I . . . now think an honorable one."[5] It would seem that Edgar Poe's future woes with money and alcohol had been foreshadowed in the even briefer public life of his parent.

Genetics might have had a part in Poe's problems with depression, an inheritable condition that, in his case, one can only infer in the absence of modern clinical verification. It does seem likely, however, that Poe's father was afflicted with that mental state and that such a predisposition affected his sons. Both Edgar and brother Henry showed signs of a similar constitution. In any event, to make matters worse, David Poe absconded in late July 1810 when son Edgar was just eight months old. His disappearance reduced the family to still more abject penury and social declension. Elizabeth Poe had to rely on her acting skill when life in the early American theater was a study in poverty, discrimination, and even contempt. When a Richmond theater caught fire and killed seventy-two patrons, the religious folk of the town considered the tragedy a just punishment from God. Throughout their married life, the Poes, like many others on the stage, had been compelled to hold benefits—basically charity gatherings—to survive.

Unable to spend her time simply caring for her babies, Eliza, as she was called, had assumed more than two hundred roles.[6] With "wide-open mysterious eyes" and thick curls, she was a versatile and popular actress, but

5. *Enquirer* (Richmond), 21 September 1810, in *The Poe Log: A Documentary Life of Edgar Allan Poe, 1809–1849*, ed. Dwight Thomas and David K. Jackson (New York: G. K. Hall, 1987), 9; George Poe Jr. to William Clemm Jr., 6 March 1809, ibid., 5–6 (quotation) and 7.

6. See John C. Guilds Jr., "Poe's Mother and Foster-Mother: An Interpretive Study" (master's thesis, Duke University, 1948), 10–4, 37.

we know little of her family's medical and emotional history. Reared in an English stage family, Eliza had lost her father when she was only two and her mother when she was just nine. The early parental deaths, though, seem not to have diminished her spirits. Poe's inheritance from her was less a predisposition to madness than a tendency toward theatricality, a kind of dramatic narcissism. Even if that trait has no biological roots, certainly Eliza's life story, as others told her son about it, would have its effects on his sense of who he was.

Eliza's biography discloses her adventurous spirit. At fifteen she married a teenage actor named Charles Hopkins, and they performed in plays together until his death on 25 October 1805. Eliza remarried on 14 March 1806. Her new husband, David Poe, left the prospects of a legal career for the stage. The newlyweds took parts in Boston and then joined a Richmond troupe. With a natural stage presence and strong singing voice, Eliza was by far the greater success of the two. A critic gushed, "On the first moment of her entrance on the Richmond boards, she was saluted with plaudits of admiration, and at no one moment has her reputation sunk." Then her second husband, a failure on or off the boards, vanished. After acting in a dreary and taxing succession of towns as far south as Charleston with the two infants in tow, Eliza became desperately ill. The crisis that would shape Poe's character more than anything else in his life occurred not long after she returned to Richmond with little Edgar, born in Boston on 19 January 1809. His sister Rosalie came into the world in the fall of 1811. (The eldest son, William Henry Leonard Poe, had been left with grandparents in Baltimore.)[7]

In early November at Mrs. Osborne's boardinghouse, Elizabeth lay dying of pulmonary tuberculosis—what was then called phthisis, which signified the spitting of blood. Luke Noble Usher (a name little Edgar never forgot), his wife, and other stage friends sadly attended the dying actress. In the midst of the deathbed scene, the children, "thin and pale and very fretful," as a contemporary reported, were given a liberal feeding of bread soaked in gin, laudanum, and other spirits so that they might sleep. An old nurse who continued in service to the children for years thereafter steadily applied such palliatives as a way, she said, "to make them strong and healthy." Her ministrations probably did more harm than good. Elizabeth Poe died on 8 December, and little Edgar was taken into the room to see his "sleeping" emaciated mother for the last time. Apparently he was allowed

7. Thomas and Jackson, eds., *Poe Log*, 10–5.

to remain with the corpse the entire night and was separated from it only in the morning.[8]

That occasion left a sensation if not an actual memory that lingered forever in his mind. An ashen corpse would become a familiar image in his writing.[9] Only several months more than two years old, the child had no means to verbalize such a loss at the time. Art, however, can prove a creative memorial of past tragedy. The living corpses of "The Premature Burial," as well as the animated dead in "The Fall of the House of Usher" and "The Case of M. Valdemar," had a clear relationship to Poe's early acquaintance with terror, grief, and a sense of abandonment. Union with the dead seemed more real than love in flesh and blood. Was a memory of that night beside the dead Eliza, however vaguely recalled, the source of the closing stanza of "Annabel Lee"? "And so, all the night-tide, I lie down by the side / Of my darling—my darling—my life and my bride, / In the Sepulchre there by the sea, / In her tomb by the sounding sea."[10]

According to analyst Robert Jay Lifton, early anxiety of parental separation may have a macabre effect on a child. He argues, "Separation is the paramount threat from the beginning of life and can give rise, very early, to the rudiments of anxiety and mourning." Particularly during the second half of a child's second year (Poe's age when his mother died), the child, once exposed to death of human beings or even animals, finds in sleep, in pain, in cuts and bruises, what Lifton calls "death equivalents." Within a year or two more, "the child shapes an increasingly formed notion of being or becoming dead." Lifton might have used Poe's tales to illustrate how the adult may reconstruct the past in metaphor, symbol, and situation through the imagery of horror and loss. Lifton continues, "The child now ruminates in endless detail about people who had 'gone away for *good*.'" They have died by some act of violence—a burning house, falling walls, or sadistic doctoring. Or else they have become "permanently still, 'asleep for good' because," Lifton asserts, "they can't breathe anymore."[11]

Poe would spend his life writing about loss in exactly Lifton's terms. He dreaded the thought of dying but also of losing hold of those upon whom

8. Ibid., 14.
9. Maria Bonaparte, *The Life and Works of Edgar Allan Poe: A Psycho-Analytic Interpretation*, trans. John Rodker (1933; reprint, London: Imago, 1949), 7.
10. *Complete Tales and Poems of Edgar Allan Poe*, 958.
11. Robert Jay Lifton, *The Broken Connection: On Death and the Continuity of Life* (New York: Simon and Schuster, 1979), 68, 69; J. Gerald Kennedy, *Poe, Death, and the Life of Writing* (New Haven: Yale University Press, 1987), 94.

he depended. When he was six years old, Poe's hysteria emerged in a dramatic way. The little boy was traveling on horseback with his favorite uncle, Edward Valentine. As they approached Staunton, Virginia, the pair passed a forlorn-looking family cemetery. The child, riding behind, shrieked uncontrollably. Uncle Edward moved him in front to hold him tight. "They will run after us and drag me down" into their graves, the boy wailed.[12] He had heard of such malevolent ghosts from the black house servants, but the roots of his distress ran much deeper.

The kind of anger, remorse, guilt, and dread that Poe was later to exhibit in his adulthood parallel the nightmarish imaginings of any child in mourning—a fear of being left isolated and swallowed up in the earth. D. W. Winnicott, the British psychiatrist and pediatrician, offers the case of Peter, an eleven-year-old boy. Peter had been brought to him for analysis. While sailing with his son, Peter's father had drowned, but Peter had luckily survived the accident. After several sessions, the youth reported a complicated and terrifying dream in which he entered a church where three coffins rested. A body from one of them arose as a ghost with a waxen face that looked as if it belonged to a drowning victim. Did the ghost intend to return him to a scene of death from which Peter had miraculously escaped? Whether the child's fantasies are happy or fearsome, as Winnicott, John Bowlby, Lifton, and others suggest, his desperate hope of fashioning something credible or at least expressive of inner thoughts may be the seeds of later creativity.[13]

To deal with the emotional turmoil, the child Poe could not have looked for succor from his father, David. Poe later told friend and novelist Nathaniel Beverley Tucker that within weeks of Elizabeth Poe's death, David Poe, also a victim of tuberculosis, apparently followed her to the grave—still far from the children he had deserted.[14] Long since departed from his wife's side, he never had any sustained relationship with his three children. Nor did Poe's adoptive family offer steady comfort to Edgar, grieving for his mother. At age twenty-five the beautiful but childless Frances Allan and her up-and-coming merchant husband, John, took Edgar to their ample house

12. Hervey Allen, *Israfel: The Life and Times of Edgar Allan Poe* (New York: George H. Doran Co., 1926), 1:61.

13. See Donald W. Winnicott, "A Child Psychiatry Case Illustrating Delayed Reaction to Loss," in *Drives, Affects, Behavior,* 2 vols., ed. Max Schur (New York: International Universities Press, 1965), 2:212–42, as cited in John Bowlby, *Attachment and Loss: Sadness and Depression* (New York: Basic Books, 1980), 3:321–7.

14. See "11 December? Norfolk, Virginia? David Poe, Jr. dies," *Poe Log,* ed. Thomas and Jackson, 15.

and met his material needs. The William Mackenzies, another Richmond family, adopted Poe's sister Rosalie. Rumor had it that Rosalie was not the daughter of Elizabeth's wayward husband but rather a consequence of adultery. Within a few days, the Allans had the Reverend John Buchanan christen their new charge Edgar Allan, adding their name as an emblem of his new status.

As he grew up, Poe showed signs of the melancholy that would affect him so deeply later. The household itself was marked by gloom. Frances Allan was remembered by friends for her hypochondria and "habitual pessimism."[15] Poe could be imperious, unapproachable, solitary, shunning friends and wandering off by himself. One contemporary reminisced that he was often "singularly unsociable in manner." Another remembered that, presenting always the "same sad face," young Poe "laughed heartily," and when he did, it "seemed to be forced."[16] In his mid-teens, Poe was much attracted to the beauty, musical voice, and charm of a fellow schoolmate's mother, Jane Stanard, wife of a future judge. She supplied him with maternal comfort. Unfortunately she suffered from severe depression. Her condition had been growing worse, then quite suddenly she died. To Poe, her demise seemed almost a repetition of the death of his mother, whom this young matron had replaced in his affections. In 1831 he published the poem "To Helen" that suggests how deeply he grieved:

> Helen, thy beauty is to me
>   Like those Nicéan barks of yore,
> That gently, o'er a perfumed sea,
>   The weary, way-worn wanderer bore
>   To his own native shore.
> On desperate seas long wont to roam,
>   Thy hyacinth hair, thy classic face,
> Thy Naiad airs have brought me home
>   To the glory that was Greece,
>   And the grandeur that was Rome.

In these memorable lines, Poe's biographer Marie Bonaparte sees intimations of his "mournful return to the mother, who, for him, would always be one who was dying or dead." Yet the poet is an intimate part of the poem, which seems to refer as much to the narrator as to the object of his narcissis-

---

15. Guilds, "Poe's Mother," 124.
16. Thomas Bolling and Creed Thomas in *Poe Log,* ed. Thomas and Jackson, 75.

tic adoration. As Bonaparte observes, Poe's lifelong conviction about the nature of love is summarized in a couplet he wrote when just twenty: "I could not love except where Death / Was mingling his with Beauty's breath—"[17]

While deprived of a fully satisfactory relationship with "Fanny" Allan, his adoptive mother, Poe was even more estranged from his austere, unloving foster father. Widely rumored to be an unfaithful husband, John Allan added little to domestic happiness in his household.[18] Although a submissive child in his early years, Poe turned rebellious in his teens, much to his foster father's vexation. Little did he understand how hard Poe, then fourteen, had taken the death of Jane Stanard. Even if sympathetically called upon to do so, Poe himself might have been unable to articulate his feelings. Further adding to Edgar Poe's unhappiness, Fanny Allan was a semi-invalid, "never clear of complaint," as her husband once declared.[19] In 1824 Allan confided to Edgar's elder brother, Henry, that Edgar "does nothing & seems quite miserable, sulky & ill-tempered to all the Family." He continued, "The boy possesses not a spark of affection for us, not a particle of gratitude for all my care and kindness toward himself."[20]

Allan's attitude toward his foster son was shaped in part by his own experience with an elder kinsman. A meanspirited uncle had put Allan early to work in his Richmond store rather than permitting him a chance for schooling. Certain of his own forbearance, Allan claimed to have given Edgar a better education than he had himself received. Still worse than Poe's lack of gratitude, Allan complained, the boy was too self-centered to show even the barest affection for his sister. "If Rosalie has to relie [sic] on any affection from him," the disgruntled father added, "God in his mercy preserve her."[21] Rose was emotionally and perhaps mentally handicapped. Unlike early-orphaned Rudyard Kipling, who shared an affectionate rela-

17. After 1 April 1823, in Thomas and Jackson, eds., *Poe Log*, 57; 30 April 1824, ibid., 59; Bonaparte, *Life and Works of Edgar Allan Poe*, 21–2; Martin Bickman, *The Unsounded Centre: Jungian Studies in American Romanticism* (Chapel Hill: University of North Carolina Press, 1980), 61–2.

18. Bonaparte, *Life and Works of Edgar Allan Poe*, 27.

19. Kenneth Silverman, *Edgar A. Poe: Mournful and Never-Ending Remembrance* (New York: Harper, 1991), 26.

20. John Allan to Henry Poe, [?] November 1824, in *Poe's Brother: The Poems of William Henry Leonard Poe*, ed. Hervey Allen and Thomas Ollive Mabbott (New York: George H. Doran, 1926), 21.

21. John Allan to Henry Poe, [?] November 1824, in *Poe's Brother*, Allen and Mabbot, eds., 21.

tionship with his sister, Edgar never warmed to Rosalie. Yet only a few doors separated them in their youthful years in Richmond. "Edgar could never love me as I do him," Rosalie once sighed, "*because he is so far above me.*" She died in a shelter for the homeless in Washington, D.C., in 1874 and was buried in a pauper's grave.[22]

Poe's relationship with Allan deteriorated still further when he began his first year at the University of Virginia. Notwithstanding his ward's excelling in language studies—German, French, Italian, and Latin—John Allan refused to pay off a mounting accumulation of debts that Poe incurred. American university life, particularly at Charlottesville, was more expensive than the non-collegiate Scotsman understood. Immature and only seventeen upon entering college, Edgar made matters worse with his own extravagances of fancy waistcoats, "Best Gilt Buttons," and gambling. As the adopted son of a Scottish merchant and the son of an actress, Poe may have become highly sensitive to his social inferiority to other young gentlemen of the planter class and sought to be more like them. After less than a year, Allan refused to pay for any more semesters.[23] Money lenders pursued the student back to Richmond. Threatened with warrants and arrest and receiving no help from Allan, Poe denounced his foster father, whom he claimed to have overheard saying that he "had no affection for me."[24] Poe's impulse was constantly to test his father's love and concern. Invariably he showed an emotionality that the old Scotsman found highly vexing. Sometimes he tried to hurt Allan's feelings: "*Your* love I never valued." On other occasions he cried for either love or funds—or both. These commodities Poe claimed to need urgently. He grew desperate: "I am in the greatest distress and have no other friend on earth to apply to except yourself." A month later, he tried again, only more strenuously. He begged Allan "not to leave me to perish without leaving me still one resource."[25] Allan's answer was usually to send small monetary aid but to give no sign of love.

In fighting his guardian, Poe was acutely conscious that insofar as Allan was concerned he was dishonoring his parents and himself. That angry crossing of conventional boundaries—subjecting the family to the whispers of neighbors—became one of the most important tropes in his stories. In so

22. Silverman, *Edgar A. Poe,* 126, 423 (quotation), 442–6.

23. Thomas Bolling, quoted in *Poe Log,* Thomas and Jackson, eds., 75; Silverman, *Edgar A. Poe,* 29–30, 34 (quotation); Guilds, "Poe's Mother," 102.

24. Silverman, *Edgar A. Poe,* 35 (quotation).

25. Poe to John Allan, 18 November, 15 December 1831, in *The Letters of Edgar Allan Poe,* ed. John Ward Ostrom, 2 vols. (Cambridge, Mass.: Harvard University Press, 1948), 1:48.

many of them he dwells on the delights of vengeance for the sake of personal gratification and honor, but almost always shame for his own misdeeds overwhelms the narrator. As J. Gerald Kennedy has noted, "In tale after tale the Poe narrator manifests . . . ambivalent feelings: toward cherished women, he harbors an implicit hostility; toward irritating males he feels an unlikely affection. Yet, his acts of cruelty always result in the narrator's self-disgust and remorse."[26]

Poe's use of aristocratic and medieval settings for posing such issues is a clear signal of how deeply he was immersed in the antique conventions of honor and shame. A single story, "Metzengerstein," sufficiently illustrates the point. The tale concerns a young baron, Frederick von Metzengerstein of Hungary, whose parents had died when he was a mere infant. Totally self-absorbed, the haughty and friendless recluse, we are told, indulges in every sort of debauchery and form of cruelty. The baron victimizes his servants. At the climax of his atrocities, none of which Poe specifies in lurid indulgence, he conspires to have the stable of a rival noble family, the Berlifitzings, set afire. While the flames mount, Frederick, seated in his hall, notices that a great, curiously marked horse in an ancient tapestry has turned toward him and come alive. He leaps from the room in panic to encounter his equerries at the gate. They are barely able to hold a horse of similar temper, a fugitive from the raging conflagration nearby. The servants at Castle Berlifitzing disclaim ever having seen the horse before, even though it is marked with the letters W. V. B. on its forehead, the initials of the old Count Berlifitzing. One evening Metzengerstein awakens to ride into the forest on his mount. In his absence, his castle, like that of his enemy, is fiercely engulfed by fire, and the domestics cannot extinguish the inferno. The horse and rider return. At a fierce gallop that the baron cannot halt, the powerful steed bears its dissolute master into the heart of the fire.[27]

Little imagination is required to identify the horse as a metaphor denoting Authority, indifferent and merciless. It may be just retribution for the baron's sins, but punishment of the self is part of the emotional pattern that Poe both illustrated in his stories and felt as a man. Redemption, grace, salvation—these Christian principles that permit a sense of hope and release— almost never appear in his work. They certainly do not emerge in this story. At the base of the matter was Poe's resentment of John Allan, but the fic-

26. Kennedy, "Violence of Melancholy," 544.

27. I have followed the interpretation of David M. Rein, *Edgar Allan Poe: The Inner Pattern* (New York: Philosophical Library, 1960), 9–16.

tional horse might be called a screen image, a double representation of both a child's anger and of patriarchal willfulness. In this story, as in others, Poe creates a setting of romanticized aristocracy. He did so not only because such representations fit the popular Gothic mode but also because Poe saw himself in a similar light—a nobleman shamed but rebelliously proud to the point of self-destruction. Son of a drunkard, grandson of a Revolutionary hero (who had fallen into bankruptcy in later years), Poe was in a sense recapitulating in grimly romantic terms his familial biography.[28] An imagined revenge against the foster father was a form of release for the writer. Yet Count Berlifitzing, the emblem of a senior's power over the young, would always win in the end.

Likewise in the better-known story "The Cask of Amontillado," Poe has Montresor seek vengeance against Fortunato for the many insults and shows of contempt he has had to bear. They are unnamed. Yet the language betokens the impulses behind the southern cavalier conventions of challenge and duel. Both names, Montresor and Fortunato, mean practically the same thing, so that there is the sense of doubleness of identity. Persecutor and victim are almost interchangeable. One is full of malice, the other is a drunken sot, easily beguiled. The mandates of honor and shame are thus not so clearly differentiated but together perform a partnered dance of defiance and death. Montresor has always turned the other cheek, or so he claims, as Poe liked to think he did in relation to his foster father John Allan. The narrator of the story, Montresor "vowed revenge" because of the "thousand injuries of Fortunato I had borne as I best could."[29] Poe assumed that his readers shared his presumptions and would intuit why the narrator Montresor felt justified and why these insults made his own behavior— immuring Fortunato in the catacombs—acceptable. One may speculate that Poe expected his audience to accept Montresor's logic. At the same time, readers would justly think the narrator obsessional to the point of insanity.

Even in the fiction of "The Cask of Amontillado," however, Poe would not confront the father directly. There are no fathers or sons anywhere in the Poe stories or poems. Yet the desire to "punish with impunity" repre-

28. Poe to John Allan, 4 February, 10 March, 20 May 1829 in *Letters of Poe,* ed. Ostrom, 1:13–7; John Allan to John H. Eaton, 6 May 1829, in *Poe Log,* Thomas and Jackson, eds., 91–2; for contrast to the mixed recommendation of John Allan, see Colonel James P. Preston to Eaton, 13 May 1829, ibid., 93.

29. Edgar Allan Poe, "The Cask of Amontillado," in *Tales and Sketches, 1843–1849,* vol. 3 of *Collected Works of Edgar Allan Poe,* ed. Thomas Ollive Mabbott (Cambridge, Mass.: Belknap Press, 1978), 1256.

sents the wishes of the resentful child against the powerful parent. It is scarcely a wonder that Poe's most avid readers are those in their teenage years. In the story, before Fortunato's death, the transgressor must come to see the error of his ways. Montresor entices his "friend" into the bone-lined family crypt underneath his mansion to taste from the pipe of Amontillado. "'I drink,' I said, 'to the buried dead that repose around us.'" Abruptly, he chains his nemesis to the side of the damp vault. With a mason's trowel Montresor walls up the besotted captive. Fortunato fusses at first but then falls silent after desperately crying "*For the love of God, Montresor!*" The last sound that the narrator hears is the jingle of Fortunato's fool's bells on the cap of his carnival costume. The silence that follows breaks the once playful bond and friendly exchange between them: "My heart grew sick— because of the dampness of the catacombs." Montresor's excuse is meant to ring hollow. Instead, we are to understand at the end that the avenger has gained from his act little genuine "satisfaction." That word was a dueling term almost uniformly invoked to demand vindication on the field of honor for insult. Montresor has become a psychological victim of his crime. He is no less a prisoner of his deed than Fortunato. Even fifty years afterward, he must revisit the horror in a confession to the reader.[30] The tangle of identities and issues of dishonor, anger, and contrition with which Poe coped with his filial concerns against the father fell under his artistic control in a masterful way.[31]

Poe's preoccupation with honor and dread of shame placed him well within the southern literary framework, even though he lived most of his adult life in New York and Philadelphia, quite apart from the slave South. Despite the self-imposed exile, he remained always conscious of his southern and allegedly noble roots. To cousin William Poe of Augusta, Georgia, Poe explained in 1840 that he relied chiefly upon "the South" to promote his career: "If I fully succeed in my purpose, I will not fail to produce some

30. *Complete Tales and Poems of Edgar Allan Poe*, 274–9; see also Kennedy, *Poe, Death, and the Life of Writing*, 139–41. Kennedy's interpretation does not relate the story to Poe's conflict with his father, but stresses the theme of doubling. Other interpreters see it as Poe's revenge against a set of critics. But in a sense Poe's fight with them originated psychologically in his anger against anyone asserting authority in a peremptory way—a return to the struggle against early losses.

31. See Silverman, *Edgar A. Poe*, 316–17; Daniel Hoffman, *Poe Poe Poe Poe Poe Poe Poe* (New York: Doubleday, 1972), 220–1. On doubling, see John T. Irwin, *The Mystery to a Solution: Poe, Bourges, and the Analytic Detective Story* (Baltimore: Johns Hopkins University Press, 1994), 5–6, 24–9, 229–30.

lasting effect upon the growing literature of the country [the South], while I shall establish for myself individually a name which that country 'will not willingly let die.'"[32] Such sentiments were not uncommon in that romantic era, but they reveal a rather juvenile naiveté in Poe. Eventually the prediction did come true, but scarcely in Poe's lifetime as he anticipated.

Despite that childlike quality in his writing, Poe was sufficiently alienated as a gifted intellectual to see the destructive aspects of honor and humiliation, so long the governing principles of a master-slave society. Yet he scarcely hoped to overthrow southern conventions and habits. After all, however much he rebelled in life and in art against the rubrics of honor, he knew no other ethical system. A third story, "William Wilson," even more autobiographical than the others, helps to illuminate. "Men usually grow base by degrees," Poe has his narrator say, "[but] I passed with the stride of a giant, into more than the enormities of an Elah-Gabalus."[33] The story concerns the doubleness of human identity, a theme to be encountered more than once in these pages. It also reveals the subtle interplay between power and helplessness. The narrator is driven to kill his double, who never leaves him alone and imitates his every action. Eventually, he plunges a sword into his nemesis. As he dies, the second Wilson whispers, "*You have conquered, and I yield. Yet henceforward art thou also dead—dead to the World, to Heaven, and to Hope! In me didst thou exist—and, in my death, see by this image, which is thine own, how utterly thou hast murdered thyself.*"[34]

In this story and in many others, the "I" in "William Wilson" has no history, no outside associations, no kinspeople. We do not even learn exactly what he looks like. As Jonathan Auerbach observes, "The typical Poe narrator impresses us less as a fully fledged person, in fact, than as a disembodied voice, sheer nervous energy seeking to order itself by trying to maintain control over the tale being told." Nearly always, the reader ends up surmising more than the narrator admits. Somehow, there was a very odd lack of self-knowledge in these narrators. They do not seem aware of the most obvious connection between the events described and their own inner feelings. The link between the writer and his first-person speaker seems very fragile and unresolved.

Poe's most famous and favorite poem, "The Raven," reveals this volatile

32. Poe to William Poe, 15 August 1840, in *Letters of Edgar Allan Poe,* ed. James A. Harrison (1902; reprint, New York: AMS Press, 1965), 18:55.
33. "William Wilson," in *Complete Tales and Poems of Edgar Allan Poe,* 626.
34. Ibid., 641.

state of affairs in the relation of author and narrator. Through it we infer much more about the author's wrestling with despair than he ever intended. In fact, in "The Philosophy of Composition," he throws his readers off the scent with a technical and objective analysis that exposes his poetic artifices as if he were explaining the mechanics of a backstage prop. His approach resembles a magician's in revealing how he performs his tricks. By that means Poe creates a distance between himself as creator and the feelings that the poem actually describes. *Who,* not what, is the Raven—whom does it symbolize with its parrot-like repetition of "Nevermore"? As Poe observes in his essay, the answer is in the poem's last lines:

> And the Raven, never flitting, still is sitting, still is sitting,
> On the pallid bust of Pallas just above my chamber door;
> And his eyes have all the seeming of a demon's that is dreaming,
> And the lamplight o'er him streaming throws his shadow on the floor;
> And my soul *from out that shadow* that lies floating on the floor
> Shall be lifted—nevermore.[35]

The Raven is the representation of the narrator's—and, I would argue, the poet's—own melancholy. The poem is only ostensibly about Leonore, the student's mistress mentioned in the middle stanzas. Her death is the occasion for his despondency. But the source of that sorrow lies not simply in grief over a dead lover. Mourning over the loss of a loved one is psychologically a temporary wound that, to some degree at least, eventually heals. Under ordinary circumstances, the intensity of lamentation gradually recedes. The Raven's permanent installation at the end of the poem signifies a sorrow beyond any healing. The location of the confrontation between man and bird drives home the point. The room where the student is seated is, of course, the narrator-poet's own body. (No distinction seems to separate artist and speaker.) Yet the narrator never sees that the chamber he occupies is his own head. Poe leaves that observation to the reader. He argued that theatrical obfuscation was best for the intended effect of horror, and he saw the necessary setting as "a close *circumspection of space*"—like a body, a tomb, and, in the poetic idiom, a dreary scholar's chamber. But the poet may have had other reasons for selecting that locale. Often writers have chosen to place their characters in cramped, confined spaces because melan-

35. Edgar Allan Poe, "The Philosophy of Composition," in *Essays and Reviews* (New York: Viking Press, 1984), 25; "The Raven," in *Edgar Allan Poe: Poetry, Tales, and Selected Essays* (New York: Library of America, 1984), 81–6.

cholia feels to them as constricting, suffocating as if they were in some kind
of lockup. For instance, William Styron in *Darkness Visible* describes why
he has the black rebel in *The Confessions of Nat Turner* tell his story from
a prison cell. Styron felt "impelled" to borrow this setting from the suicidal
Albert Camus's *The Stranger*. In that novel, the hero, Meurseult, is awaiting
his execution in a cell. Walker Percy's insane protagonist Lance Lamar in
Lancelot is similarly imprisoned. Returning to Poe, the caged figures in so
many of his tales—some of them literally walled-in—are all victims of the
demonic nature of the illness that afflicted their creator. It is despair itself
that imprisons.[36]

Those artists who have suffered from severe mental collapse have often
imagined their illness not only as a particular location but also a specific
creature of dread. "I have a black melancholia tearing at my roots or eating
like the Spartan fox at my vitals," John Gould Fletcher, an early-twentieth-
century southern poet, wrote a friend.[37] Greatly afflicted by the malady,
Winston Churchill called the mood his "black dog." Sylvia Plath referred to
it as "the groveling image of the fearful beast in myself" and the "demon of
negation." For writers the figure of a demon is frequently invoked to represent madness, isolation, emptiness, and it appears in the closing stanza of
"The Raven." Walker Percy called his family's mental distress "the sweet
beast of catastrophe." For these writers as well as many others so afflicted,
depression had to be fought minute by minute with a "stoic face" and "a
position of irony," as Plath reminded herself in her journal.[38]

Poe employs the specific image of a bird to signify the agony of melancholy, which representation, like that of a demon, may be readily found in
both contemporary and in modern artistic work. Vincent van Gogh's painting of crows flying over a field of yellow stalks has been so interpreted. The
French poet Charles Baudelaire touched on the same theme more than once,

36. Poe, "Philosophy of Composition," 23–4; Jonathan Auerbach, *The Romance of Failure: First-Person Fictions of Poe, Hawthorne, and James* (New York: Oxford University Press,
1989), 25; William Styron, *Darkness Visible: A Memoir of Madness* (New York: Random
House, 1990), 21. See also Gavin Cologne-Brookes, *The Novels of William Styron: From Har-
mony to History* (Baton Rouge: Louisiana State University Press, 1995), 223.

37. Quoted in Ben F. Johnson III, *Fierce Solitude: A Life of John Gould Fletcher* (Fayetteville: University of Arkansas Press, 1994), 238.

38. Anthony Storr, *Churchill's Black Dog, Kafka's Mice, and Other Phenomena of the
Human Mind* (New York: Grove Press, 1988), 76; Walker Percy, *The Last Gentleman* (New
York: Farrar, Straus, and Giroux, 1966), 16; 1 October 1957 entry in *The Journals of Sylvia
Plath*, ed. Ted Hughes and Frances McCullough (New York: Dial Press, 1982), 177; Anne Ste-
venson, *Bitter Fame: A Life of Sylvia Plath* (Boston: Houghton Mifflin, 1989), 114–5.

but particularly when he wrote, "No tears for me. I'd rather have / ravenous birds reduce this mortal girth / And in my flesh peck out a cave." William Styron could make the same claim. He describes his own descent into madness as if there were something specifically menacing about the presence of birds. Vacationing at Martha's Vineyard, he was emotionally struck down while watching "a flock of Canadian geese honking above the trees ablaze with foliage." Usually, he writes, such "a sight and sound . . . would have exhilarated me." On this occasion, though, he "stood stranded there, helpless, shivering." He was acutely aware that his mind was racing out of control and that he was unable to re-gather himself.[39] In *Lie Down in Darkness,* Styron has his young suicidal heroine, Peyton Loftus, react in terror to imaginings of birds: "They followed me, prissing along with their stiff-legged gait and their noiseless, speckled wings."[40] In his famous essay, Poe mentions that the student-narrator was not only troubled by notions of "self-torture" but also by superstition. Although he fails to specify the superstition, he was probably referring to the old southern folk-warning that a bird flying into a house meant that a sudden death was about to occur—in this case, perhaps the student-narrator's.[41]

So grim an interpretation of the Raven's poetic meaning is further supported by its location in the room. The bird sits, appropriately, on the bust of Pallas Athena, the goddess of the intellect. In his customary disingenuous style, Poe throws dust in the reader's eyes by claiming that he chose "Pallas" simply because it was a mellifluous, poetic term (the word "Pallas" is a reminder of "pallid," a fittingly morbid adjective). But the way the bust functions in the poem belies such guilelessness. The statue resides on a shelf above the student-narrator's own head. Pallas Athena, of course, sprang from the head of Zeus; she was the seat of learning and wisdom, according to ancient Greek mythology. The ancients believed that emotions resided in the heart, not head, but in Poe's time it was understood that the brain carries all mood and thought, rational and otherwise.

According to Poe's poetic exegesis, this mindless, loveless, carrion beast at first amuses the student. This is another of Poe's efforts to distance himself from the emotional reality in the poem. Actually, the poem by no means

39. Charles Baudelaire, "The Carefree Corpse," in *Complete Poems,* trans. Walter Martin (Manchester, Eng.: Carcanet: 1997); William Styron, *Darkness Visible,* 46.

40. William Styron, *Lie Down in Darkness: A Novel* (New York: Viking, 1951), 382.

41. See Henry B. Cumming to Julia A. D. Cumming, 29 September 1825, Hammond-Bryan-Cumming MSS, South Caroliniana Library, University of South Carolina, Columbia, S.C.

offers so lighthearted a moment even at the start. Instead, the Raven has invaded the soul of the poet just as it has the narrator's, and shows no intention ever to leave. At first, the occupant of the room expects that he can shoo it out the window from whence it had entered. As Poe admits in his later explication, the student gradually realizes that he is "impelled . . . by the human thirst for self-torture" to keep probing the motives of the bird. But what is this yearning to inflict injury—"self-torture"—upon one's own self? In "The Philosophy of Composition," Poe makes it seem a natural motivation. Surely it is not—at least as a constant force in the psyche. The Raven torments the figure in the poem with his repetitive taunt—echoes that remind us of Poe's own compulsively repetitive behavior—his bouts of drunkenness, repeated quarrels with others, and other signs of fragile self-control. The black creature is not at all separable from the narrator himself. Rather, the representation of the poet's despair is an indwelling part of his identity that only *seems* invasive. Yet it is there, lying in wait all the time, ready to destroy life itself.

In addition to the theme of unwholesome dejection that the Raven symbolizes, Poe experimented with the ambiguities of honor. That Manichean construction of ethics posed glory against disgrace. The polarities were in a sense parallel with the dichotomy between mania and depression, between a sense of omnipotence and a feeling of complete worthlessness. From the Spanish Golden Age and Shakespeare to the late nineteenth century, most dramatic works dealt in one way or another with principles of honor and the perils of dishonor, whether for heroes in battle or heroines under threat of rape or seduction. In an essay on poetry, Poe, always the romanticist, closed his search for sublimity with an elegiac poem by Motherwell, in which an old cavalier croaks, "Deathe's couriers, Fame and Honour call / Us to the field againe."[42] In December 1846 his child-wife Virginia lay dying of consumption and malnutrition in an unheated cottage near New York City. Yet Poe was reluctant to accept the help of friends to escape the dishonor of being a ward of "public charity."[43] His sense of independence, upon which his identity as a man of honor rested, mattered more than her well-being.

Poe's notion of honorableness culminated in a worship of ancestors. In fact, he worshiped them in a manner that psychoanalyst Karen Horney

42. Edgar Allan Poe, "The Poetic Principle," in *Selected Writings of Edgar Allan Poe,* ed. Edward H. Davidson (Boston: Houghton Mifflin, 1956), 485.
43. Allen, *Israfel,* 2:724.

would identify as a problem of grandiosity. General David Poe, his grand-father, had been a Revolutionary War hero and a quartermaster general in Washington's army. From his slender resources, he had supplied five hundred dollars to clothe the troops of General Lafayette. The sacrifice won him high posthumous praise when the general visited the United States in 1824. In September 1814, General Poe had further distinguished himself in the defense of Baltimore against the British invaders.[44] From such glories, Edgar Poe derived as much sense of self-importance as William Faulkner later did with regard to his great-grandfather, the swashbuckling Confederate hero, Colonel William Clarke Falkner.

In 1843, a Philadelphia journal published a highly inaccurate biography of Poe. Drawing on Poe's misrepresentations, the gullible author of the article wrote that he had come from "one of the oldest and most respectable families in Baltimore." The dynasty included naval heroes and connections with "the most illustrious of Great Britain." As Poe's biographer Kenneth Silverman observes, however, the reality was less impressive. The old general was a dry-goods storekeeper whose speculations forced him to insolvency in 1805. Other distortions of Poe's imagining had his tubercular parents dying under the same roof, when, in fact, they had been long separated. The wealthy John Allan, his adoptive father, had named Poe "his sole heir," the article announced. Actually young Poe had been stricken from the will. Further, Poe pretended a matriculation at Charlottesville that lasted three years instead of the actuality—a mere eight months. Inspired by his brother Henry's travels, he claimed to have joined the Greek cause against the Turks and to have escaped perils in Russia, thanks to the help of Henry Middleton, the American minister to the Court at St. Petersburg.[45] At least when William Faulkner boasted of war wounds, daring dogfights over France, and other outlandish fantasies, he did not have them advertised in the papers.[46] Both of these sufferers from what appears to have been chronic depression adopted fictions in their self-presentations. Psychoanalyst Karen Horney calls this impulse a substitution of "grandiose ideas for attainable goals." The purpose, she surmises, is to cover "unendurable feelings of nothingness." The lies become "the pillar" upon which "self-esteem rests."[47]

44. Entries for 12–13 September 1814 and 8 October 1824, in *Poe Log*, ed. Thomas and Jackson, 22, 60–1.
45. Meyers, *Edgar Allan Poe*, 38.
46. Silverman, *Edgar A. Poe*, 196–7.
47. Karen Horney, *The Neurotic Personality of Our Time* (1937; reprint, New York: W. W. Norton, 1964), 223, 224.

*   *   *

No less important to Poe than his adherence to the honor code as well as alienation from it was his preoccupation with art itself—but with a purpose different from that of other contemporary southern writers. His fixation with madness raked him down until his death. Yet dread of going mad was itself a prominent feature in his artistic scheme. Almost as if he anticipated the coming of Sigmund Freud, he probed the depths of the mind and entered a world of irrationality, shame, remorse, rage, and vulnerability. "Were I called on to define the term 'Art,'" Poe once wrote, "I should call it 'the reproduction of what the Senses perceive in Nature through the veil of the Soul.'"[48] Later in the century the poet Baudelaire hailed Poe for exposing "the primordial perversity of man."[49]

Thus Poe was the first southerner to recognize in himself and his art what Edward Engelberg calls "the Unlived life." As Allen Tate observed, Poe "represents that part of our [southerners'] experience which we are least able to face up to: the Dark Night of Sense." Indeed, Poe's outlook on life was very southern, very conservative. Slavery and slaveholding bothered him not at all. He proposed so many negatives—the transiency of life, the puniness of human creatures in the natural order, the improbability of progress, the limits of human rationality, and the dangers of democracy and consequent disorder. How could there be a world without the necessary gradations of status? Poe argued that "in efforts to soar above our nature, we invariably fall below it." The words reveal both the antiprogressive ethos of southern intellectuals like himself and his own bitter experience as a compulsive manic-depressive. According to critic Robert D. Jacobs, in Poe's literary world the poet, despairing over the limitations of art, "finds himself in a state of everlasting grief concerning the human predicament, at his 'inability to grasp *now,* wholly, here on earth, at once and forever, those divine and rapturous joys of which, *through* the poem, we attain to but brief and indeterminate glimpses." (The internal quotation, writes Jacob, is from Poe, "The Poetic Principle.") Emphatically Poe claimed that melancholy was "the most legitimate of all the poetical tones."[50] His use of vague abstrac-

48. Edgar Allan Poe, "Marginalia" (June 1849), quoted by Robert Regan, "Introduction," in *Poe: A Collection of Critical Essays,* ed. Robert Regan (Englewood Cliffs, N.J.: Prentice-Hall, 1967), 6–7.

49. Baudelaire quoted by Sidney Kaplan, "Introduction to *Pym,*" in *Poe: A Collection of Critical Essays,* ed. Regan, 146.

50. Poe quoted in Robert D. Jacobs, "Poe and the Agrarian Critics," in *Southern Renascence: The Literature of the Modern South,* ed. Louis Rubin, Jr., and Robert D. Jacobs (Balti-

tions and Gothic forms proved an effective way to hide the autobiographical sources of his writing. He did not wish to reveal himself to the reader any more than William Faulkner did. Poe argued strenuously that "literary criticism" had to comment solely "upon *Art*" and nothing else.[51]

Some critics, however, have claimed that Poe was preoccupied with a different agenda. Edmund Wilson contends that the story "The Descent into the Maelström" embodies "a metaphor for the horror of the moral whirlpool" into which, with some justification, Poe had, as we know from more explicit stories, "a giddy apprehension of going down." But the story symbolizes the descent into the depths of despair and madness, not moral degeneracy in a corrupted commercial and slaveholding American republic. Likewise "The Pit and the Pendulum" has a larger meaning that conforms with the melancholiac's own impression of unremitting despair. Andrew Solomon, a novelist who describes his own descents into emotional hell, writes of the feelings of a fellow sufferer, Ted Instead. Hospitalized thirty times in seven years, Instead describes his sensations when in the throes of dejection: "It's like my head is in a vise, squeezing together. All I can do is obsess on the negative, and the pain is petrifying and physical. It's like I'm in a locked room and I can't get out and the walls are closing in and I'm being compressed and destroyed under the pressure."[52] Instead's account lends credence to this interpretation of the moving sides of the pit in Poe's short story. "I shrank back—but the closing walls pressed me resistlessly onward. . . . I struggled no more, but the agony of my soul found vent in one loud, long, and final scream of despair," Poe writes. At the last moment, he rescues his narrator in "The Pit and the Pendulum" from the final terror of death.[53]

Curiously, the perils of insanity found so frequently in Poe's work have been misinterpreted. One critic, for instance, has called "The Fall of the House of Usher," published in 1839, an exploration of "an enclosed planta-

---

more: Johns Hopkins University Press, 1953), 41, 43; James A. Harrison, ed., *The Complete Works of Edgar Allan Poe* (New York: G. D. Sproul, 1902), 14:198 (quotation); Edward Engelberg, *Elegiac Fictions: The Motif of the Unlived Life* (University Park: Pennsylvania State University Press, 1989); Allen Tate, "The Angelic Imagination: Poe as God," in *Collected Essays* (Denver: Alan Swallow, 1959), 432.

51. Jacobs, "Poe and the Agrarians," 46.

52. Andrew Solomon, "Anatomy of Melancholy," *New Yorker* (January 12, 1998): 55; Edmund Wilson, "Poe at Home and Abroad," in *A Literary Chronicle: 1920–1950* (New York: Doubleday, 1956), 75.

53. *Complete Tales and Poems of Edgar Allan Poe*, 257.

tion world—the 'garden of the chattel.' "[54] According to this view, Poe was allegorizing the coming sectional conflict. Such writers as Richard Wilbur have more plausibly argued that it was a "dream of the narrator in which he journeys 'into the depths of the self.'" Actually D. H. Lawrence came closer to the truth when remarking that the story centered on the individual personality "in a great continuous convulsion of disintegration." In his recent study of the Gothic tradition, Matthew Brennan persuasively suggests that Poe anticipated Carl Jung in his depiction of "the narrator as the dream ego, Roderick Usher as his shadow and Madeleine as his anima" or female component in his character. Throughout the story the mood of utter depression is sustained. The stress upon Roderick's emaciation, the appearance of the mansion itself as a human skull, with its "vacant eye-like windows," underscore the starved nature of the narrator's own depleted soul.[55]

With the menace of insanity as its basic theme, the story's dreamlike quality and abstraction are deliberate evocations. The tale of Usher's fall takes place in the realm of the imagination—but with a remarkable inner reality. The reader is not meant to contemplate matters of public policy regarding slavery but rather the hazards of irrationality, which is represented by the fear of premature burial. The idea of suspended animation and burial, in that twilight time when scientific medicine had just begun to advance, had popular appeal. Death remained the all-too-frequent outcome of most medical interventions. In the story, Usher's thoughts are confused. There is no certainty, no security anywhere; the center of being will not hold and madness or death is pending. In a life of sorrow and storm, the narrator stands terrified as he witnesses a cloud taking the shape of "a demon in my view."[56] One can imagine Poe himself was well acquainted with such phantasms and the fear they provoked. He once told a publishing colleague, who must have been perplexed, "I believe that demons take advantage of the night to mislead the unwary—although you know, I don't believe in them."[57] Intellectually he may have been telling the truth as he perceived it. On an emotional plane, however, he knew those impish creatures all too well.

In the hands of another writer such a link between imagination and real experience might seem far-fetched. Yet nearly every Poe interpreter finds

54. Simpson, *The Dispossessed Garden*, 65–71.

55. Matthew C. Brennan, *The Gothic Psyche: Disintegration and Growth in Nineteenth-Century English Literature* (Columbia, S.C.: Camden House, 1997), 135 (Wilbur quotation),136, 139; D. H. Lawrence, *Studies in Class American Literature* (1923; New York: Viking, 1961), 65.

56. Davidson, ed., *Selected Writings of Edgar Allan Poe,* 53–4.

57. Quoted in Silverman, *Edgar A. Poe,* 76.

similar interconnections in Poe's life and art. For instance, John Irwin observes that the Poe narrator, particularly the detective-criminal C. Auguste Dupin, is often estranged from his "illustrious family." Like Poe himself, he lives in semi-mad isolation. He is so completely divorced from the world that life seems confined to womblike security. The death of Poe's child-wife and cousin Virginia Clemm, only thirteen when he married her, figures in "The Murders in the Rue Morgue." Poe's love for his little family—the mother Maria Clemm and her daughter—was always ambivalent. He had managed at last to create a secure domestic group able to fill his emotional needs. Yet the women thrust upon him financial responsibilities that in the poorly paid profession of writing he could not meet. "One can well imagine," writes critic John Irwin, "that at moments Poe thought the price he had paid for domestic stability was too high and resented" anyone who stifled "his independence." Yet he felt ashamed of his own disloyalty to a mother and daughter who loved him.[58] The artist in Poe found expression for these difficulties in the gruesomely vivid descriptions of violence against both daughter and mother in "The Murders in the Rue Morgue."

As a depressive and alcoholic, Poe faced problems that may have been complicated by sexual impotence. That failure in the marital bed is perhaps represented in "Morella," "Berenice," and "Eleanora," in which the hero has either not engaged in lovemaking or has done so with too little blessing from the god "Eros." Poe's women are never happy for very long. Yet they scarcely articulate any frustration about the sexual inadequacies of their partners. That subject would have violated the Victorian code of reticence, which would not be broken for another half century or longer. Even Roderick Usher's infatuation with his sister is presented without reference to carnal longings by either party, dead or alive.[59] To break into autobiography on such a subject would scarcely do for any nineteenth-century American writer, most particularly a southern one for whom the posture of manliness was intensely prized and failures tucked away from the public eye.

Conventional about sex, Poe had no desire to deal with the subject, yet he grasped a different truth of the human condition: that madness is inheritable. In "The Fall of the House of Usher," for instance, Poe has Roderick Usher appear to the narrator as one subject to "an incoherence—an inconsistency . . . an excessive nervous agitation" such as Poe himself so often experienced. "His voice varied rapidly from a tremulous indecision . . . to

58. Irwin, *Mystery to a Solution*, 237.
59. Tate, "Our Cousin, Mr. Poe," in *Collected Essays*, 460; Irwin, *Mystery to a Solution*, 236.

that species of energetic concision . . . which may be observed in the lost drunkard. . . . It was, [Roderick] said, a constitutional and a family evil, and one for which he despaired to find a remedy." Usher is subject to "a host of unnatural sensations" and "a morbid acuteness of the senses."[60]

At some level Poe surmised that his own condition may have been familial in nature. He was most curious about his genealogy and loved to think he had such powerful medieval ancestors as some of the figures in his Gothic tales.[61] These connections would have added a special cachet, a romantic coloring to a genetic predisposition for the madness that he knew. Neurological and genetics work over the last twenty years, particularly with studies of twins separated early from each other, confirms the transmission of mental ailments through the genes.[62] We do not know with certainty that Poe's father was a depressive, but the indications are that he was. If so, the chances of the son being also afflicted, according to recent research, were almost one in three.[63]

A combination of parental losses and a genetic predisposition rendered Poe a victim of emotional collapse. For him it was most perplexing to account for his episodes of alcoholic abuse and madness. He wrote a poem titled "Alone" to express the sentiment. It begins: "From Childhood's hour I have not been / As others were—I have not seen / As others saw." He could find no joy; he could express no love. The poet traces the origin of his sorrow to his youngest years—at "the dawn of a most stormy life" from whence began "the mystery that binds me still." Throughout all the seasons and in all the places he has been, he is haunted by "a demon in my view."[64] Besides being a common signifier of depression in literature, that demon also represented anger against others as well as the self. Poe's preoccupation with retaliation against enemies in both his life and in his fictional representations is itself an indication of a deep level of fury that he could neither master nor understand. Though he craved notice and praise no matter how slight, he

60. *Complete Tales and Poems of Edgar Allan Poe,* 234–5.

61. Sarah Helen Whitman to Maria Clemm, 17 April 1859, in *Letters of Edgar Allan Poe,* ed. Harrison, 17:428.

62. See Kay Redfield Jamison, *Touched with Fire: Manic-Depressive Illness and the Artistic Temperament* (New York: Free Press, 1993), 193.

63. See Ming T. Tsuang and Stephen V. Faraone, *The Genetics of Mood Disorders* (Baltimore: Johns Hopkins University Press, 1990); Nancy J. C. Andreasen and Arthur Canter, "The Creative Writer: Psychiatric Symptoms and Family History," *Comprehensive Psychiatry* 15 (March/April 1974), 123–31.

64. "Alone," in *Complete Tales and Poems of Edgar Allan Poe,* 1026.

was savage in his criticism of literary mediocrity wherever he found it. A few months before Poe's death, a writer retaliated with some doggerel: "With tomahawk upraised for deadly blow, / Behold our literary Mohawk Poe! / Sworn tyrant he o'er all who sin in verse— / His own standard, damns he all that's worse. . . ."

Poe's battle against the literary establishment of New York and Boston three years before his death was itself a form of suicide. Although he never was as solitary and friendless as popular opinion supposed, the fracas cost him friends and induced him to live for a time in relative exile, thirteen miles out of New York at the village of Fordham. It was there that his wife, Virginia Clemm, expired in 1847. Surrounding her death was the turmoil of anonymous, poisonous letters delivered to Poe's doorstep. In retaliation Poe published gossip that he had no license whatsoever to air. The New York columns were filled with insults back and forth.[65] Still worse, after the death of Virginia Clemm, his mental health deteriorated with increasing speed. Manic-depression sometimes grows steadily more serious as the years pass, particularly if it is accompanied by alcoholism.[66]

Poe's attempted suicide with an overdose of laudanum, taken at a Providence, Rhode Island, hotel in November 1848, was the climax of his distraction. The widower had been courting Sarah Helen Whitman, a woman of intellect but older than himself. She had fallen in love with him and always remained a champion of his character. Yet she had the good sense to refuse his proposal of marriage. He fell to heavy drinking and sent her a note so hysterical in character that she worried about his dangerous "state of mental perturbation." Sarah Whitman feared that at any moment some calamity might erupt, as she later recalled. Poe had to be treated by a physician who found "symptoms of cerebral congestion." Her description of a scene shortly after the aborted suicide illustrated his frenzied mood. "A Mr. McFarlane, who had been very kind to Poe during the night" at the hotel, she recalled, "persuaded him" to sit for a daguerreotype.[67] Afterward, Mrs. Whitman reports, he arrived at the home of her mother "in a state of wild & delirious excitement, calling on me to save him from some terrible impending doom.

65. Sidney P. Moss, *Poe's Major Crisis: His Libel Suit and New York's Literary World* (Durham: Duke University Press, 1970); poem from *Holden's Dollar Magazine,* January 1849, quoted in Killis Campbell, *The Mind of Poe and Other Studies* (Cambridge: Harvard University Press, 1933), 59.

66. Jamison, *Touched with Fire,* 250.

67. The daguerreotype, incidentally, gives visible evidence of Poe's mental collapse. It is part of the Richard Gimbel Collection, Philadelphia Free Library.

The tones of his voice were appalling & rang through the house." Her mother had to deal with him for two hours before Mrs. Whitman appeared, and "he hailed me as an angel sent to save him from perdition." When she went to prepare strong coffee for him, "he clung to me so frantically as to tear away a piece of muslin dress I wore."[68]

In the afternoon Poe calmed down. His swings of mood, however, were clearly growing worse, and it engendered grave anxieties about the future. Soon afterward, he reported, "I went to bed & wept through a long, long, hideous night of despair." He woke at dawn and tried to walk off his mood "in the cold, keen air—but all *would* not do—the demon tormented me still." He dreaded that, unless he rid himself of his "fearful agitation," he would again try to kill himself or become "hopelessly mad."[69]

Certainly among the factors that burdened Poe's inclination to melancholy and suicide was his residence in the North. He was the only major southern poet or short-story writer to locate himself in the midst of that alien part of the country. In a period when the sections were growing ever more antagonistic, as his biographer Arthur Hobson Quinn remarks, "Poe's impulsive, excitable nature, his keen sense of personal honor and his contempt for purely material values, were not likely to endear him to the metropolis where standards were being based more and more upon commercial prosperity." Moreover, in his acerbic reviews and published comments, he had carelessly alienated the reigning New England poets—Henry Wadsworth Longfellow, James Russell Lowell, Ralph Waldo Emerson. The New York artistic circle was even less well disposed, to put the matter mildly. As an exile who felt increasingly isolated, Poe determined in 1849 to resettle in Richmond but once there felt immediately desperate and anchorless. He wrote his mother-in law, Maria Clemm, in New York, "It seems to me that I would make any sacrifice to hold you by the hand once more, and get you to cheer me up, for I am terribly depressed. . . . When I am away from you I am too miserable to live."[70] He found it impossible to live tranquilly in either sectional homeland but moved back to New York City.

Still more important in Poe's final slide into madness was the death of Virginia Clemm two years earlier. The loss had found poignant expression

68. Helen Whitman to John Henry Ingram, 25 October 1875, in *Poe Log,* ed. Thomas and Jackson, 766.

69. Edgar Allan Poe to Annie L. Richmond, 16 November 1848, in *The Letters of Edgar Allan Poe,* ed. Ostrom, 2:401–3.

70. Quoted in Arthur Hobson Quinn, *Edgar Allan Poe: A Critical Biography* (Baltimore: Johns Hopkins University Press, 1998), 616, 619.

in his poem "Ulalume" (1847), which Quinn considers Poe's most fully real-ized artistic expression. The poet mourns not only because the beloved is gone but because her death has robbed him of his essential existence—his soul. The poem explores forgetfulness, collapsed hope, delusion, and death. Each verse brilliantly records the poet's measured approach to Ulalume's tomb, a site to which he had brought her remains exactly one year before, "in the lonesome October / Of my most immemorial year." It is marked by somber repetitions, the reappearance of Poe's demon, and the coming of au-tumnal gloom:

> Then my heart it grew ashen and sober
>   As the leaves that were crisped and sere—
>   As the leaves that were withering and sere,
> And I cried: "It was surely October
>   On *this* very night of last year
>   That I journeyed—I journeyed down here—
>   That I brought a dread burden down here—
>   On this night of all nights in the year,
>   Ah what demon has tempted me here?
> Well I know, now, this dim lake of Auber—
>   This misty mid region of Weir—
> Well I know, now, this dank tarn of Auber,
>   This ghoul-haunted woodland of Weir."

In the poetic tongue, the onset of winter traditionally has been the season of darkest mood. Poe's lines bring to mind William Alexander Percy's "The Fifth Autumn," in which the poet walks by another river under the autum-nal trees, whose "brown leaves had fallen in slow spirals." The early-twenti-eth-century Mississippi poet of loss and unfulfilled desire confesses, " 'The fifth autumn is upon me,' I said, / 'And I have not forgotten.' " [71]

By some remarkable coincidence Poe died on 8 October, the month that had been the date for "Ulalume," published two years before. The circum-stances of death indicated an almost suicidal determination to abuse his health. After leaving New York by steamer, Poe, who had not tasted alcohol for some months, apparently ran into some old drinking associates in Balti-more. During the "terrible debauch" that ensued, he lost his trunk and

71. "Ulalume," in *Works of Poe*, ed. Harrison, 951–4; Quinn, *Poe*, 532–3; Bertram Wyatt-Brown, *The House of Percy: Honor, Melancholy and Imagination in a Southern Family* (New York: Oxford University Press, 1994), 207.

clothing. An acquaintance discovered him in a tavern, disheveled, soiled, and completely incoherent from alcohol. He and others took Poe to the Washington Medical College. There he remained until his death some hours later. The causes were certainly related to his binge drinking—possibly alcohol poisoning. Or more indirectly, he might have died from exposure to the cold and damp of the streets while out of his mind from drinking and depression. According to a recent speculation, he might even have been bitten by a rabid vermin or dog. Whatever the circumstances, his self-abandonment was evident in his erratic conduct.[72]

In a deep stupor upon his arrival at the hospital, Poe remained almost comatose for a time. When he woke, shaking uncontrollably, he entered a phase of "constant talking." John J. Moran, the attending physician, reported that he held "vacant converse with spectral and imaginary objects on the walls." When the doctor suggested that friends would soon contribute to his well-being, Poe cried that the best they could do for him "would be to blow out his brains with a pistol—that when he beheld his degradation he was ready to 'sink in the earth.'" A violent delirium followed. Just before he died, he moaned, "*Lord, help my poor Soul.*"[73]

Poe's struggle with life, sexuality, death, insanity, and artistic representation of themes aided immeasurably in establishing the tradition of alienation and loss with which so much of southern literature has ever since been endowed. Thanks in part to Poe, re-creating down-to-earth facts in an attempt at pure realism was not the southern way. Rather, he added to the overlay of romanticism so dear to the southern mind but chose to concentrate on the most joyless, the most negative, aspects of that dominant paradigm. Ironically, his treatment of death, dying, and lost love appealed to female poets and novelists, of both North and South, perhaps more than to the men. Mark Twain would make considerable fun of the death's head school in his portrait of Emmeline Grangerford in *The Adventures of Huckleberry Finn* and her memorable "Ode to Stephen Dowling Botts, Dec'd." Her "tributes" were so facilely rendered that "neighbors said it was the doctor first, then Emmeline, then the undertaker." Twain had based the satire on the popular versifier Julia A. Moore, the "Sweet Singer of Michigan." There were, how-

72. See John Evangelist Walsh, *Midnight Dreary: The Mysterious Death of Edgar Allan Poe* (New Brunswick, N.J.: Rutgers University Press, 1998).

73. Silverman, *Poe,* 432–4; Dr. John J. Moran to Maria Clemm, 15 November 1849, and William T. D. Clemm to E. R. Reynolds, 20 February 1889, in *Poe Log,* ed. Thomas and Jackson, 845–7.

ever, scores of others—Eleanor Percy Lee of Mississippi and Catherine Ann Warfield of Kentucky among them. They all trod Poe's lachrymose path to the graveyard.[74]

Given his poor moral reputation, it is hardly a wonder that Poe's immediate impact was greatest among the disaffected intellectuals of France and Russia. Drawn by the abstract, classically philosophical manner of Poe's Gothicism, such French poets as Charles Baudelaire, Stéphane Mallarmé, Arthur Rimbaud, and Paul Valéry acclaimed Poe's rapport with their own sense of alienation. Baudelaire may have felt a special affinity for the American, partly because he, too, had been reared in a well-to-do household but forced into what he interpreted as undeserved penury by unsympathetic, loveless parents.[75] Dostoevsky's plot in *Crime and Punishment* (1866) was prefigured in Poe's "The Tell-Tale Heart" (1843). The latter story concerns an obsessive murderer of an old man. The victim groans in terror, but his cries for mercy only inflame the criminal to do the motiveless deed. Even when three policemen arrive, the protagonist complacently shows them around the house, proudly convinced the crime was flawless. But before their departure, the narrator-killer can no longer pretend innocence and blurts out a self-defeating confession in an agony of guilt-ridden terror.[76]

Thanks in part to Poe, memorialists, thinkers, poets, and fiction writers in the South experimented, however tentatively, with an introspective approach. The culture of silence about the half-conscious world that inhabits us all prevented truly open exploration. Nonetheless, the foundations of southern pessimism, preoccupation with death and violence, suicide and incest, and other tragic circumstances were there from the start. As Poe's sad history discloses, the theme of elegy, exile, and threat of madness reaches back long before William Faulkner wrote *The Sound and the Fury*.

74. Mark Twain, *The Adventures of Huckleberry Finn* (Boston: Houghton Mifflin, 1963), 87–8. See Tom Quirk, *Coming to Grips with Huckleberry Finn: Essays on a Book, a Boy, and a Man* (Columbia: University of Missouri Press, 1993), 27; Julia A. Davis Moore, *The Sentimental Song Book* (New York: Platt & Peck, 1912); Bertram Wyatt-Brown, *The Literary Percys: Family History, Gender and the Southern Imagination* (Athens: University of Georgia Press, 1994), 59–87.

75. Lois Davis Vines, "Poe in France," in *Poe Abroad: Influence, Reputation, Affinities,* ed. Louis Davis Vines (Iowa City: University of Iowa Press 1999), 11; Bonaparte, *Life and Works of Edgar Allan Poe,* 669–97; Meyers, *Edgar Allan Poe,* 286.

76. Feodor Dostoevsky, *Crime and Punishment,* ed. George Gibian and trans. Jessie Coulson (1964; reprint, New York: W. W. Norton, 1975); Poe, "The Tell-Tale Heart," in *Complete Tales and Poems of Edgar Allan Poe,* 303–6.

II

SECTIONALISM, WAR, DEFEAT

2

Literary Fire-Eaters:
A "Culture of Failure"
Tucker, Hammond, and Ruffin

I here declare my unmitigated hatred to Yankee rule—to all political, social & business connection with Yankees—& to the Yankee race. Would that I could impress these sentiments, in their full force, on every living southerner, & bequeath them to every one yet to be born! May such sentiments be held universally in the outraged & down-trodden South, though in silence & stillness, until the now far-distant day shall arrive for just retribution for Yankee usurpation, oppression, & atrocious outrages—& for deliverance & vengeance for the now ruined, subjugated, & enslaved Southern States!
                    —Edmund Ruffin

POE was mad. Yet among the thinkers and belletrists of the South he was scarcely alone in that respect. None of the three writers discussed in this chapter proved as distracted as he. Yet their gloom, sense of thwarted ambitions, and vehemence sometimes bordered on unreason, almost to the point of clinical hysteria—what in the nineteenth-century medical accounts was described as neurasthenia. The condition involved physical problems and affective disquiet.[1] In fact, one of the most curious aspects of southern liter-

1. "Hysterical Men" in Elaine Showalter, *Hystories: Hysterical Epidemics and Modern Media* (New York: Columbia University Press, 1997), 62–77; F. G. Gosling, *Before Freud: Neurasthenia and the American Medical Community, 1870–1910* (Urbana: University of Illi-

ary history is the frequency with which a reactionary temperament was paired with depression during the pre–Civil War era.[2] The number of leading secessionist thinkers with deep-seated emotional problems defies easy analysis. I have particularly in mind Nathaniel Beverley Tucker, James Henry Hammond, Edmund Ruffin, and their intellectual cohorts, who shared their melancholy and their resentment of feeling disengaged from the rest of elite society. Michael O'Brien argues that these southern thinkers became intensely involved with Romantic ideas, unchecked by the counter claims of the neoclassical philosophies, which the European intelligentsia did not fully relinquish. Quite persuasively he notes, "Romanticism had special appeal for those who felt themselves on the periphery." In this respect, the antebellum southern intellectual elite resembled the Russians, who also embraced the Romantic mentalité with special "eagerness."[3]

This untrammeled Romanticism seemed to have a stifling effect on southern intellectual sensibility. After all, at the same moment in history, the northeastern intelligentsia flourished—Nathaniel Hawthorne, Henry Thoreau, Ralph Waldo Emerson, Herman Melville, and such lesser lights as Bayard Taylor, Washington Irving, and William Cullen Bryant. In contemporaneous Great Britain and France, Thomas Carlyle, John Stuart Mill, George Eliot, the Brontës, Charles Dickens, Gustave Flaubert, Baudelaire, Paul Valéry, and Stéphane Mallarmé were exploring new realms of human consciousness. Perhaps the need to preserve slavery did hobble the southern imagination, but other authoritarian societies developed less derivative and more stimulating literary cultures. Even czarist Russia, with its censorship, intrusive police, and serf system, was the home of Pushkin, Gorchakov, Gogol, and Turgenev, and later Tolstoy and Dostoevsky. A slavish dedication to the precepts of honor that held southerners in the iron grip of communal conformity inhibited free expression and turned disenchantment and

---

nois Press, 1987), 9. Gosling notes, "Neurasthenics were not insane—indeed many occupied important positions in business and society—but they suffered both mentally and physically. They complained of vague symptoms such as insomnia, headache, fatigue, dyspepsia, depression, and other ailments that prevented them from keeping up their former pace of life."

2. Tucker, Hammond, and Ruffin were not the only depressives belonging to the radical secessionist wing of the intelligentsia. See, for instance, Douglas Ambrose, *Henry Hughes and Proslavery Thought in the Old South* (Baton Rouge: Louisiana State University Press, 1997) and Bertram Wyatt-Brown, "Modernizing Southern Slavery: The Proslavery Argument Reinterpreted," in *Proslavery Thought, Ideology, and Politics,* ed. Paul Finkelman (New York: Garland Publishing Co., 1990). Others include William J. Grayson and George Frederick Holmes.

3. Michael O'Brien, *Rethinking the South* (Baltimore: Johns Hopkins University Press, 1988), 50.

alienation toward enemies abroad and not toward self-examination. Although choosing a later period to classify the southern literary scene as a "culture of failure," Lewis Simpson has coined a useful term. The date for its application should be moved backward to the antebellum period.[4]

No less important than the degree of parochial limits that southerners imposed on themselves was the southern intellectuals' tendency to perceive politics, rather than the creation of art, as the central issue. As Drew Faust first handsomely disclosed in A Sacred Circle, men of mind threw their inner worries upon a political canvas. They did so, however, not merely as a way toward power but as a form of emotional release from the alienation they felt within. That was the key to their common mindset.[5] In any event, anger, frustration, and projection of inner turmoil onto other objects or individuals, real and fictional, boiled up in the fire-eaters' rhetoric.

Most of these disunionist thinkers were polemicists without much interest in consciously literary expression. As David Donald observes, Edmund Ruffin's diary, which filled twenty-five manuscript volumes of 4,100 pages, was "no document of first-rate literary quality."[6] Nonetheless, these gentlemen of means and education must be treated with seriousness, though not for their artistic merits. They had few. Rather they were important in developing an antebellum southern mindset and therefore have appeared in nearly all works discussing the intellectual life of that era.[7] However artlessly, they wrote and spoke about the chief issues of their times, most especially the need to preserve their civilization, which rested on slavery, against

4. Lewis Simpson, The Fable of the Southern Writer (Baton Rouge: Louisiana State University Press, 1994), 12, 72.

5. Drew Gilpin Faust, A Sacred Circle: The Dilemma of the Intellectual in the Old South, 1840–1860 (Baltimore: Johns Hopkins University Press, 1977). Cf. Eric H. Walther, The Fire-Eaters (Baton Rouge: Louisiana State University Press, 1992), 6–7, which argues that there were more differences than similarities among the secessionist leaders. I find almost all of them angry, autocratic, honor-obsessed, and yet fatalistic souls.

6. David Donald, "The Diary of Edmund Ruffin," New York Times Sunday Book Review, 24 September 1974, 2.

7. Extended remarks on all three of these writers appear in Faust, Sacred Circle; Clement Eaton, The Freedom-of-Thought Struggle in the Old South (1940; New York: Harper & Row, 1964); Rollin G. Osterweis, Romanticism and Nationalism in the Old South (1949; Baton Rouge: Louisiana State University Press, 1967); William R. Taylor, Cavalier and Yankee: The Old South and American National Character (New York: George Braziller, 1961); Louis D. Rubin, Jr., The History of Southern Literature (Baton Rouge: Louisiana State University Press, 1985); Fred Hobson, Tell about the South: The Southern Rage to Explain (Baton Rouge: Louisiana State University Press, 1983); Richard Gray, Writing the South: Ideas of an American Region (1986; reprint, Baton Rouge: Louisiana State University Press, 1997).

a changing and hostile world. For most of them the obvious answer was
withdrawal from a contaminating union with the free states. They deemed
it a holy mission to arouse the South and alert it to the perils ahead. Their
unhappy cause outlasted their lifetimes, the devastating midcentury war,
and the troubled peace that followed. The fire-eating polemicists helped to
establish the regional literary tradition, however disappointing it was,
which only the most restive artists of the late nineteenth century had the
temerity to challenge. The two Virginians in the group, Edmund Ruffin and
Nathaniel Beverley Tucker, directly united fiction writing and radical political advocacy. (William Gilmore Simms, of course, was also a writer of tales
and narrative poetry; his contribution to southern letters, though, is treated
separately in the upcoming chapter.)

Nathaniel Beverley Tucker of Tidewater, Virginia (1784–1851), was the
first among this small group of zealots to advocate secession through the
vehicle of fiction. Like Ruffin, his successor in the field, Tucker loyally
served as a polemicist and propagandist for his home state. Behind Tucker's
rages against abolitionists, northern politicians, and the alleged tyranny of
central government, lay a record of death and gloom in family history. Despite strong aristocratic roots on his mother's side and high prestige on his
Bermudan father's, he admitted in 1839 to a relation that he had always felt
himself "an alien to my family." In 1792, Tucker's half brother Randolph
died in New York City while attending Columbia. Three years later, his
brother Thomas contracted a fatal disease. The most recent infant addition
to the family died the following September. In 1796 Tucker lost his eight-
year-old sister, and then Richard Randolph, another older half-brother, suddenly took ill. He expired in June of the same year.[8]

Above all other travails for Tucker, though, was the death of his mother
when he was only four. To that event, he later attributed his surrender to
"stupefying melancholy" and his compulsive dwelling upon "dark and
gloomy subjects." How greatly he had missed her gentleness and love, he
later recalled. If she had lived, he mourned, she would have recognized his
specialness, and he would not have felt the heavy hand of "severity . . .
harshness & oppression" to which his father, St. George Tucker, and teachers subjected him. Added to these woes was the departure of the family from
a plantation with its luxuries to Williamsburg, where his father began to
teach law at the College of William and Mary. The change of locale fright-

8. Faust, *Sacred Circle*, 24; Robert J. Brugger, *Nathaniel Beverley Tucker: Heart over Head in the Old South* (Baltimore: Johns Hopkins University Press, 1978), 26.

ened and exasperated the lonely, motherless child. He had left, he later reminisced, a garden of Eden and found himself in a hellish place where "I
almost learned to hate everyone with whom I had to do," most especially
his censorious and, he thought, loveless father.[9]

The accumulation of these blows, rather than just the maternal loss,
seemed to have prompted Tucker's sullen, belligerent demeanor, obstinacy,
and defiance toward teachers and classmates at school in Williamsburg. He
was determined to set himself apart from the high academic achievements
of his older brother Henry, whom he thought his father blindly idolized and
preferred over himself. Also hobbling his self-esteem was his subjection to a
disconcerting stammer. Tucker excelled at school only when a topic interested him, but otherwise mocked and ignored what he did not like. Professor Tucker was at a loss to know how to handle his obstreperous son.[10]

Later, as a law student at William and Mary, Tucker continued to be an
indifferent, sullen scholar. He found legal topics too dry, whereas history
and philosophy intrigued him. His half brother, the famous eccentric politician John Randolph of Bizarre, became one of his closest friends. A common bond might have been a mutual despondency. Not only did Randolph
and Tucker share a tendency to dramatize their angst, but Judith Randolph
felt the same throes of perturbation. She was the widow of Richard Randolph, another of Tucker's half brothers. On one occasion, John Randolph
urged Tucker to visit Bizarre to help him with "the task of soothing her
wounded spirits."[11] They had good reason to worry about her. Along with
Judith's sister, Nancy, Richard Randolph was implicated in 1792 in a case
of alleged infanticide and incest. For his part, Richard won acquittal, but
only by the exertions of attorneys Patrick Henry, John Marshall, and Alexander Campbell. It was a defense team that even O. J. Simpson might have
envied. Four years later, Richard died quite mysteriously and unexpectedly,
leaving the Tucker-Randolph households as gloom-ridden as ever.[12]

Adding to his distress, Tucker found his early law career at Charlotte
Court House lonely, unrewarding, and tedious. He fell into a serious depression. Tucker even confessed to his forbidding father how he could neither
sleep night after night nor shake off self-recriminations and doubts. He once
declared, as if yearning for a future session on the psychoanalytic couch,

9. Brugger, *Tucker*, 6, 12; Faust, *Sacred Circle*, 25 (quotation).

10. Faust, *Sacred Circle*, 25; Brugger, *Tucker*, 6–7.

11. Brugger, *Tucker*, 26.

12. Robert Davidoff, *The Education of John Randolph* (New York: W. W. Norton, 1979),
100–4.

"There are few in this world qualified to minister to the distempers of a mind like mine. I have always felt myself a stranger to this world, where I have rarely found any who could understand me, and enter into my feelings and keep pace with my thoughts."[13]

Dependent on his father's blessing and advice—often not taken—Tucker was stunned when St. George Tucker brusquely rejected his son's talk of impending matrimony. In his opinion the young attorney lacked the resources and the maturity for such a step. Marriage to Polly Coalter was postponed. Young Tucker reacted to parental intervention and to lack of success in the courtroom by blaming society or his father, not himself. The state of his law practice, however, was scarcely his father's fault. Ever the snob, Tucker was simply too fastidiousness about the cases he would take. It did not suit him to deal with the lower classes and their troubles before the bench. Did he not have an abundance of breeding, a sense of honor, and illustrious ancestors that should draw clients to his shingle without having to huckster his skills? Despite this lofty pose, however, Tucker all his life sought his identity in the opinions of others, a common practice in the Old South. "Everything with me," Tucker confessed, "depends upon the estimation in which I may be held."[14] Given the vagaries of popularity, it is easy to see how that approach may well have prompted volatile oscillations of mood.

Restive and hoping for a fresh start, Tucker and his bride Polly Coalter, whom he finally married, resettled near St. Louis, in the territory of Missouri. In the early 1820s, he became a judge and, for once in his life, enjoyed power, prestige, and life in general, despite losing two young children to illness. He resigned the judgeship, however, over a small local dispute. In the late 1820s, recuperating slowly from a serious dental infection, he grew ever more intemperate in language and quarrelsome with opponents. Yankee politicians, he protested, were "bloated vampyres sucking at the heart's blood" of the agrarian South and perverting the central government to satiate their greed. Robert Brugger, his biographer, puts the issue well: "Tucker's hatred of 'yankeys' was a kind of antisemitism without Jewry, a hobbyhorse that observers noted he was riding, and a response to perceived wrongs and 'foreign' values growing uglier."[15]

    13. Faust, *Sacred Circle,* 26.
    14. Quoted in Faust, *Sacred Circle,* 43. On the psychology of honor, see Bertram Wyatt-Brown, *Southern Honor: Ethics and Behavior in the Old South* (New York: Oxford University Press, 1982), esp. 46–7.
    15. Brugger, *Tucker,* 78.

Although scarcely reaching a point of violence or bizarre hallucination, Tucker's vituperations exceeded the bounds of ordinary political discourse, outrageous though that often was. Certain that the Nullification issue was the harbinger of the breakdown of the union with the despised Yankees, Tucker welcomed a chance to return to Virginia. There, he thought, the real battle against the northern foe should be initiated. With alacrity he took the chair of law at William and Mary, rejoicing at the chance to fill his formidable father's former role.[16]

In his capacity of instructor to the young, Tucker swiftly moved away from St. George Tucker's mildly antislavery position. Quite self-consciously in filial rebellion, he announced, "[We must] hold ourselves always on the alert to defend . . . [slavery] with tongue and pen."[17] Soon he was bristling with rage against the dishonorable calumnies of northern churchmen like Charles Grandison Finney and the small but vocal band of abolitionists. They sought, he contended, to obliterate the South in the name of a "Christian Charity and Brotherly Love" but had in mind slave insurrections and bloodthirsty chaos.[18] In 1836, in an effort to defeat Martin Van Buren, the northern Jacksonian leader, Tucker produced the novel *The Partisan Leader*. Hastily written and sloppily imitative of Sir Walter Scott's Scottish formulae, the tale is almost unreadable today. It closes with Virginia winning "her independence" with "the solid banner of her sovereignty" lifted "from the dust."[19]

Such banal sentiments indicated the problems in the creative literature of the region that southern men of mind had to resolve. Lacking much sense of the complexity of the human condition, Tucker in *The Partisan Leader, George Balcombe*, and in his journal essays showed little originality or cleverness. Instead he relied on the conventions of honor and the alleged villainy of the shameless Yankee. In the lofty, wooden language that romancers cherished, Tucker has the eponymous hero of *George Balcombe*, half Virginia gentleman and half grisly frontiersman, criticize a companion for being too self-effacing about his lineage. Balcombe boasts, "Is it not a higher honour to be sprung from a race of men without fear and without reproach—the ancient cavaliers of Virginia?" In the novel, such men were incapable of bending a knee to pretended authority. These valiant southerners were

16. Ibid., 79–90.
17. Ibid., 107.
18. Ibid., 110.
19. Nathaniel Beverley Tucker, *The Partisan Leader: A Tale of the Future* (1836; Chapel Hill: University of North Carolina Press, 1971), 392.

ready, even impatient, to pour "out their blood like water," and disperse "their wealth like chaff" when patriotism demanded sacrifice.[20] The views in the book represented Tucker's own position. No sign of introspection or self-examination intruded in his writing. His love for and resentment of his father, his frustrated rivalry with Henry Tucker—his elder brother and highly esteemed Virginia judge—and the early deaths of his mother and some of his siblings left their marks on his temperament. He raged against enemies as a way to release an anger that could find no other outlet.

Tucker's polemical writings against the Union reached a climax in the 1850 crisis. For years he had complained that Virginia's political leaders had cut him out of their deliberations. A combination of Whigs and Democrats in his congressional district named him an alternate delegate to the secession-headed Nashville Convention. Henry Wise, the chief delegate (who later became Virginia's governor on the eve of war), demurred so that the venerable Tucker could take his place. The old professor exulted that, despite his obscurity in the state and even in much of his own political district, he was at last on his way to major influence. Traveling through Cincinnati, where Irish brogues and thick German accents drove English speaking into the streets, as it were, the traveler despaired. Savage immigrants were fast overrunning American civilization.

In Nashville, Tucker caught up with former governor James Henry Hammond of South Carolina, and other secession zealots. Tucker discovered that he was one of the few radical participants to insist that a southern manifesto emerge from the convention's deliberations. The document that Tucker wanted ratified would have required concessions from the northern majority—stipulations assuring the perpetuation of slavery and the upholding of southern honor and power in national councils. If Congress denied the demands, Tucker advocated, the slave states should immediately withdraw. The convention, however, was safely in the hands of moderates. They sought only a return to the peaceable ways of past political compromises. When he had the chance to address the throng at the Methodist church meeting-hall, Tucker spoke of the ominous Yankee conspiracy that inspired the compromise measures of 1850. Unless the plots against slavery were checked, he warned, the nation would soon fall into the hands of merchant princes like those of old Venice. With enormous wealth in the hands of a small cabal, the vast majority of Americans would find themselves unem-

20. Quoted in Taylor, *Cavalier and Yankee*, 320–1.

ployed and in abject penury. Peaceful secession, he promised, was the sole solution.[21]

The forensic effort met no success. Tucker's voice was reduced to a scratchy whisper. In his passion, he skittered into incoherence. The outworn classical references, heady fare, perhaps, for his college students, won him no converts. A post-convention visit to Hammond's plantation Redcliffe did not lift Tucker's sagging spirits. Hammond's neighbors condescended to him—then in his late sixties—as if he were no more than an inoffensive old fool. Tucker returned to Virginia, but his reception there was scarcely pleasant. Published in the state papers, his Nashville Address blemished his reputation. To make matters worse, a "rabble of low demagogues," Tucker worried, were in the meantime pushing a new mobocratic constitution upon the state that would lessen the influence of the wise and good in the Tidewater counties. Power would accrue to the western, nonslaveholding region over the Blue Ridge mountains. Thoroughly discouraged, Tucker reported to Hammond, "I know [the constitution] will prove at once insolent and base." It would turn the Old Dominion over to "her enemies, persecutors & Revilers."[22]

The only hope left, Tucker concluded, was to arouse South Carolina to renewed boldness. He beseeched Hammond to help enlist the European powers in funding a rebellion against the United States. Otherwise, abolitionist conspiracies would widen in scope and effect. Tucker's plans for counterstrokes swelled ever more fantastically. He implored his compatriot to insist upon the unceremonious ousting of Carolinian officials who were perfidiously administering federal laws. Abolitionists caught in the state, Tucker demanded, had to be hanged forthwith. Re-enslave all free African Americans who failed to leave South Carolina, he suggested. Make it a capital crime to escape from slavery. Toward the end of his life in midsummer 1851, Tucker wrote Hammond, "There is Hope in Desperation, in despair none." Almost poignantly, the aging professor asked Hammond what use were old and decrepit men such as he? All they could do, he grieved, was "to lead forlorn hopes," die, and be buried, with "their bodies to be marched over by younger men." Perhaps these fresh troops could reap the harvest that Tucker's dying generation had sown.[23]

Not long after penning these dark thoughts, Tucker died. He did not see

21. Brugger, *Tucker*, 184–7.
22. Ibid., 188–9.
23. Ibid., 194.

the fruits of his rhetorical and fictional labors to sever the Union. Seldom in a cheerful state of mind, Tucker had judged his life a failure, and from the perspective of his contribution to the intellectual life of the South, his sentiment has validity. If he had lived longer, though, Tucker would have had still greater reason to mourn.

Like Tucker, James Henry Hammond did not survive to see the vanquishing of an independent Southland. Both shared the same spirit of pessimism and alienation that found its angry ventilation in defense of slavery and advocacy of southern self-reliance. Yet Hammond was more of a realist than the romantic law professor of Virginia. In the late 1850s he grew increasingly aware of northern might and southern weakness. By then it was too late to win nationhood for the slave states, he reasoned. Strict adherence to the precepts of honor might require a reckless disregard of consequences. Hammond was shrewd enough to seek less drastic solutions. In a speech at Barnwell, South Carolina, in 1859, Senator Hammond pointed out to a throng that the South's political strength had always won battles when its people were unanimous in their determination. He proposed a reknitting of old ties with northern conservatives. Although the northern press reacted favorably to his remarks, secession stalwarts quickly denounced his apparent betrayal of his former cause. In any event, the course he proposed was no longer possible. Northern conservatives recoiled from southern disunionist truculence.

Shortly after Abraham Lincoln's election in November 1860, James Chesnut of South Carolina and Robert Toombs of Georgia relinquished their Senate seats. Hammond did likewise. He wrote his son Marcus that resignation from office had become "an epidemic and very foolish. It reminds me of the Japanese who when insulted rip open their own bowels. . . . God knows the end."[24] South Carolina and soon the whole South would follow suit, he predicted. Sensible as his later views were, Hammond proved to be no less alienated, self-destructive, and even paranoid than the others in this unhappy cluster of thinkers.

Unlike most others in this study of dejection and intellectuality, Ham-

---

24. James Henry Hammond to Marcus C. M. Hammond, 12 November 1860, in Carol Bleser, *The Hammonds of Redcliffe* (New York: Oxford University Press, 1981), 88; see also James Henry Hammond to William Gilmore Simms, 13 November 1860, quoted in Drew Gilpin Faust, *James Henry Hammond and the Old South: A Design for Mastery* (Baton Rouge: Louisiana State University Press, 1982), 358.

mond had not lacked parental guidance and solicitousness. Far from it. His father provided his son with one moral admonishment or demand after another. While lacking the virtues he required of his offspring, he set criteria for achievement almost impossible for anyone to have met. The purpose was to force the youngster to accumulate all the successes that had eluded the old man. The young Hammond smarted from knowledge that his father, a New Englander, stood low on the local social ladder. He was a school teacher, often in debt, and ineligible for much recognition among the wealthy. Not surprisingly, though highly intelligent and handsome, the younger Hammond did not gain much sense of self-possession.

Pressed by Elisha Hammond and treated to frequent lashings, James Henry grew up torn between a rebellious urge to be himself and a desire to please his exacting father. He described his early turmoil in harrowing terms: "From my earliest recollections I now remember that I had nightmares & before I was 17 years old I had confirmed indigestion . . . that paralyzed intellect and shattered nerves." A lifetime of inner conflicts would be his undoing. As late as 1848, he mused, "I still fear myself that my acting may give out some day." His sense of inauthenticity undermined outward self-confidence and drive. "I often think I should be better off," he wrote, "if I had one of those thrashings my Father used to bestow on me—rather liberally, I thought then."[25] The sting of the lash might have made him feel more in touch with reality.

Determined to make a success at everything he did, Hammond adopted forms of coercion to serve his ends. They show how desperate he was to exercise control over others, as if to regain in adulthood the sense of self-mastery that his father had apparently taken from him as a child. He led an exploitative sex life. Quite possibly he sexually assaulted his roommate at college. After his marriage, he took on slave mistresses and abused the innocence of his nieces by marriage. As Louis Rubin observes, "He was a driving fury of self-aggrandizement, a political ideologue, a highly indulgent sensualist, a tyrannizing father and domineering husband."[26]

Yet Hammond had great gifts, even if they were employed in a doomed cause. His famous address in 1858, remembered for the phrase "Cotton Is King," was a powerful defense of the South's labor regime. Hammond's

25. Quoted in Faust, *Hammond*, 12, 13.
26. Louis D. Rubin, Jr., *The Mockingbird in the Gum Tree: A Literary Gallimaufry* (Baton Rouge: Louisiana State University Press, 1991), 86.

Letters on Slavery (1844), a response to abolitionist attack, was also masterful and widely circulated.[27] Contemporaries acknowledged his abilities and
expected him to rise perhaps as high in the country's estimation as John C.
Calhoun. Yet Hammond retained a pernicious ambivalence about success.
He yearned for it, needed it, but fear of friends deserting him, fear of his
lack of self-control and drive, fear of the future, raked him downward. Early
in his career, he mused, "And is life worth so much? Yes. No. I cannot de-
cide. Life without honor is the deepest damnation. Not to do your duty is
dishonor. To do your duty—wins honor—Destroys health—makes life a
burden. Thus we reason & the world works in a circle."[28]

For fifty years Hammond's diary remained hidden from public scrutiny
and, long after his death, was open solely to friends of Les Inabinet, head
archivist of the South Caroliniana Library in Columbia, and to interested
members of the Hammond clan. Then, in 1988, historian Carol Bleser
gained permission to publish the diary. In this remarkably candid if not truly
self-knowing document, Hammond offers almost stereotypical complaints
of the depressive personality. For instance, he protests in 1852, "I am left
alone. My mother never comes to see me. My wife never even sends a message unless it something to annoy me [she had uncovered his affair with
Louise, a slave]. Friends I have none. . . . I crawl about, and no one knows
what I suffer . . . and will not heed my complaints."[29] Nor did he have the
solace of religion: "I have not a Christian's hopes nor feelings. The comforts
of Religion are wholly wanting to me. As to the world, I am surrounded and
hemmed in by people entirely incapable of appreciating me."[30] During the
Civil War, as Sherman was preparing to begin the March to the Sea, Hammond may have accelerated his own death. He was already ill with hyper-
tension or cardiac problems, but an overdose of laudanum contributed to
his demise ten days later.[31]

27. Some of Hammond's speeches and letters have been thought historically significant
enough to be reprinted. See Clyde N. Wilson, ed., *Selections from Letters and Speeches of the
Hon. James Henry Hammond of South Carolina* (Spartanburg, S.C.: Reprint Co., 1978).

28. Quote from Hammond's Diary, February 14, 1839 or April 12, 1836, Hammond
MSS, Library of Congress, in Lawrence T. McDonnell, "Struggle against Suicide: James Henry
Hammond and the Secession of South Carolina," *Southern Studies* (Summer 1983):123.

29. Entry for June 7, 1852, in Carol Bleser, ed., *Secret and Sacred: The Diaries of James
Henry Hammond, A Southern Slaveholder* (New York: Oxford University Press, 1988), 255.

30. Entry for January 29, 1848, ibid., 188.

31. McDonnell, "Struggle against Suicide," 136–7; Edward Spann Hammond to Harry
Hammond, The Last Moments of J. J. Hammond, November 13, 1864, in Bleser, ed., *Secret
and Sacred,* 299–301.

Hammond had no more ambition to be remembered for his literary achievements than Ruffin or Tucker. Yet he, too, represented a style of the conservative, romantic southern mind, infused with the same ardent love of honor and yearning for reputation that gripped others in Faust's Sacred Circle. The outward and visible signs of the honorable hero were deeply ingrained in his character. But that style of behavior was self-defeating. Once he bitterly complained that his hospitality—signal of a magnanimous, honorable gentility—had not won him the applause that it should have. Instead, he insisted, it aroused jealousy among his rivals for office and helped to account for his humiliating defeat in his run for the U.S. Senate in 1846. "[John Laurence] Manning could not conceal it," Hammond seethed in his diary. "He built his home in Clarendon to beat me and he endowed a scholarship in College because I had presented to it a lot of land." But Hammond thought he had had the last word: "I beat them *in their own line*—furniture, balls, & dinner parties." They were all, he cursed, "purse-proud fools, who claim positions which God has not given them the intellects to win or to hold." (Hammond admitted, though, that the scandal about his sexual play, while state governor, with General Wade Hampton's teenage daughters contributed to the Senate-seat loss.)[32]

Unable to break from the cultural constraints and romantic honor-consciousness of his times, Hammond made as little use of his talents as Tucker had. None of these figures added much strength to southern letters. Nonetheless, they cannot be dismissed. They represented what the planter class stood for in cultural terms: defense of slavery, pursuit of a romantic conservative resurgence, religious orthodoxy, and radical dissent from the growing unity of the nation under northern advance in population, politics, and economic development. Recognizing the juggernaut of northern progress, gentlemen thinkers like Hammond, Tucker, and Ruffin had substantial reason to worry about the future.

Edmund Ruffin was the only one of these three ideologues to survey the rise and agonized loss of southern independence. In April 1861, eager to witness the moment of Confederate creation, Ruffin hurried to Charleston. There he joined the Iron Brigade of the Palmetto Guard facing Fort Sumter. General P. G. T. Beauregard selected that unit to begin the bombardment. The Iron Brigade elected Ruffin to be "their instrument" in setting off the first charge. "Highly gratified by the compliment to perform the service," he re-

32. Bleser, ed., *Secret and Sacred*, 174.

ported in his diary, "the shell struck the fort, at the north-east angle of the parapet."[33] For Ruffin, association with the young heroes of the artillery battery in Charleston Harbor had made all those years of seemingly fruitless agitation for disunion worth the effort.

Like the others in the Sacred Circle, Ruffin came to his radical convictions about southern secession through the fires of personal sorrow and resulting anger and desire for vengeance. Just as Tucker's long battle against northern conspiracies had roots in his own death-haunted family past, so too did Ruffin bear a heavy familial burden. Unanticipated fatality had been a constant presence in the Ruffin clan of Virginia. Epidemics of dysentery, typhoid, malaria, measles, smallpox, and diphtheria that had once held the seventeenth-century Virginia population nearly below the rate of natural increase seemed still to be holding sway in the Ruffin family's neighborhood.

Edmund Ruffin's father and grandfather were both the sole survivors in their respective families. The only fact the adult Edmund Ruffin knew about his mother was her name. She had died in his infancy. Not one of her kinfolk had survived to give the growing youth any information. When his father remarried in 1799, he chose a wife from the aristocratic Cocke family, whose record of early death matched his own family's roster. The second marriage produced for the young Ruffin three half sisters and a brother who was sixteen years his junior. In 1810, when Ruffin, sixteen, was attending William and Mary College, his father died. In terms of kin and family of natal origin, Ruffin was left entirely alone. More often emotional distress rather than physical debility afflicted the gloomy thinker, as it had in Tucker's case. A lonely, grieving child, Ruffin took his father's death very hard, as might be anticipated in a teenager. Like Tucker, he complained that in his youth he had suffered "neglect, slight, and contempt."[34]

After his father's passing, Edmund Ruffin became the charge of his uncle Thomas Cocke, a learned recluse whom he quickly and ardently came to love. In 1840, however, Cocke killed himself. In an autobiography, Ruffin offered details of the death scene and then minutely examined his own reaction to the tragedy. After a lengthy search for the missing planter, Ruffin's son discovered the nearly headless body in a thicket hidden from the house.

33. Entry for 12 April 1861, in *The Diary of Edmund Ruffin: Toward Independence October, 1856–April, 1861,* 3 vols., ed. William Kauffman Scarborough (Baton Rouge: Louisiana State University Press, 1972–89), 1:588.

34. Quoted in Faust, *Sacred Circle,* 33; "Gallery of Industry and Enterprise: Edwin Ruffin, Agriculturalist," *DeBow's Review* 11 (1851): 431–6.

"The corpse," wrote Ruffin, "was seated upright, in a natural posture." Cocke's back was resting against an ancient oak tree, and his "right hand, blackened with the burnt gunpowder[,] showed that it had grasped the gun near the muzzle." Cocke had removed his shoe to use the big toe to pull the trigger. Ruffin described the result of that last action: "Pieces of the scull [sic] some of them black from the burnt powder, and the brains were scattered all around." Ruffin helped to gather fragments. As might be expected, the event profoundly affected him. He wrote, "Long will it be before the vividness" of the scene "will be erased from the memory of those who saw it." At night for years to come, Ruffin confessed, his "painful feelings & shattered nerves" made him feel "almost afraid to look around, lest the object which so dwells on my mind's eye should be more palpably present, & thus demand of me more strongly & sternly than does my own heart, 'Why did you to make no effort to prevent this deed?'" At first, though, he admitted to a sense of denial and "dull & torpid feelings . . . hardness of heart." Terror and guilt were uppermost. Ruffin thought that if only he had been more direct and confrontational when Cocke hinted that he thought life meaningless, he could have drawn him back from the brink. No doubt his initial denials of feeling stemmed from his earlier parental losses, now repeated. Gradually, however, Ruffin surrendered to "remorse" and "grief." He vowed to "write down the strange and horrible circumstances" so that he would never forget them and ever be reminded how it felt to lose one's capacity to feel.[35]

Of course, Ruffin was flagellating himself unfairly. It is true that suicides can be prevented *in some instances* by improving external conditions and engaging in close conversation. At some point, the determined suicide, however, will do the deed regardless of vigilant care-taking. Cocke's situation, one might speculate, fell into the latter category. He had written a note that Ruffin later found. "When I look forward, even hope itself suggests no relief," the suffering Cocke explained. "I find myself not only a burthen on myself, but entertain no hope that my permanence in this world can essentially aid my dear children." He threw his decision to end it all before God

35. David F. Allmendinger, Jr., ed., *Incidents in My Life: Edmund Ruffin's Autobiographical Essays* (Charlottesville: University Press of Virginia, 1990), Appendix 2, 179, 184–5; see also David F. Allmendinger, Jr., *Ruffin: Family and Reform in the Old South* (New York: Oxford University Press, 1990); David F. Allmendinger, Jr., "The Early Career of Edmund Ruffin, 1810–1840," *Virginia Magazine of History and Biography* 93 (April 1985):127–54; William Kauffman Scarborough, "Introduction," in Ruffin Diary, ed. Scarborough, 1:xv–xlv.

and commended his soul to "the Mercy of Heaven."[36] Ruffin had an example set before his eyes—how to do it and why.

Years later, further troubles returned Ruffin's mind to the bleak prospect of extinction. In the intimacy of his diary, the Virginian recorded a series of unrelenting family deaths in the 1850s that left him susceptible to thoughts of his own end. In 1859, aware of declining health and increased deafness, he remarked that he had little desire to undergo a "wearisome passage of time" that would "make my life too long." After witnessing the triumph of secession, which he had so long advocated, he spoke of mortality, not joy. "I have now lived long enough," he asserted.[37] On 4 October 1859 Ruffin's daughter Mildred was married. It was, Ruffin sighed, "a dismal time for me." He elaborated, "If I had died five years ago, how much of unhappiness would have been escaped!" Ruffin was left to his own devices—just as he had been when a child. It was a state of existence that held little appeal: "I fear that I am now about to enter that condition of idleness & wearisomeness which I always dreaded—which I have until now kept off by keeping my mind occupied with some study or pursuit."[38] Ruffin thought seriously of doing away with himself.

Then came news of John Brown's raid at Harper's Ferry in October 1859, and Ruffin once more found hope for his disunionist dream.[39] He traveled to the subsequent trial of the conspirators in Charlestown, Virginia, and went on to Washington to confer with slave-state politicians about the crisis. With spirits revived, he began feverishly to write a novel about the breakup of the Union, titled *Anticipations of the Future, to Serve as Lessons*

36. Allmendinger, ed., *Incidents in My Life,* 185. Kay Redfield Jamison, *Night Falls Fast: Understanding Suicide* (New York: Knopf, 1999), 268–74, points out that sophisticated training in suicide prevention can make a difference, but the techniques were scarcely available to Ruffin at the time. Neurological factors may predispose individuals with low serotonin levels or other kinds of chemical imbalances in the brain to severe depression, which in turn may spark thoughts of suicide. Jamison cites, for instance H. van Praag, "Depression, Suicide, and Metabolism of Serotonin in the Brain," *Journal of Affective Disorders* 4 (1982): 275–90. See this and other references in Jamison, *Night Falls Fast,* 370–1.

37. Entry for October 18, 1859, in *Ruffin Diary,* ed. Scarborough, 1:348. This "calmness" was a signal of a deeper depression than he realized, a numbness that indicated a repression of anger and grief betokening his later suicide. I am indebted to David F. Allmendinger, Jr., *Ruffin: Family and Reform,* esp. 169–84, but the author does not suggest that Ruffin may have suffered from an unremitting depression. His preoccupation with death suggests a morbid tendency, however, and clearly the Ruffins were aware of his state of mind.

38. Entry for 4 October 1959, ibid., 1:346.

39. Entries for 19, 21, 23, 24, 25 October 1859, ibid., 1:348–50.

for the Future. His "plan," he noted in his diary, was to recount the exciting events through the words of a London newspaper correspondent covering the second administration of President William H. Seward. In Ruffin's imagination, Seward was the most fanatical of the hated Republican leaders. His purpose was to show how submission to such a fate would mean for the slave states "virtual bondage to the North."[40]

To reveal the possibility of slow erosion of southern rights, Ruffin paints a picture in his novel of an increasingly antislavery Congress and President Seward gradually enfeebling the South with high tariffs, restrictions on slavery, and antisouthern Supreme Court appointments. Abolitionists like Wendell Phillips and Hinton Helper of North Carolina take federal posts. Southerners thought that Helper's *The Impending Crisis* was a work of sheer treachery. Ruffin has him appointed a "Receiver of the Lands Office."[41] Ruffin's fictional southerners are at first incapable of bold action. The moral risks that failure of nerve in the border states make worse is the "lesson" Ruffin sought to preach. Though discontented, the upper South slaveholders remain "silent and subdued and sullen."[42] By the time southerners awaken fully to their peril, Seward has split up the northern states into smaller units until they control a three-fourths senatorial majority. By that means slavery could be constitutionally abolished through the amendment process. In 1868, with the upper South still uncommitted to secession, the six states of the Deep South withdraw. South Carolina seizes Fort Sumter in Charleston Harbor, where, indeed, the first shots of the war did occur. Finally aroused, the people of the upper South join their brethren against Federal invasion. With grim pleasure, Ruffin describes how Union troops and sailors on burning warships meet ghastly ends in warring against the brave "Southrons." Despite abolitionist conspiracies to incite slave rebellions, slaves reject the opportunity for freedom to stay loyally in thralldom. Even fugitive slaves return South to find their old masters or, failing that, someone else. With much satisfaction the fire-eating novelist depicted the economic ruin of northern commerce and industry because of the disruptive war and the loss of southern trade. New York City is practically razed in bloody riot and anti-abolitionist fury—a prefiguring of the anarchy that did strike the city in 1863. After only six months, the North sues for peace. In-

40. Entry for 1 March 1860, ibid., 1:408.
41. Edmund Ruffin, *Anticipations of the Future, to Serve as Lessons for the Present Time: in the Form of Extracts of Letters from an English Resident in the United States, to the London Times, from 1864 to 1870* (Richmond, Va.: J. W. Randolph, 1860), 38.
42. Ruffin, *Anticipations of the Future,* 33.

dependence for the slave states is assured. Ruffin's war is short—a six-month affair—and relatively painless for the South. New England is thoroughly humiliated because its midwestern allies are so impressed with southern success that they seek to join the slave states in a new confederation.

Anticipations of the Future came to over four hundred pages, but it was obviously more polemic than art. In its impassioned prose, especially toward the end, it has an almost manic energy, as if Ruffin himself had shed for a time his corrosive pessimism. Even in the midst of war, when he was once more enveloped in gloom because of relentlessly bad military news, he took pleasure in reviewing his 1860 fantasy. In 1836, Ruffin had read Tucker's *The Partisan Leader* upon its first appearance. In 1864 he reread it with much more interest. In his diary, Ruffin remarked that Tucker's fiction had not received much attention twenty-five years earlier, and "it had nearly passed into oblivion." Upon its republication during the war, however, it was "praised, not for its real & great merit, but as being generally & remarkably prophetic of the subsequent incidents of secession—which it certainly is not—though as much so as could be expected from a fore-teller so much earlier than the supposed events." Ruffin mused that his own work was far inferior in execution and literary invention. Yet he congratulated himself on being the more accurate forecaster of events. He closed his thoughts on the matter by hoping that both novels would earn a place in a Confederate literary canon some time later.[43] That outcome was not to be.

Ruffin was happy and excited while composing his disunionist fantasy. Yet the indifferent reception that greeted the publication of *Anticipations* beckoned him toward a renewed sense of futility. Only four hundred copies were disseminated, some of them given away or sent out for review. In his diary, he bemoaned his lack of success: "It is to me a mortifying truth, that, instead of being . . . welcome, my book has been scarcely noticed, & its very existence seems to be ignored by the public, even in the more southern states, where, if no where else, I expected notice & approval."[44] At the same time, Ruffin was busy corresponding with other secession leaders. He wrote William L. Yancey that Alabama must step into the vanguard of disunionism, complimenting him for possessing the talent, prestige, and eloquence to rouse the lower South to its duty. Ruffin, though, could not hide his own sense of alienation and inadequacy. "Already & for years past in a differ-

43. Entry for 3 October 1864 in *Ruffin Diary,* ed. Scarborough, 3:592–3.
44. Entry for 21 February 1861, ibid., 1: 554.

ent & far less effective mode," he confided to Yancey, "I have labored (by writing & publishing my views), to influence the public mind in this great object—but with small success" because of his "obscure name & position, & limited powers."[45]

While lamenting public indifference to his novel, Ruffin took heart in the outrage throughout the South that greeted Lincoln's presidential victory. A real war was about to begin. Momentarily the prospect lifted him from an inner rage he never fully understood. Euphoria proved short lived. Death once more ravaged the Ruffin household. Biographer David Allmendinger observes that Edmund Ruffin was the parental exception in knowing his children as well as he did. All the other Ruffin progenitors, back to 1700, had not lived long enough to rear all their children. "From the time the family first settled in Prince George County, only his great-grandfather had known more than one grandchild," Allmendinger reports.[46] Having already lost an infant daughter and son years before, Ruffin between 1844 and 1861 buried his wife, four daughters, two grandchildren, and a favorite daughter-in-law. Then, in the midst of the civil conflict, two granddaughters and another daughter died. Ruffin was surprised at the "calmness, & insensibility with which I received the news of [Mildred's death]." She had been his "most beloved remaining child." Also, his grandson Julian Beckwith was killed in 1862 defending Richmond at Seven Pines.[47] That was a blow of special magnitude. The young soldier had been peering over the top of his artillery unit's redoubt when a shell literally beheaded him.

All Ruffin's expressions of grief were confined to a journal that he showed no one in his lifetime. Instead, he turned his rage against adversaries—chiefly Virginia politicians, Yankees, and abolitionists—all of whom he categorized as dull-witted wretches. During a period of unhappiness over familial losses, Ruffin began writing up his private thoughts—as his sole employment, he said—as if to fill a deep void in his life. Gradually he relinquished life—no longer walking for exercise or enjoying visits of friends. Instead, he sat "alone," as he once put it, "with my own wearisome thoughts as companions." In 1864 he remarked, "Every day of my life is a continuation of the same unvarying affliction of *ennui*—wearysomeness [*sic*] of everything, including life itself. There is for me no alleviation, no

45. Edmund Ruffin to William L. Yancey, 29 October 1860, ibid., 3:635.
46. Allmendinger, *Ruffin: Family and Reform*, 60. See also William Kauffman Scarborough, "The Ruffin Family," in *Ruffin Diary*, ed. Scarborough, 2:xxiii–xxvi.
47. See also entry for 24 July 1863, in *Ruffin Diary*, ed. Scarborough, 3: 81–2.

remedy, until death shall relieve me."[48] Yet such were the circumstances of Ruffin's era that, even in this secretive form, he did not explain the sources of his agony—if indeed his conscious mind knew them. He confined himself to being no more introspective or confessional than he would "with any of my intimate & confidential friends, or of my own children."[49]

Having symbolically begun a war that he so strenuously hoped for, Ruffin had to watch helplessly as his dream of retribution against the Yankees faded over the next four years. The country he loved had become a bloodied and despoiled victim of its own folly, a calamity that he did not wish to survive. Perhaps the self-destruction that he so often contemplated was being played out in his mind in the immolation of the South itself. He ended his own life, 18 June 1865, after the surrender of Edmund Kirby Smith, the last general officer to lay down arms. Ruffin left a testament, quoted in the epigraph for this chapter, that cursed the forced reunion and revealed once again his wrathfulness against life, against nation, against reality. The rest of his final words heaped further curses on the victors: "May the maledictions of every victim to the malignity, press with full weight on the perfidious Yankee people & their perjured rulers." He especially damned the invaders and their record, as he put it, of "robbery, rapine & destruction, & house-burning, all committed contrary to the laws of war on non-combatant residents & still worse on aged men & helpless women."[50]

As if it were all part of some inevitable scheme, Ruffin faced the end of the Confederacy and that of his own life with a surprising sense of deliberation and calmness of manner. In his journal, Ruffin wrote that he had devoted two months of reading and contemplation to the idea. He had only delayed the decision because of impending family nuptials and the arrangement of affairs, as well as "some matters of public importance, after the surrender of Gen. Lee's army, which I desired to know the end of." But the trans-Mississippi armies also surrendered.[51]

During that period, Ruffin studied the history of the Ancient Near East and the Holy Scriptures to find religious answers to the prospect of self-destruction. He pondered the mass self-slaughter of the Jews in 70 A.D. in

48. Entry for 6 January 1864 and 2 April 1864, ibid., 3:303 and 384. "I am anxious," he wrote, on May 27, 1859, "to keep employed, & writing is my only employment." (Ibid., 1:xxiii and 304.)
49. "Introduction to the Attempt," October–December 1856, in *Ruffin Diary*, ed. Scarborough, 1: 5–20.
50. Entry for 18 June 1865, ibid., 3:946.
51. Entry for 16 June 1865, ibid., 3:945.

their war against the Romans. When all hope had vanished, he wrote in his diary on 16 June, fathers and husbands slew their wives and children and then turned the swords on themselves at Jotapata, Joppa, Gamala, and Masada. They had broken no Mosaic law, Ruffin took satisfaction in noting. He rationalized that most Christian martyrs had more or less willed their own deaths—"voluntary acts of self-sacrifice." Besides, neither the Old nor New Testament prohibited suicide. Ruffin also reasoned that he could do no more for his family than he already had. Plantations Beechwood and Marlbourne were in ruins, his extensive library scattered or burned. Living in his son Edmund's house was a dependency that degraded him. Ruffin argued to himself that he was now useless—too old in body, too damaged in spirit to add anything to the world's or his family's material and intellectual storehouses. Self-destruction was injurious to the survivors only if they had not been otherwise provided for. Satisfied that nothing further encumbered his departure from life, he went upstairs to his bedroom at ten o'clock on the morning of 18 June, intending to end his existence. Some well-wishers arrived, however, and he wanted no one about the house except family when the deed was done. Finally, the guests left. At 12:15, he was prepared to carry out the plan. The first attempt failed. A loud concussion rang out. The cap had not ignited the powder. Alarmed by the noise and suspecting what had happened, the women below ran out of the house to call the men in the fields. Meantime, Ruffin replaced the cap. On the second try, the firearm worked properly, and Ruffin was dead before anyone could climb the stairs.[52]

Kay Redfield Jamison, a specialist on manic-depression and suicide, writes that something ignites the self-destructive act—some event or series of events of a disturbing nature.[53] But behind the obvious and immediate source of Ruffin's anguish—the loss of the Confederate cause—other and more determinative factors may have predisposed this sufferer toward self-dissolution. Certainly Thomas Cocke, a man he considered highly moral, had offered him an efficient example. Ruffin imitated his guardian's exact procedure. Over the years Ruffin had ruminated about Thomas Cocke's deadly resolve, but he had long been impressed with how the old planter had been so intent to seize governance over his own destiny. Orphans feel

---

52. Entry for 16 June 1865, ibid., 3:941–5; Betty L. Mitchell, *Edmund Ruffin: A Biography* (Bloomington: Indiana University Press, 1981), 255–6. Curiously, the season for suicides seems to be late spring and early summer in many countries, including the United States, and the pattern falls away from July to December. See Jamison, *Night Falls Fast*, 207.

53. Jamison, *Night Falls Fast*, 200.

deprived of control over their lives by the insecurity attending sudden parental losses. Once grown, Ruffin sought to fill that deficiency by his own exertions.[54] He would not let fate take charge. He had to be in command of his
life—and of his death. Ruffin placed himself in a sitting position, putting his
back firmly against the chair, just as Cocke had situated himself with his
back resting against the oak. Ruffin then pointed the muzzle of the rifle at
his face. He did not remove his shoe to use a toe but, improving on Cocke's
method, applied a forked stick to pull the trigger.

Reasons for living were there to be seized had Ruffin so wished. He knew
that the new Unionist government in Richmond and in Washington had no
intention of hanging him or imprisoning his relations. Even he was surprised
that the freedmen had gone back to working—and for less subsistence than
he figured they had received as slaves. Loving kinfolk surrounded him, and
grandchildren's laughter and tears animated the household.[55] But fear of old
age, dread of starting over almost from scratch without the strength of heart
to do it, and his own sad history—these factors found voice in his final out-
cry against the detested Yankees and the Union. That testament of hate was
hardly less rueful than the deed itself. The impulse to commit suicide is often
a form of irrationality, if not insanity, and those suffering in its grip should
be treated as humanely as possible. But a loathing of his fellow Americans
on the order to which Ruffin elevated it can never be judged ennobling or
inventive. Such patently uncontrolled ire and sectional bile was to stain the
literary culture of the South for years to come, even when mellowed down
to the sentiments of the "Lost Cause." Projecting fears and monstrous
dreams of destruction upon a political landscape could not create art. Yet it
affected the southern literary climate as a whole.

54. For some clinical observations on childhood loss and later problems of depression and
suicide, see Donald W. Winnicott, "A Child Psychiatry Case Illustrating Delayed Reaction to
Loss," in *Drives, Affects, Behavior,* 2 vols., ed. Max Schur (New York: International Universities Press, 1965), 2:212–42; Alistair Munro, "Parental Deprivation in Depressive Patients,"
British Journal of Psychiatry 112 (1966):443–57; M. J. Gay and W. L. Tonge, "The Late Effects of Loss of Parents in Childhood," *British Journal of Psychiatry* 113 (1967):753–59; O. W.
Hill and J. S. Price, "Childhood Bereavement and Adult Depression," *British Journal of Psychiatry* 113 (1967):743–51; Alistair Munro, "Some Familial and Social Factors in Depressive Illness," *British Journal of Psychiatry* 112 (1966):429–41; Martha Wolfenstein, "Loss, Rage,
and Repetition," *Psychoanalytical Study of the Child* 24 (1969):432–60.

55. Allmendinger, *Ruffin: Family and Reform,* 171–6; entries for 17 July 1862 and 5 January 1863, in *Ruffin Diary,* ed. Scarborough, 2:378–9 and 531; Ruffin to Edmund, Jr., 17 May
1864, ibid., 3:426–27; and entry for 7 June 1864, ibid., 455.

Edgar Allan Poe
*Courtesy Rare Book
Department, The Free
Library of Philadelphia*

Edmund Ruffin
Courtesy Virginia Historical Society

James Henry Hammond
*From a copy, courtesy of South
Caroliniana Library, University of
South Carolina, Columbia*

William Gilmore Simms
*From a copy, courtesy of South
Caroliniana Library, University of
South Carolina, Columbia*

Mirabeau B. Lamar
*Courtesy Austin History Center,
Austin Public Library*

Abraham Lincoln
*Courtesy Illinois State
Historical Library, Old State
Capitol Building, Springfield,
Ill., 62701*

Theodore O'Hara
*Courtesy The Filson
Historical Society,
Louisville, Ky.*

Sidney Lanier
*Ms. 7, Sidney Lanier Papers, Special
Collections and Archives, The Johns
Hopkins University*

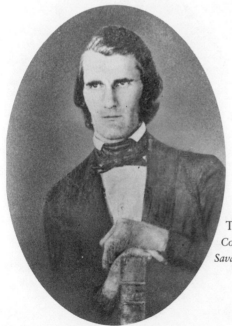

Thomas H. Chivers
*Courtesy Georgia Historical Society,
Savannah, Ga.*

Abram J. Ryan
Frontispiece from Abram J. Ryan,
Poems: Patriotic, Religious, Miscellaneous
(New York: P. J. Kennedy & Sons, 1896)

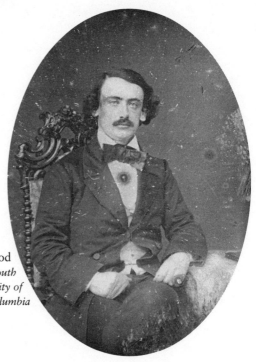

Henry Timrod
From a copy, courtesy of South
Caroliniana Library, University of
South Carolina, Columbia

3

The "Golden Goal" Unachieved
William Gilmore Simms & Co.

The spirit was within him, & he strove,
Unqualified by base desire or deed,
Most nobly though perchance he never won,
The golden goal he sought.
—William Gilmore Simms

FROM the beginning of the Cavalier South, roughly 1830, the region's belletrists seldom wrote in an overtly autobiographical, self-revealing style. Nevertheless, along with Poe, they helped to set in southern letters a tradition of social, intellectual, and emotional alienation. Michael O'Brien has observed that by and large they were "not a happy crew" and the "tone of antebellum southern romanticism" was so gloomy that these thinkers were seemingly preparing themselves for the coming "disaster of war."[1] Unlike the interior struggles and goads that tormented Poe, however, their anguish most visibly arose from external factors—their relationship to planter society at large. But the same pattern of intrinsic alienation that Poe experienced also appeared unmistakably in their lives to a lesser but still significant degree.

1. Michael O'Brien, *Rethinking the South: Essays in Intellectual History* (Baltimore: Johns Hopkins University Press, 1988), 51.

Such developments might appear as scarcely southern in character. Intellectuals are a suspect lot in nearly every culture—in the police state of czarist Russia and even in prudish and closed-minded England. Writers from Lord Byron to Oscar Wilde keenly felt the lash of condemnation. The bells of melancholy tolled mournfully throughout the works of many artists in Western society, especially when romantic subjectivity opened new but not yet wholly self-revealing expression. But there was a difference between the southern form of dolor and that, for instance, of Puritan New England. Literary critic Lewis Simpson argues that "a culture of alienation"—that is, a separation of the intellectual from his or her social and political surroundings—was a northern phenomenon. That sense of apartness affected, he rightly observes, the outlook of Nathaniel Hawthorne, Herman Melville, Henry Thoreau, Walt Whitman, Emily Dickinson, and others who created the New England Renaissance. Indeed, some of these writers also had reasons early on for feelings of abandonment that left them scarred by grief for the rest of their lives. Nathaniel Hawthorne lost his father, Nathaniel Hathorne, when the child was almost four. A sea captain who was seldom ashore, Hathorne died in Surinam from yellow fever in 1808. Many of Hawthorne's stories reflected the repressed anger and sense of isolation that his father's death helped to create in him. Writing, for him, as well as for others who have heeded the literary calling, was at least in part a later response to unresolved mourning. As his biographer Edwin H. Miller phrases it, in his last, semi-autobiographical fiction, *Septimius Felton,* Hawthorne struggled "like Jacob with an elusive demon to tell and at the same time not to tell his life story."[2]

Although southern antebellum writers generally came from respectable people, the northern ones were, paradoxically, more aware of their ancestors' prominence, a status almost aristocratic or as close to it as Americans were ever likely to reach. But that lineage could be a source of guilt as well as pride. "Let us thank God for having given us such ancestors; and let each successive generation thank him, not less fervently, for being one step further from them in the march of the ages," Hawthorne observes in one of his stories.[3] He had in mind the cruelty, superstition, and self-satisfaction of his progenitors, most notably John Hathorne, the justice who presided over the

2. Edwin Haviland Miller, *Salem Is My Dwelling Place: A Life of Nathaniel Hawthorne* (Iowa City: University of Iowa Press, 1991), 496.

3. Nathaniel Hawthorne, "Main-Street," in Nathaniel Hawthorne, *Tales and Sketches* (New York: Library of America, 1982), 1039.

infamous Salem witch trials and saw to it that wandering Quakers were thoroughly thrashed in the streets. Hawthorne's sense of alienation arose partly from his distress with New England narrow-mindedness, a bequest from the prior generations of Hawthornes.

Preoccupied with the defense of slavery, the South, Simpson contends, could not, or at least would not, permit a division of high intellect from the popular mind. Southern alienation was much more personal in nature. It was not based, to borrow from Simpson, upon a "pastoral reaction to modernity" as the world became more commercial, industrial, urban. The South had yet to undergo such a rapid state of change.[4] When southern writers expressed their dissent from modernity, they identified it with northern commercialism, usury, absurd utopian theories, belching smokestacks, clanking industrial wheels. For their part, these writers' frequent complaint against fellow southerners centered on the illiteracy of the poor and the indifference of the hunting and fishing rich to matters of culture. The southern conservative dissenter thought that the world of eighteenth-century noblesse oblige offered an ideal counterpoint to modern crassness. John Pendleton Kennedy's ironic, Polonian novel *Swallow Barn* and William Gilmore Simms's nostalgia for a more heroic, Revolutionary past in his historical romances revealed such a tendency. Writing to an editor of a brand-new magazine designed for southern ladies, Simms pronounced his sad conviction about the journal's prospects: "When I sit down to write for a Southern periodical . . . I do so under the enfeebling conviction that my labors and those of my editor are taken in vain;—that the work will be little read, seldom paid for, and will finally, and after no very long period of spasmodic struggle, sink into that gloomy receptacle of the 'lost and abused things of earth.'" On an earlier occasion of similar discontent, Simms had likewise allowed such diffidence to affect his way of thinking about himself: "I have been an exile from my birth, and have learned nothing but to drudge with little hope, and to think and feel and act for myself."[5]

Henry Augustine Washington of Virginia lamented that even the well educated among his compatriots could scarcely name even one or two of the commonwealth's "colonial heroes." He thought such blatant ignorance

4. Lewis Simpson, *The Dispossessed Garden: Pastoral and History in Southern Literature* (1975; reprint, Baton Rouge: Louisiana State University Press, 1983), 35.

5. William Gilmore Simms to James Henry Hammond, 20 May 1845, in *The Letters of William Gilmore Simms,* 6 vols., ed. Mary C. Simms Oliphant, Alfred Tylor Odell, and T. C. Duncan Eaves (Columbia: University of South Carolina Press, 1953–82), 2:515; Simms to P. C. Pendleton, 1 December 1840, in *Simms Letters,* ed. Oliphant et al., 1:202.

below the "dignity and importance" that such knowledge required. Washington relished the notion that Virginia's "*Landed Aristocracy,*" men who had "descended from the nobility of England," had developed American liberty from feudal sources. His approach was more flattering to his home state than critical; he marveled at an evolution toward ever greater egalitarianism, albeit solely for whites.[6] By and large southern authors like Washington had to reject too much of the fast-changing world of modernity. They were incapable of satirizing or excoriating the sins of their region in a public way.

Despite recent questioning of the point, southern romantic literature was no match when compared with the inspired literary outpouring in New England. Some have blamed the meager quality of southern fiction and poetry on the need to defend an outworn institution. That seems unlikely. Rather, it was the inability of southern authors—Poe aside—to experiment with new modes of articulation. To break with traditional ways was to risk regional betrayal, it would seem.

A spirit of censorship prevailed throughout the South. Suppression of antislavery materials in the mails, the denial of free speech in the academies, colleges, and pulpits, and the general suspicion of strangers and new ideas were all part of the popular reaction to northern criticism. W. W. Holden of the *Raleigh Standard* editorialized that he and fellow newsmen had "uniformly rejected the isms which infest Europe and the Eastern and Western States of this country. Newspapers devoted to socialism, or to social equality, nihilism, communism or to infidelity in any of its shapes or shades, could not live in the atmosphere of North Carolina." In the words of one historian, "an intellectual blockade, a *cordon sanitaire,*" surrounded the slave states. Indeed, intellectual historians must continue to recognize this factor in the nineteenth-century cultural life of the slave states.[7]

The issue of slavery, however, did not alone turn the southern purveyors of culture away from deep examination of the human condition. Rather, a major deterrent for imaginative excellence was the stifling of their own hearts. The threat of losing manhood and respect was an obstacle not to be lightly dismissed. Southerners who could not claim a degree of virile honor-

6. Henry Augustine Washington, "The Social System of Virginia," in *All Clever Men, Who Make Their Way: Critical Discourse in the Old South,* ed. Michael O'Brien (Athens: University of Georgia Press, 1992), 245.

7. Simpson, *Dispossessed Garden,* 66; Mary Ann Wimsatt, *The Major Fiction of William Gilmore Simms: Cultural Traditions and Literary Form* (Baton Rouge: Louisiana State University Press, 1989), 6. Holden and Eaton quoted in Clement Eaton, *The Freedom-of-Thought Struggle in the Old South* (1940; New York: Harper & Row, 1964), 336.

ableness would lose all favor in the eyes of peers. That sense of masculine respectability rested largely in the hands of relatives and neighbors. Therefore almost everyone was a willing participant in a society that required all its members to conform or suffer unpleasant consequences, the outcome being a suppression of genuine individuality whenever it might arise.[8]

Men of mind like Simms were so stricken by a sense of exile to the fringes of society that their isolation seemed to inhibit artistic experimentation, which, one might imagine, would further distance them from the ideals of acceptability. As a result, scarcely any of Simms's contemporaries are remembered outside academic cloisters today. Instead, the southern antebellum writers slavishly hewed to the English gentry style of discourse and genres. Especially popular in fiction were Gothic and sentimental romances in the mode of Sir Walter Scott, stately essays on travel or similar themes, and discursive critiques of literature, philosophy, theology, economics, and science, usually rendered accessible to the unspecialized reader. To be sure, northeastern novelists and intellectuals did likewise, but rebels and iconoclasts had begun to question the Boston and New York artistic constrictions.

Recently scholars have challenged the long-held view of southern intellectual mediocrity.[9] Yet W. J. Cash was not far from the mark in declaring that the Old South had no one comparable in philosophy "to set beside Emerson and Thoreau; no novelist but poor Simms to measure against the Northern galaxy."[10] Southern letters produced little above the respectable, the conforming, or the average of what could be read in the pages of the *Edinburgh Review* abroad, and the *North American Review* in Boston. But should that standard be the one to set before the astonishing outpouring of great literature in the Age of the Regency and Victoria? In his study *Beneath the American Renaissance,* David Reynolds explains how significant the lesser lights of literature were in stimulating the creativity of the major free-state artists. "Literariness," Reynolds argues, grew out of "a full *assimilation* and *transformation* of key images and devices" that the more ordinary writers of their times produced.[11] The diversity and clamor of northern re-

---

8. See Bertram Wyatt-Brown, *Southern Honor: Ethics and Behavior in the Old South* (New York: Oxford University Press, 1982).

9. See "Preface to the Brown Thrasher Edition," and "Introduction," in O'Brien, ed., *All Clever Men*, ix–xv and 2, 24.

10. Eaton, *Freedom-of-Thought Struggle;* W. J. Cash, *The Mind of the South* (1941; New York: Knopf, 1991), 96–7.

11. David S. Reynolds, *Beneath the American Renaissance: The Subversive Imagination in the Age of Emerson and Melville* (New York: Knopf, 1988), 7.

forms and movements were stimulants not found in the South. Civil society, although fast developing in the closing prewar years, was much weaker in the South than in the North. A few southern urban centers replicated many of the associations and voluntary activities to be found in profusion in the North. Nonetheless, the regional countryside and hamlets offered little.

The slave states had no counterpart to the intellectual upsurge that New England and New York were nourishing. While Emerson hailed the principle of associationism as a trend "pregnant with ethical conclusions," southerners, with an impotent sense of puzzlement and even outrage, mocked the northern proliferation of societies, clubs, and agencies to improve, uplift, and celebrate.[12] The immediate abolitionists like Parker Pillsbury, Nathaniel P. Rogers, and Theodore Weld, whom the white southerners despised, won Emerson's praise as the iconoclastic ranters who "reinforced the city with new blood from the woods and the mountains."[13] Even Hawthorne and Melville, who were opposed to antislavery agitation, exploited it not to extol slavery but to satirize and comment upon their own society. Moreover, a novel like George Lippard's *The Quaker City* set Melville to work on *Pierre,* not in imitation but in a tangential leap of imagination.[14]

Similar interactions between the reformers (if they existed in any number at all) and the top echelon of artists in the South did not exist. Years ago Clement Eaton revealed the self-imposed censorship that hobbled the artistic and even political imagination in the region. Those few who doubted the efficacy and morality of slavery had to feel the sting of reproach or worse. Angelina Grimké of South Carolina, for instance, had been exiled in the 1830s for her heretical views on slavery. In the North, she wrote with great economy and skill for the antislavery cause and the equally radical movement for women rights.[15] She certainly had no admirers, no imitators, in the South.

12. Ralph Waldo Emerson, *Essays and Lectures* (New York: Library of America, 1983), 159.

13. Ralph Waldo Emerson, *The Complete Works,* 12 vols. (Cambridge, Mass.: Riverside Press, 1903–04), 7:95.

14. Reynolds, *Beneath the American Renaissance,* 81 (quotation), 83.

15. See Stephen Howard Browne, *Angelina Grimké: Rhetoric, Identity, and the Radical Imagination* (East Lansing: Michigan State University, 1999); Eaton, *Freedom-of-Thought Struggle.* In spite of Michael O'Brien's intelligent and sensitive appreciation of the southern antebellum thinkers, I affirm Eaton's essential points: that blind Christian faith replaced the enlightened skepticism of the prior generation; that defense of slavery (and southern honor or self-idealization) drained serious attempts at self-criticism, and that intellectual life itself did not have the strength to wrestle with difficult issues. Cf., for instance, Michael O'Brien, "Intro-

A major factor in the production of lackluster southern literature had to have been the relative weakness of the second and third rate writers. In the North, the vast growth of a mass media was changing the whole character of public discourse. Pamphlets, tracts, broadsides, and especially penny newspapers like James Gordon Bennett's *New York Herald* with their strident emotionalism and coverage of murders introduced a newly literate generation to the habit of daily reading, particularly in the big cities. Edgar Allan Poe transformed Mary Rogers, who was murdered in Hoboken, into Marie Roget. He once remarked that the penny press had changed American culture "probably beyond all calculation."[16] Melville and Poe both avidly read the scurrilous columns. The former came across an account of the freakish destructiveness of a white whale in the penny press. The Virginian exile discovered a story of a human-like raven in the same tasteless, unlikely source. Probably the Revs. Thomas Dew, James H. Thornwell, or even William Gilmore Simms, did not subscribe to such lowly fare. In the onslaught of new patterns of news and popular language, the inflexible older forms of discourse, which the southern intelligentsia preferred, fell away.[17] Yet Simms himself was quite capable of accurately rendering the dialects of the Gullah black, the mountain white, the frontiersman—much to the distress of fastidious critics.[18]

William Gilmore Simms, whose reputation has greatly risen in recent years, must be regarded as the founder of professional fiction-writing in the South if not in America as a whole. Like so many other writers whom we encounter in these pages, his literary ambitions and extraordinary prolixity grew out of unhappy experiences in his early life. His mother died when he was very young, and his father disappeared from his life not long afterward. Although Simms was to marry twice into wealthy families, misfortunes, both fancied and actual, dogged him all his life. Like his equally alienated friends William Grayson and James Henry Hammond, he perceived himself as an outsider. "All that I can claim is this," he once complained, "that what I am I am in *spite of friends,* of fortune, and all the usual aids of the ambitious

duction: On the Mind of the Old South and Its Accessibility," in *All Clever Men,* ed. Michael O'Brien, 1–25.

16. Poe quoted in Reynolds, *Beneath the American Renaissance,* 171.

17. Ibid., 7, 173.

18. See John Caldwell Guilds, *Simms: A Literary Life* (Fayetteville: University of Arkansas Press, 1992), 43–75.

. . . I have never known what was cordial sympathy, in any of my pursuits among men."[19]

One reason for that sense of exile was the way that Simms's father had abandoned him. An Anglican immigrant from County Antrim, Ireland, William Gilmore Simms Sr. had much to mourn during his son's early years. His wellborn Charleston wife, Harriet Singleton, died in childbirth in 1808. The newborn son followed its mother to the grave soon after. Within a week, it was said, the Irish merchant's hair turned white. Even before these losses, he and Harriet had buried their second son, leaving alive only the child named for his father. As if these heartbreaks were not agonizing enough, his business in Charleston was declining precipitously. Drained of hope and deep in gloom, Simms saddled his horse and departed from a city that he heartily resented. Years later he told his son, "Do not think of Charleston. . . . Charleston! *I know it only as a place of tombs.*"[20]

A melancholy, brooding soul, the senior Simms left his son in the care of the child's maternal grandmother and headed to Tennessee. There he became a cavalry officer in Andrew Jackson's forces, successively fighting the Creeks, the British at New Orleans, and the Seminoles in Florida. The novelist Simms's lifetime interest in the history of the Southwest and his stories of heroics on the frontier had much to do with the direction his absent parent had taken so long before.[21] Perhaps aware of the emotional legacy that his father had bequeathed, Simms recognized that despite the senior Simms's adventurous career, he was "too sensitive a man not to suffer frequent touches of despondency & gloom."[22]

The novelist George Meredith once proposed that most artists were "deprived of a normal, happy and healthy childhood" with the result that they felt compelled "to compensate themselves for their lack of companionship and outward incident by an early life of dreams and fantasies."[23] The situation could be put in much more positive terms. According to psychiatrist George Pollock, the artistic impulse may be a form of liberation from bereavement. For others, Pollock suggests, there is no completion of the mourning process. Yet the making of art might prove to have therapeutic

19. Alexander S. Salley, "Biographical Sketch," in *Simms Letters,* ed. Oliphant et al., 1:65.

20. Oliphant et al., eds., *Simms Letters,* 1:lxxxi.

21. William P. Trent, *William Gilmore Simms* (Boston: Houghton, Mifflin, 1892), 4–6; Salley, "Biographical Sketch," in *Simms Letters,* ed. Oliphant et al., 1:lx.

22. Oliphant et al., eds., *Simms Letters,* 1:160.

23. Felix Brown, "Bereavement and Lack of a Parent in Childhood," in E. Miller, ed., *Foundations of Child Psychiatry* (London: Pergamon, 1968), 437, 443, 445 (quotation).

value even when it fails to cure. A Finnish analyst concludes that the imaginative temperament can evolve from the very need to repeat the work of mourning.[24]

As in the case of William Gilmore Simms, the death of a parent, an often precipitating incident, is likely to be more traumatic than what a mother or father undergoes in dealing with the demise of a young boy or girl. With greater knowledge of the world and its troubles, the adult can ordinarily expect to rear other children, even though the initial loss is searing. Yet for a small child like Simms, the absence of a parent or significant nurturer could become nothing less than an emotional amputation. When he lost his mother by death and then his father by absenteeism, a part of his dependent self was lopped off.

No one would prescribe parental disappearance as a way to initiate artistic skills. Even in the absence of traumatic loss, some children are equipped—or burdened—with unusually sensitive antennae, so to speak. As one analyst reports, such youngsters "tend to dramatize and mythologize their histories: to distort the people and events of their past through fantasy and exaggerated emotional intensity." Everyone recalls his or her past in highly colored terms. The analyst contends, however, that "this tendency seems to be exaggerated in artistically creative people."[25]

Simms's Grandmother Gates soon noticed that her charge had an extraordinary gift of imagination. Nevertheless, she expected that he would prepare himself for a medical career. Unfortunately she mismanaged the considerable estate that her son-in-law left behind. He possessed two town houses, twenty-five slaves, and over five hundred acres of farmland. There was sufficient money to give the boy first-rate instruction. A miserly soul, Grandmother Gates, however, sent him to cheap and discreditable common schools where the instructors, Simms later remarked bitterly, "taught me little or nothing. One old Irishman, during one year, taught me to spell, read tolerably, and write a pretty good hand. He was the best, and he knew little." In fact, Simms later condemned the whole Carolinian school system of his youth. It was, he declared, "worthless and scoundrelly." The teachers,

24. George H. Pollock, "The Mourning Process, the Creative Process, and the Creation," in *The Problem of Loss and Mourning*, ed. David R. Dietrich and Peter C. Shabad (Madison, Conn.: International Universities Press, 1989), 27–60. Hägglund is cited ibid., 30.

25. Leon E. A. Berman, "An Artist Destroys His Work: Comments on Creativity and Destructiveness," in *Creativity and Madness: Psychological Studies of Art and Artists,* ed. Barry Panter, Mary Lou Panter, Evelyn Virshup, and Bernard Virshup (Burbank, Calif.: Aimed Press, 1995), 75.

not the students, played truant, not appearing sometimes for half a week. Politicians, who feared rasing taxes and saw no advantage in preparing commoners for any professional occupation, did little to improve the educational system. The poor should spend their lives, low-country opinion averred, as laborers or farmers.

Despite such narrow-minded impediments and a lengthy apprenticeship in an apothecary's shop, young Simms discovered imaginative literature and immersed himself in the works of Scott, Byron, and Moore. In his acute loneliness he found solace in stirring his imagination through voracious reading late into the night.[26] Moreover, his grandmother offered further dreamy exhilaration in telling tales of ghosts and goblins and anecdotes about her harrowing childhood experiences during the Revolution, stories that Simms never tired of hearing repeated. Occasionally his father wrote from the distant frontier and supplied his son with fantasies of the venturesome life that could await his joining up with his parent.

Although devoted to his maternal grandmother, Simms remembered enduring a wretched time in childhood. "Sickness, and suffering, and solitude / Crouch'd o'er my cradle," he mourned poetically.[27] Death had reached him as a youngster too many times. And there were still more trying times ahead. In 1816, when Simms was ten, his father, having achieved some financial and emotional stability, sent James Simms, his brother, to retrieve his son in Charleston. Grandmother Gates refused to surrender him. Uncle James then tried to kidnap him on the street, but young Simms shrieked in panic. Neighbors rushed to the rescue. A court battle ensued with prominent lawyers representing the father and his mother-in-law. Unable to resolve the dispute, the judge asked Simms to name his preference. Thus he was allowed to remain with his grandmother. The decision, however, must have been very taxing on the emotions of so young a child. He had to have been torn between his idolization for his distant, Irish father and his wild and virile life in the Southwest and his love for the stern, penny-pinching but affectionate Grandmother Gates. In his mature years, Simms thought he had chosen disastrously. The consequences, he claimed, were to his "irretrievable injury." He had selected safety over the opportunity to strike out into the unknown in the company of a father whom he worshiped as a frontier hero. Moreover, he later thought, the choice amounted to a repudiation of his father. Certainly that early decision helped to create later a sense of alienation in

26. Trent, *Simms*, 5.
27. Salley, "Biographical Sketch," in *Simms Letters*, ed. Oliphant et al., l:lxii.

his relationship to Charleston—and even to himself. Perhaps he felt femi-nized; he had not seized the so-called manly course when it was tendered.[28]

The decision made Simms's misery worse. Alexander Salley, a descen-dant, declared, "The sense of intolerable isolation from family ties was so intense with him that it haunted him almost to the point of obsession." Along with the death of his mother and two younger siblings, infants Har-riet and James, and the absence of his father, he had reason to feel aban-doned.[29] Alone much of the time, often ill with childhood diseases, Simms was unathletic and even unable to swim. In a published piece, he described how a boy of special genius refused to play sports with other schoolmates. He preferred to read and dream. They refused to see his superiority and thought him a snob. "As he stands alone in his objects," Simms wrote, "he is soon isolated among his associates. This isolation produced gloom . . . and a morbid feeling of resentment." When others were laughing, he was "sad and thoughtful," and "solitary when they crowd together."[30]

Simms imagined a life at sea would restore his confidence in his masculin-ity. William P. Trent, an early (and overly critical) biographer, described how he sought "to commune" with the sea "as with a mysterious being, that had affected his imagination more powerfully than had anything else in nature." Rather than follow the mariner's life, however, Simms decided to reunite with his father in the West. At the close of 1824, when Simms had just forsaken medicine for the law, he arrived at his father's plantation near Georgeville, Mississippi. The trip reestablished a bond with his father and provided him with firsthand experiences of a rough male world that he would later interpret in the romantic and heroic literary idiom of the day.

Nevertheless, Simms refused to take up the life of action that his father preferred. He would not live the hero's life but would write it instead. He returned to Charleston to marry, settle into a literary career—and yet never find satisfaction in his troubled life.[31] Simms plunged into voracious study of South Carolina's colonial and Revolutionary history, from which source he drew his fiction. As Louis Rubin observed, "Simms's extraordinary zeal for Southern and particularly for South Carolina history grows in intense

28. Guilds, *Simms*, 9–10. I am indebted to John Guilds for these insights. Quotation in Simms to James Lawson, 29 December 1839, in *Simms Letters*, 1:161.

29. Salley, "Biographical Sketch," in *Simms Letters*, ed. Oliphant et al., 1:lxii.

30. Quoted in Drew Gilpin Faust, *A Sacred Circle: The Dilemma of the Intellectual in Old South, 1840–1860* (Baltimore: Johns Hopkins University Press, 1977), 28.

31. Trent, *Simms*, 13 (quotation), 12–8.

ways out of his wish to identify himself with his community's past."[32] Yet one of the factors in Simms's alienated disposition was a never gratified yearning for acceptance that only a revolution in the mind-numbing social climate of his native city could ever make possible. No matter that his histories and historical novels sang the past glories of South Carolina's valor and the endurance of its people. His villains were not one-dimensional figures but showed signs of generosity, sagacity, and humanity.[33] Simms's attention to the flaws of character that even stolid heroes might exhibit earned him little standing in the local hierarchy. Simms often complained that there was no circle of literati in Charleston. To offer a serious topic for conversation was to invite the listeners "to slink off as if from a contagious distemper," he confided to a friend. A poet was regarded as "little less than a nuisance," an opinion that exiled him, he protested, to "the coventry in which we labor." The dismal circumstances, he confessed, made him feel almost numb—"dull & fatigued" and even too listless to reach for the pen at times.[34]

The historian John Mayfield points out that Simms "tried to be both critic and celebrant of southern culture—no easy task."[35] There is almost a sense that Simms felt the way Faulkner's Quentin Compson did about his

32. Louis D. Rubin Jr., *The Edge of the Swamp: A Study of the Literature and Society of the Old South* (Baton Rouge: Louisiana State University Press, 1989), 93.

33. For a spirited defense of Simms's literary stature, see Davidson, "Introduction," in *Simms Letters,* ed. Oliphant et al., l:xxxi–lxxxix. See also the fine works listed below for the reintroduction of Simms to contemporary scholars: John Caldwell Guilds and Caroline Collins, eds., *William Gilmore Simms and the American Frontier* (Athens: University of Georgia Press, 1997); John Caldwell Guilds, ed., *"Long Years of Neglect": The Work and Reputation of William Gilmore Simms* (Fayetteville: University of Arkansas Press, 1988); John Caldwell Guilds, ed., *The Simms Reader: Selections from the Writings of William Gilmore Simms* (Charlottesville: Southern Text Society, University Press of Virginia, 2001); James E. Kibler Jr., *The Poetry of William Gilmore Simms: An Introduction and Bibliography* (Spartanburg, S.C.: Reprint Co., 1979); James E. Kibler Jr. *Pseudonymous Publications of William Gilmore Simms* (Athens: University of Georgia Press, 1976); Mary Ann Wimsatt, *The Major Fiction of William Gilmore Simms: Cultural Traditions and Literary Form* (Baton Rouge: Louisiana State University Press, 1989); Charles S. Watson, *From Nationalism to Secessionism: The Changing Fiction of William Gilmore Simms* (Westport, Conn.: Greenwood Press, 1993); Jon L. Wakelyn, *The Politics of a Literary Man: William Gilmore Simms* (Westport, Conn.: Greenwood Press, 1973).

34. Simms to James Lawson, 1 November 1830, in *Simms Letters,* ed. Oliphant et al., 1:8, 9.

35. John Mayfield, " 'The Soul of a Man!': William Gilmore Simms and the Myths of Southern Manhood," *Journal of the Early Republic* 15 (Fall 1995): 484.

relationship to his native region—the classic love-hate relationship. Like Faulkner himself, he could not escape nor break away to live up North in more intellectually congenial surroundings. At the same time, Simms's antipathy, as it sometimes was, against his native city cannot be taken as entirely accurate. Charleston printers produced his books, the bookstores carried them, and the reading public bought and admired them. Like other depressives he sought unstinting acclaim as if it were invariably his due. He was externalizing his fury against himself for not meeting the impossible standards that unresolved mourning induces. Yet Simms's unhappiness with Charlestonian high culture was at the same time a spur to experiment. Sometimes he could be very bold. In 1841 he published a story titled "Caloya; or, The Loves of the Driver" in a magazine. The tale concerned life among African Americans and Indians, and critics denounced him for being vulgar and obscene. He defended the story on the grounds that even the lowliest of human beings had lives, loves, and feelings akin to those of higher rank. "No race is so very low," he argued, "as to deprive them of the power to excite this interest in the breasts of men." The artist has every right to analyze "their modes of life, passions, pursuits, capacities and interests." After all "the great writers" would have little to say were they barred from exploring "the deadly sins of man." In fact, "*A Writer is moral only in proportion to his truthfulness.*"[36]

These were brave words, but Simms was too conventional to carry the defiant message further than the reading public would allow. In some quarters he was already thought to be too prolix, vulgar, unrefined. He seemed to relish depicting murderous horrors, unredeemable villains, good folk who prove corrupted by the search for riches, and oath-swearing protagonists. Such characterizations of how men and women behaved were truly literary assets, but critics often withheld applause, to Simms's further despair. Still worse, fellow southerners appeared unwilling to recognize his genius and buy his fiction in sufficient numbers. "Carolina has been a region of tombs for me, and my worldly prosperity is by no means" secure, he wrote.[37]

Donald Davidson, the Agrarian critic, claimed that Simms's alienation from southern society was the result of "the dissociation—and consequent loneliness—of the literary artist in a society hardly aware . . . of the claims

36. Oliphant et al., eds., *Simms Letters*, 1:256, 259.
37. Wimsatt, *Major Fiction of William Gilmore Simms*, 9–10, 122–3, 143–5 (quotation 143).

of literature."[38] By no means, though, was Simms as completely separated from Charleston society as William P. Trent claimed in his biography toward the end of the nineteenth century. In fact, Simms was quite proud of his Carolinian forebears—as a grandson of the Revolutionary patriot Thomas Singleton and a descendant of members of Francis Marion's famous brigade. Yet despite his fierce defense of his native city against outside critics, he was deeply ambivalent about his position in Charleston society. He admitted that his more immediate kin were not wealthy, though certainly they belonged in good society. Still, his father had been "a discontented & forever wandering man." Certainly the Irish immigrant could not claim to be one of Carolina's grandees like John C. Wade Hampton and other men at the pinnacle of power. He had left in Grandmother Gates's hands, however, a substantial property for the rearing of his son.[39]

As a young editor in the early 1830s, Simms challenged the city's near unanimity for Nullification, a position both defiant and futile. He did so no doubt because of his father's military association with Andrew Jackson, the president whom the reigning Nullifiers reviled. In his resentment of being called a Unionist turncoat and coward, Simms seemed almost eager for a violent showdown with the aristocratic hotheads. Perhaps he hoped for a glory that he thought his father had earned in battle. Simms boasted that the members of the so-called Submission Party, to which he proudly belonged, were "thinking of war & vengeance—to the very knife. We are practicing at the broad sword & the thrust—pistols are popping up in every direction—sabre cuts & bullets have destroyed nearly all the finest trees."[40] Such bravado and yearning for military immortality would be a familiar response to challenge among southern men of letters in both the nineteenth or twentieth centuries. Often that eagerness for war and bloody results signaled an almost suicidal proclivity.

Luckily, in this instance, the political crisis between South Carolina and the federal administration passed with only the arboreal losses. So spared, Charleston society once more subsided into its customary routines. As sectional tensions heated up in later years, however, Simms, like Ruffin, Ham-

38. Donald Davidson, "Introduction," in *Simms Letters,* ed. Oliphant et al., 1:xxxv.

39. Simms quoted in Wimsatt, *Major Fiction of William Gilmore Simms,* 175; Simms to James Lawson, 29 December 1839, in *Simms Letters,* ed. Oliphant et al., 1:160.

40. Simms to Lawson, 19 January 1833, in *Simms Letters,* ed. Oliphant et al., 1:50. Rubin (*Edge of the Swamp,* 58, 59–63) considers Simms an example of a throwback to old Federalism in his support for the Union, but a few pages later recognizes his devotion to Andrew Jackson, the paladin of southern honor and military glamor.

mond, and Tucker, became an ardent secessionist at the expense of his literary imagination and productivity. In a letter to Tucker after the Compromise of 1850, he lamented Georgia's surrender "to the Submissionists," a title he once had worn as a badge of honor. If only the rest of the South had supported South Carolina when she "threw herself into the breach," Simms continued, southern rights would have been secure. Such an outcome was one the novelist had earlier sworn to resist even by his own sword. Simms's reversal from Unionism and conversion to Carolinian radicalism greatly lessened his sense of social distance from his compatriots in the state, though there did linger a perception of social inferiority. Yet Simms was finally in his element. Critic Charles Watson observes that South Carolina itself had become "a very storehouse for romance," the source of a new southern nationalism, and Simms's work reflected his home state's feelings. In his romance *The Forayers; or, The Raid of the Dog Day* (1855) and *Eutaw: A Sequel* (1856), for instance, Simms stressed the victorious outcome of the Revolution to inspire a southern thrust for independence from a tyrannous North. These were extravagant misreadings of the wide discrepancies in military, economic, and industrial power between the two American sections. Simms's concept of Revolutionary Carolinian honor had become pure, personal hubris. Yet underneath the sectional nostalgia wreathed in myth, Simms privately bemoaned, as he had all his life, the South's weaknesses. When war began and immediate Confederate independence was not achieved, Simms repeated a longstanding complaint, "It is melancholy to look about and see how resourceless we [southerners] are in intellectual power."[41]

No less important to Simms than his own disappointments in politics were the uncompensated emotional losses in his life in the last antebellum decade. The solitary years of childhood were followed by the early but lingering death of his father in 1830. Then his grandmother died. After five years of marriage, his first wife fell mortally ill, bequeathing the widower a young daughter to rear by himself. In 1836 he married the well-born Chevilette Eliza Roach. They had fourteen children. Simms, however, lived to bury all but six of them. As his biographer notes, he lost his youngest daughter in 1842; another child, just over a year old, in 1846; a son, stillborn, in 1853; his father-in-law in 1858, and then his "two brave beautiful boys"

41. Simms to Nathaniel Beverley Tucker, 27 November 1850, in *Simms Letters,* ed. Oliphant et al., 3:76; Watson, *From Nationalism to Sectionalism,* 111–5; Simms quoted in Faust, *Sacred Circle,* 142.

from yellow fever in the same year. In addition he buried two beloved wives, the second after twenty-seven years of marriage. Furthermore, he was an unlucky homeowner. He had to watch helplessly as several of his dwellings burned to the ground—the first by accident. Sherman's army not only razed his plantation house but also destroyed his sizable collection of books and early American art. Thanks to unreliable book publishers, his unstable financial situation and frequent shortage of ready cash were vexations both early and late in his life.[42]

These problems, both emotional and material, help to account for his almost frantic productivity. According to the literary critic Jay Hubbell, Simms had a "fertility of invention," much variety of themes, and an acute "sense of reality." Even though, aside from Captain Porgy, he created no memorable characters like those in the fiction of Dickens, Hawthorne, or Henry James, these virtues were well suited to the genre of nineteenth-century romance.[43] Yet he often sacrificed even these attributes in his haste to move from one project to the next. Before his death in 1870, he had composed eighty-two published works—nineteen collections of poetry, thirty-four novels, three volumes of history, two of geography, three dramas, three anthologies, six biographies, and twelve miscellanies. His occasional pieces, it is estimated, could have filled twenty more volumes. Only the English novelist Anthony Trollope could match his outpouring of work. Such an abundance suggested an unslakable ambition for fame, a need for money to keep up his social ambitions, a thoroughly exploited gift for facile writing, but also a mixture of anxiety and repressed anger. He was the typical workaholic, to borrow a current term. There is nothing at all incompatible between the sort of distress and depression that Simms experienced and a prodigious productivity. The most notable example of these two qualities is found in the composer George Frederic Handel, though he had a discipline and depth in his artistry that Simms did not fully develop.[44]

Resentment, fear, guilt, and grief—all part of a tendency to melancholy—played a very important role in Simms life. So passionate a nature as he possessed stemmed from early yearnings for a love that an absent father and deceased mother could not furnish him. Though reticent and much less in-

42. Guilds, *Simms,* 392n1.

43. Jay B. Hubbell, *The South in American Literature, 1607–1900* (Durham: Duke University Press, 1954), 597.

44. Kay Redfield Jamison, *Touched with Fire: Manic-Depressive Illness and the Artistic Temperament* (New York: Free Press, 1993), 298n63; Anthony Storr, *The Dynamics of Creation* (New York: Atheneum, 1972), 30, 213.

trospective than many other writers of his disposition, Simms spoke of this concern on at least one occasion. "I had two brothers, both dead when I was an infant," he recalled. "I grew up without young associates. I grew *hard* in consequence, hard perhaps of manner—but with a heart craving love beyond all other possessions."[45] Subject to "fits of despondency," as the editors of his letters affirm, Simms threw himself into his writing. His bouts of despair and overwork led his friend Hammond to counsel that he should study contentment, compel his unhurried slaves to labor harder, and put up "a foot more *now & then*" during his remaining years.[46] (Busy spinning out his storytelling, Simms let his plantation run itself—almost into insolvency—to the gratification of his nearly autonomous slaves.)

Sensitive about his honor, Simms admitted to Edgar Allan Poe that he did not take criticism from strangers lightly. "I need not say to you that, to a Southern man, the annoyance of being mixed up in a squabble with persons whom he does not know, and does not care to know . . . would be an intolerable grievance." To his New York editor James Lawson, he announced, "I am one of those whose mood is not to suffer quietly under either the *suppressio veri* or *suggestio falsi.*" Simms could work himself into a frenzy when he thought northern critics and fellow writers had ignored or underrated him. To a friend he denounced the "Literary Jackals, the *serviles* of the press, the petty prowlers after prey . . . the thickskulled & lily livered scoundrels—the *webb*-footed & creeping things of the mental hogstye." Possessing a pride no less stiff than Simms's, Hammond thought his closest friend was far too coarse in manner, too belligerent and tactless when criticizing his "literary rivals, and in fact, most others." Yet Simms's displays of arrogance were often at war with his equally frequent acts of generosity, especially toward young Carolinian writers like Paul Hamilton Hayne and Henry Timrod. When assessing his literary worth during an expansive mood, however, he thought that he far outshone all others. "My poetical works," Simms congratulated himself, "exhibit the highest phase of the Imaginative faculty" ever seen in America.[47]

45. Simms to John Esten Cooke, 14 April 1860, in *Simms Letters,* ed. Oliphant et al., 4:216.
46. Hammond to Simms, 10 December 1850, in *Simms Letters,* ed. Oliphant et al., 3:87n6.
47. Simms to Edgar Allan Poe, 30 July 1846 ibid., 2:176; Simms to James Lawson, 11 September 1830, ibid., 1:5; Simms to Lawson, 19 January 1833, ibid., 1:50; entry for 30 March 1841 in James Henry Hammond, *Secret and Sacred: The Diaries of James Henry Hammond, A Southern Slaveholder,* ed. Carol Bleser (New York: Oxford University Press, 1988),

A Charlestonian once quipped about him, "A genius of the *tribe terrible* is not one to take advice even from those who themselves excel." These were defects that Hammond attributed to Simms's "early education." Though Hammond himself came from a rather humble lineage, Simms, he thought, had not been reared in the fashion a gentleman should be.[48] Certainly the poet and novelist showed serious signs of undignified volatility. In his introduction to the Simms correspondence, the Agrarian literary critic Donald Davidson noted an almost universal, timeless grievance that afflicted the Old South. He called it the "phenomenon of the disassociation—and consequent loneliness—of the literary artist in a society hardly aware, or at best only casually aware of the claims of literature."[49] Simms added to that cultural deficiency his own intense mood of anguish.

Almost as if to justify his own touchiness, Simms glorified the principles of intemperate recklessness in military descriptions in his historical romances. He penned the common aspirations of his southern compatriots when he noted in *The Partisan* the bravery of the Revolutionary Carolinians, usually with a strongly patriotic flavor but marked by the complexities of changing loyalties and human failings. In pursuit of his topic, he gleaned all the current historical accounts that he could find. Also, he learned "lessons at the knees of those who were young spectators in the grand panorama of our Revolution." He visited the battle sites, read private papers, interviewed all and sundry for local color, anecdotes, and memories— whether they represented "Whig or Loyalist" positions—and tried to cover any "event, mournful or glorious—scarcely a deed, grand or savage" in local history.[50]

Simms's novels follow the customary formulations of the adventure romance with their simple dichotomies of heroes and villains. A critic notes that in *The Yemassee,* a novel about the colonial period, Simms adopted the line "Blue blood will tell." Belonging to an old English gentry family, the book's protagonist, royal governor Craven of South Carolina, uses rough language, but he embodies the Cavalier ideal. According to a recent critic,

49; Simms to Evert Augustus Duyckinck, 24 November 1853, in *Simms Letters,* ed. Oliphant et al., 3:261–2.

48. Quoted in Salley, "Biographical Sketch," in *Simms Letters,* ed. Oliphant et al., 1:lxxx; Hubbell, *The South in American Literature,* 575–6; Entry for 30 March 1841 in Hammond, *Secret and Sacred,* ed. Bleser, 49.

49. Davidson, "Introduction," in *Simms Letters,* ed. Oliphant et al., 1:lxxxv.

50. Quoted in Wimsatt, *Major Fiction of William Gilmore Simms,* 64.

Simms's heroes have a tendency to swagger about at the beginning when establishing their innate nobility and then disappear until near the end, when they return to wrap up the plot with a momentous triumph over evil that leads to the inevitable union with the heroine. In an 1838 work, *Richard Hurdis,* however, Simms adopted a less predictable approach. Writing uncharacteristically in the first person, Simms spins a tale that has elements of autobiography. His hero is no gentleman of charm, with an appropriately cavalier, sporting nature and a self-consciousness about honor. That role is assigned to Richard Hurdis's sidekick, William Carrington. Instead, Hurdis is a rough, half-roguish wanderer—more or less like Simms's pioneering father. Simms's hero thrives in the wilderness and learns lessons from a thief and murderer named Clement Foster, whom he much admires. (Foster is based on the notorious bandit and slave-stealer John Murrell of Tennessee and Mississippi.) The historian John Mayfield regards the hard-driving, ambitious Hurdis—a prefiguration of Faulkner's Thomas Sutpen—as Simms's own self-image, or at least the individual he would like to have been, a true offspring of his daring, Irish father. Thus, on one level, Simms seemed to recognize that the patrician ideal of virtuous manhood was inadequate in the commercial age that was reshaping the Old South beneath all the courtliness and aristocratic pretensions. Although he was too skilled a novelist to follow rigidly a set formula, he could well have been at least partially critical of the high-toned Carolinian world in which he had been reared and into which he had fortuitously married. That world took little notice of his intellectual powers and general worth, he thought.[51]

Simms's wrath and dread went much deeper than the ambivalence that he mildly conveyed in *Richard Hurdis.* Other novels demonstrated time and again his restless discontent, a morbid bitterness even when he varied the mournfulness with descriptions of pastoral tranquility. Americans, he publicly complained, were indifferent to the benefits of order, stability. The nervous haste to move on without completing a task was a deplorable trait that Simms declared made his fellow countrymen look "ridiculous," though in decrying this quality he was condemning his own habits. Even on short notice he could scribble out the conclusion to a novel. But he was too slipshod and headlong, as if he might otherwise have to stop and reflect on matters

---

51. William Gilmore Simms, *Richard Hurdis* (Philadelphia: Carey and Hunt, 1838); Mayfield, " 'The Soul of a Man!' " 496–8; J. V. Ridgely, *William Gilmore Simms* (New York: Twayne, 1962), 54.

that he dared not confront. "My ambition is such," he once boasted, "that having fairly rid myself of one labour, I must necessarily go on to another. I cannot be content, if I would."[52]

When the turn of fortune's wheel threatened to crush him, though, Simms fell almost into a state of apathy. In the late 1840s and early 1850s, severe droughts nearly ruined his plantation, Woodlands. Nor was Simms's fiction selling well. Abroad, bloody revolutions were undermining social order in the very bastions of Western civilization. Inaugurated in 1849, President Zachary Taylor, whom Simms had supported, proved a traitor to the South by seeking California's admission as a free state and thus depriving the South of parity in the Senate. Still worse, no one had heeded the dying Calhoun's warnings of impending disunion unless the North mended its dictatorial ways. With Calhoun dead, the passage of the Compromise of 1850 set the South adrift, as far as Simms was concerned. Bitterly he protested to Hammond, "Of politics I hear no great deal, & greatly eschew the subject. This is a transition period in which the scum must necessarily be uppermost."[53] His angry, depressed lethargy continued through much of the 1850s, so much so that his friends gossiped that for two years he was succumbing to "a morbid depression of spirits." Simms claimed that his father had warned him to expect nothing of Charlestonians, and in his despondency he averred, "I can now say the old man was right."[54]

High society, even in London or Boston, could be likewise impervious to writers and artists who thought they deserved prominence. Yet the accepted notions of southern literary inferiority mistakenly led Simms and his supporters to feel that if he moved to or had been reared in a northern city he would have won instant recognition. Reacting to this perceived injustice, Simms lashed out, blaming the planter class for an uncharacteristic listlessness that he felt in himself. Carolinian men of wealth, he scoffed, simply "fold their arms, in stupid despair, & cry 'Allah il Allah!' They yield. They submit. Hence they are submissionists" (a badge which, ironically, he had once proudly sported). Planters could easily choke the rise of a healthy native literature, Simms grieved. So long as the gentry "remains based on so many heads of negroes and so many bales of cotton," conditions would not change. As the son of a city merchant, Simms thought professional men like

---

52. Jan Bakker, *Pastoral in Antebellum Southern Romance* (Baton Rouge Louisiana State University Press, 1989), 69; Simms quoted in Guilds, *Simms,* 76.

53. Simms to Hammond, 9 June 1851, in *Simms Letters,* ed. Oliphant et al., 3:128.

54. Hubbell, *The South in American Literature,* 579.

himself needed more recognition not merely for their own advancement but for the sake of those to come after.[55]

A healthy give and take, a constructive criticism of work in progress that only a self-confident circle of thinkers could provide each other, would assure an enlivening of art. Yet Simms's complaints about the parochial-mindedness of his compatriots and the slowness of the South to see its perils within the Union also harbored a degree of self-recrimination. The conflict between seeking public power and achieving literary standing at home and abroad left him sick at times, burdened with a sense of failure for having neither objective within his grasp. He hurried from one writing chore to the next so frenziedly that he admitted not remembering earlier drawn plots and characters and failing to re-read drafts before sending the manuscript to the publisher. In 1852 he wrote his friend Hammond, "If you knew how woebegone I am made by the sight of pen & paper, you would not wonder that I do not read what I have written, but that I write at all."[56]

Indeed, his confusion over whether to pursue one career or another slowed both efforts considerably in the mid to late 1850s. Hardly a wonder, then, that as sectional tensions rose in the 1850s, the Charleston patriot grew increasingly preoccupied with the defense of the South against abolitionist meddlers, whom he accused of "an odious tyranny."[57] Like others living through the secession crisis of 1860, he loved the cliché "Whom the Gods would destroy, they first make mad." The sentiment matched his mood at least as well as it fit any Yankee abolitionist or Republican politician that Simms had in mind.[58]

Absorbed in political issues, Simms lost his creative power in the decade before the Civil War. Wracking headaches tortured him, sometimes for days. "I have none of that enthusiasm, such as I could once boast," he sighed in early 1860. "The depression is very great, & I weary of all things!" Although he deeply felt the loss of two sons from yellow fever, bad publishing results, and other complications, he recognized that he had no control over a mood arising from his own fancies: "The very imagining proves the disease to be real, & in the most dangerous region, the Brain!" He felt sur-

55. Oliphant et al., eds., *Simms Letters,* 4:226; William Gilmore Simms, "Country Life Incompatible with Literary Labor," *Southern Literary Journal,* 1837, quoted in Hubbell, *The South in American Literature,* 583–4.

56. Simms to Hammond, 18 August 1852, in *Simms Letters,* ed. Oliphant et al., 3:197.

57. Simms to William Porcher Miles, 15 July 1860, ibid., 4:230, and Simms to James Lawson, 13 November 1860, ibid., 4:266.

58. Simms to James Lawson, 13 November 1860, ibid., 4:265.

rounded by enemies: "I am myself a failure! In South Carolina I am repudiated." The complaints were clear pleas for sympathy from his friend
William Porcher Miles, to whom he addressed them, but they also revealed
his need to replenish an empty space within.[59]

Perhaps further to restock the void, he began actively defending the
South against the free states in a curious personal—and foolhardy—
crusade. On a lecturing tour of the northeastern states, the popular romancer chose to speak of South Carolina's contribution to the Revolution.
Before an audience of twelve hundred in Buffalo, November 1856, he
heaped praise on his home state's Revolutionary heroes in rapid staccato,
but accompanied his almost bullying exaltation of the motherland with insults about New England's allegedly inglorious role in the 1770s.

A reason for his indignation was an event that had taken place some
eight months earlier. During the Kansas debates Charles Sumner had ver-
bally assailed South Carolina for its supposedly pusillanimous part in the
War for Independence. Preston Brooks, congressman of South Carolina,
had responded by caning the Massachusetts senator unmercifully on the
floor of the chamber. Before the throng in Buffalo, Simms excused Preston
Brooks's attack on the grounds of extreme provocation and the southern
ideals of honor. With a note of frenzy in his voice, he hoarsely announced
that South Carolina would tolerate no further aspersions upon her "Past."
Instead she would bring down all the pillars of government in a justifiable
moment of "moral suicide." He concluded, "Forgive me, my friends, if I
have spoken warmly; but you would not, surely, have me speak coldly in
the assertion of a Mother's honour!" Though respectful, his first listeners
were nonplused and disappointed that he had turned a literary occasion into
a diatribe against them. The references to honor fell on uncomprehending
ears. Southern ideas of what constituted the essence of that ethic no longer
figured in the commercial world of the North.

Failing to moderate his truculence, Simms hastened to Rochester to repeat his harangue. From thence he took himself to New York City where a
small audience grew so hostile that he felt obliged to cancel the rest of the
tour. Wrapped in the cloak of his own preoccupations, he considered himself the injured party and the "rancorous temper of Black republicanism"
his persecutor. He moaned to friend Hammond, "My *heart* (suffer me to
have one) was *slavishly* in these topics of S.C. I could no more fling them
off from it, than I could fly."[60] Although a stalwart defender of South Carol-

59. Simms to William Porcher Miles, 18 January 1860, ibid., 4:185, 186.
60. Simms to Hammond, 8 December 1856, ibid., 3:466, 469; Ridgely, *Simms,* 122.

inian planter interests, Hammond was baffled. He could see no gains in Simms's belligerent approach but rather a shrinking away of northern conservative friends of the South.

Hammond was also alarmed about his friend's mental health, and he pressed Simms to account for his behavior: "What Demon possessed you, mon ami, to do this? I was shocked with the account of your first Lecture." Making matters even worse, in Hammond's opinion, was the inevitable failure of Carolinians to recognize Simms's sacrifice of his popularity. Congressman Brooks, who ought to have shown eternal gratitude for Simms's defense of his conduct, would reckon his effort "only a slight oblation." Hammond warned Simms that he had martyred himself "for So[uth] Ca[rolina] who will not even buy your books." Moreover, Hammond continued, Simms had unwisely turned "a little Quixotic—rather beyond Shakespeare and Petrucchio."[61] And his friend, slightly chastened, agreed. He repeated, "My mind followed my heart." Yet after all, he continued, both he and Hammond were quite incapable of escaping "from our impulses."[62] One biographer argues that Simms fell victim to his own myth-making powers.[63] More to the point, the same deep-seated sense of rage and disguised self-castigation that prompted his quarrels with critics and indifferent southern neighbors lay behind his excited belligerence on the tour. The inner rage that a melancholy state of mind customarily arouses revealed Simms's inability to know himself. Instead he projected his bleakest feelings on sectional politics.

Simms's late novels reflect the same mordant spirit. In his famous Revolutionary War novel *Woodcraft,* set in South Carolina, for instance, he depicts the sordid ruin and degenerating changes that war inflicts. The novel concerns Captain Porgy, a fat, Falstaffian, and eccentric planter, a caricature perhaps of Simms's stubborn but mild-mannered planter father-in-law. The character is a rather sexless creature, a comic version of the Ashley Wilkes type that Margaret Mitchell later made famous. Porgy is easily manipulated by a hard-driving woman, Widow Eveleigh, an antebellum Scarlett. She rejects his marital advances, being secure in her powerful singleness. She is hardly the southern die-away matron ready to give herself to the nearest gentleman in the neighborhood. Such a plot did not reflect the plantation legend as southerners felt it should be, but Simms was not wholly aware of his own departure from convention.

61. Hammond to Simms, 27 November 1856, ibid., 3:465n136.
62. Simms to Hammond, 8 December 1856, ibid., 3:469.
63. Ridgely, *Simms,* 124.

Simms's vision of the South even before the Civil War had begun was "essentially tragic." There was a premonition of doom in Simms's imagining a perfected South that had lost its soul. His attention turned toward the character of Hamlet, that tragic figure who contemplated suicide rather than confront a dead father and his demands. Hamlet, whom Simms took to be a particularly appropriate character for Carolinians to recognize as one of their own kind, suffered from a tragic flaw: "It is contemplation, speculation, thought, by which the energies of Hamlet are enfeebled."[64] Shakespeare's Melancholy Dane cannot act because he doubts himself and only arouses himself to action when honor or pride compel him to spring forward. By then, though, it is too late—just as it would be, as Simms rightly predicted, for the South as a whole. Yet in aligning Hamlet's plight with that of South Carolinians, Simms did not realize that he was describing his own melancholy. In that pre-Freudian era, he did not recognize what he might have in common with a fatherless Hamlet.

Simms's answer to the Hamlet dilemma that South Carolina faced was the celebration of honor—the Carolinians' glorious past, the sturdy virtues of a slaveholding gentry as he imagined them to be. As a writer, he felt no need to explore the interiority of personality, to question old verities, the cruelty of social restraints, or the tyranny of custom. Similarly, the careful depiction of things in ordinary life, the monotony of routine, did not appeal to him. Such matters, Simms was convinced, belonged to the future—and to a freer and more secularized culture, but one that held no charms in his eyes. The romance in which honor and manliness triumphed and villainy and godlessness were crushed before the story's conclusion best suited his purposes. Yet this orderly formula did not entirely hide his darker imagination.

Although best known for his Revolutionary series, Simms also wrote some ten volumes, many of them from first-person perspective, in which he tried to probe the depths of mental pain. (Among them is the murder/love story, *Beauchampe; or, The Kentucky Tragedy,* which Robert Penn Warren later used as the basis for *World Enough and Time.*) Simms thought these works held his best writing, yet they were marked, as critic Jay B. Hubbell asserts, by "an intensifying egotism." Simms realized, though, that his readers expected adventures. They did not want to follow "the silent progress of the thoughts, sentiments, and emotions—the passions themselves working

64. William R. Taylor, *Cavalier and Yankee: The Old South and the American National Character* (New York: George Braziller, 1961), 291, 275. In his classic study, Taylor brilliantly captures Simms's fatalism, lack of gentility, and melancholy.

as undercurrents of moods and feelings—moods which speak not, and feelings that boil for ever in fiery fountains, but are never suffered to overflow!"[65] Yet even in his more traditional books, he sometimes exhibited a willingness to defy convention. His treatment of the conquest of Indians, for example, showed a much broader level of sympathy than one might expect. In *The Yemassee: A Romance of Carolina* (1835), he identified more closely with the Indian characters, who would ultimately fail, than with the white heroes and heroines. The latter characters conformed to the sentimental conventions of the day. The Indians, however, may have represented the melancholy and loss that Simms knew but did not give full voice.[66] To some degree he was describing his own inner life in the customary, reticent way that the age preferred to what would then have been called vulgar, shameless confession.

To return to an earlier point, that same tragic note appeared in Simms's preoccupation with the figure of Hamlet. The dilemma facing the South was whether to act boldly, even rashly, or to remain inert, passive—and perhaps survive. Contemplation enfeebled Hamlet, Simms argued, just as it did the hesitant Southland. But why did Simms feel so intensely the ominous political conflict between the sections—between slavery and the Carolinian way of life and freedom and northern hegemony? Perhaps he knew that the coming struggle was the same issue that he had faced when a youngster before the judge. He had then chosen security and grand-maternal care over entry into the challenging and completely male world of his father in Mississippi. In later years he bitterly regretted that decision, however, and perhaps in urging the South to action he was hoping to rectify his own earlier passivity, which he considered a great mistake. The historian William R. Taylor points out that Simms's counsel to fellow southerners grew increasingly unrealistic, the mutterings of a crank or crackpot, as when during the war he urged P. G. T. Beauregard to dress Confederate soldiers as Indians to frighten the Yankee troops. Knowing his own ambivalence and oscillations between lust for action and love of contemplation, Simms dwelt on a problem that he had faced all his life—"the dangers of melancholy and introspection," as Taylor puts it. Simms confessed to Hammond, "Reverie . . . perhaps the most grateful of mental exercises, is . . . dangerous . . . and beguiles perpetu-

---

65. See W. R. Jilson, "The Beauchampe-Sharpe Tragedy in American Literature," *Kentucky Historical Society Register* 36 (January 1938):54–60; Hubbell, *The South in American Literature*, 592.

66. Wimsatt, *Major Fiction of William Gilmore Simms*, 55–6.

ally into provinces which make it daily more & more ungrateful to return to the earthy."[67]

If Simm's vision of the coming conflict and its resulting ruin of the South had had the power of clairvoyance, it would have been remarkable indeed. Instead, Simms thought the South could do pretty much what it pleased. His conservative friends up North reassured him that only a minority of Yankees approved of abolitionism or followed Republican principles. After the Civil War, which destroyed his world and demolished his aspirations, Simms loyally repudiated his former disapproval of southern life. Instead he defended the city of his birth, where the war had begun. "Charleston, sir, was the finest city in the world," he admonished a visiting Yankee skeptic. He went on to describe it as "the flower of modern civilization. Our people were the most hospitable, the most accomplished, having the highest degree of culture and the highest sense of honor, of any people . . . of any country on the globe."[68]

By the time of this solemn defense of the people who had so often before wounded his pride, Simms had watched his wealth, his beloved Woodlands, and many of his kindred and friends, including James Henry Hammond, vanish from the earth. In fact, Hammond's death in late 1864 pitched Simms into the deepest despair. In a poetic tribute, Simms mourned that Hammond, the teacher of wisdom, had "tilled a barren soil" that had brought forth no welcome response from the "coarse crowd" of his fellow Carolinians but only "exile" as reward for "years of toil." "So all earth's teachers have been overborne," Simms preached, no doubt seeing himself likewise scorned and rejected amidst a "clamor, 'Crucify!'" These sentiments reinforced Simms's longstanding, bleak appraisal of his own role both in war and peace: "I was fated like Cassandra to speak the truth with nobody to listen."[69]

Yet for one who had suffered wrathful bouts of gloom, sometimes too severe to permit his writing, Simms achieved in his closing years a remarkable acceptance of fate. In March 1868, Simms lost a favorite grandchild who took ill with the croup. "The little life was reft from it in two brief days of illness," he sorrowed. The mother, Simms's eldest daughter, herself feeble, in danger of a miscarriage, and stricken with grief, refused to leave her chamber. "Yet, through all this," he wrote editor Henry Barton Dawson, "I

---

67. Quotations in Taylor, *Cavalier and Yankee*, 295, 296.
68. Simms quoted in Hubbell, *The South in American Literature*, 584–5.
69. Quotations from Simms in Faust, *Sacred Circle*, 142–3.

am now writing harder than ever, in the hope to avert a foreclosure of mortgage upon the house in which my son in law & daughter reside, and in a
room of which I find my temporary shelter now."[70]

As he sat at his desk in a small brick outbuilding beside the blackened
chimneys and charred timbers of Woodlands, he wrote two successive seri-
als, *Voltmeier; or, The Mountain Men* and *The Cub of the Panthers,* as well
as some fragments—a total of over three thousand pages in just a little more
than a year. The serial style of publishing paid better than the bound novel.
Increasingly hobbled by the pains of aging, a poor stomach and deteriorating kidney, and bowed by grief, he filled page after page, day after day, night
after night. Writing his fellow novelist and friend John Esten Cooke of Virginia, he announced that he had finished 660 pages, with only 3,400 more
to complete. But, he moaned, "I write with difficulty, with heart sore, head
heavy, brain dull. I am overtasked & badly paid." His output belied his self-
pity, but his complaint of low pay was valid. Indeed, Simms, "threatened by
a general mortgage," was about to be turned out of his lodgings. It was as
if storytelling in the old romantic mode was the only means to keep friend
Death from the door. To the aspiring poet Paul Hamilton Hayne, he wrote,
"I am rapidly passing from a stage where you young men are to succeed me,
doing what you can. God grant that you may be more successful than I have
been." The golden goal, he knew, was lost forever. With its lack of psychological realism and its improbable twists of plot, the romance was still suitable for boys, but Simms knew his era was over. "I am weary, Paul," he
continued to his friend Hayne. "And having much to say, I must say no
more; but with love to all, God be with you in mercy."[71] Simms died on June
11, 1870. When his body was being prepared for burial, Paul Hayne recalled in 1885, one of Simms's old female admirers had reported, "I made
garlands of laurel and bay, and wove too a cross of white immortelles,
which I placed in the poor emaciated hands of the corpse, *the fingers of
which refused to take any other position than their natural one, drawn up
as if to write!*"[72]

*   *   *

70. Simms to Henry Barton Dawson, 9 March 1868, in *Simms Letters,* ed. Oliphant et al.,
6:267.

71. Simms to John Esten Cooke, 9 May 1868, John Esten Cooke MSS, Perkins Library,
Duke University.

72. Simms to Paul Hamilton, 2 January 1870, in *Simms Letters,* ed. Oliphant et al., 5:290;
"Introduction," *The Writings of William Gilmore Simms Centennial Edition,* ed. John Caldwell Guilds, 5 vols. (Columbia: University of South Carolina Press, 1969), 1:xxix.

The mantle of romance that Simms had worn for half a century passed on to John Esten Cooke. The Virginian was the author of the best-selling *Surry of Eagle's Nest* (1866). In 1867, on the basis of that success and a solid reputation from pre–Civil War novels about eighteenth-century Virginia, Cooke had reminded himself, "I hope to become the writer of *the* South, yet! Big ambition."[73] Like *Surry, Mohun,* its successor, made the Cavalier vs. Roundhead myths, which suffused all of Cooke's work, into Civil War legend. In these narratives, Stonewall Jackson, Turner Ashby, and the recklessly brave cavalry officer J. E. B. Stuart, Cooke's cousin, become larger-than-life paladins. By writing of the deaths of Jackson and Stuart, Cooke sought to enact a sacred obsequy honoring the great but fallen Confederate cause: "These two kings of battle had gone down in the storm, and, like the knights of Arthur, I looked around me with vacant and inquiring eyes. . . . Jackson! Stuart!—who could replace them?" The obvious answer was no one. Lewis Simpson puts the matter well: Wrapped in the cloak of rhetorical nostalgia, "the metaphysical southern nation" grew out of "a sable antebellum civilization centered in the harmonious pastoral plantation and the beneficent institution of chattel slavery." To question that proposition was deemed nearly an act of treason.[74]

Simms's work and that of Cooke as well as other romancers were engaged in a process of collective mourning. Even a northern writer, Constance Fenimore Woolson (treated in a later chapter) recognized the common southern keening: Thousands of our soldiers could not have lost their lives for no reason or purpose. In her poem of 1874, "At the Smithy," Woolson has a blacksmith, a veteran and father of sons all killed in the war, remark to a customer: "I can't make it plain / To my mind that my four boys have died all in vain." In authoring similar sentiments, Cooke earned the gratitude of readers like Edward V. Valentine of Richmond. We must exalt "our own Virginia worthies," Valentine intoned. Cooke, he wrote the novelist, portrays them as heroes—an excellent notion "in order that the world may not go back into a prosaic, commonplace, money-worshiping barbarism. I have said that I thought Stuart the last Cavalier this world would ever see." So long as novels like *Surry* and *Mohun* appeared, Cooke's corre-

73. John Esten Cooke, "Literary Record: March 1867–April 1868," p. 2, John Esten Cooke MSS, Duke University.

74. Ritchie Devon Watson Jr., *The Cavalier in Virginia Fiction* (Baton Rouge: Louisiana State University Press, 1985), 157–8; Lewis P. Simpson, *The Fable of the Southern Writer* (Baton Rouge: Louisiana State University Press, 1994), 77.

spondent insisted, the proper image of nobility and heroism would still inspire the young.[75]

The Scottian style, however, was beginning to cloy, and in later efforts, before his death in 1886, Cooke tried to mix some realism with the usual formula. Nevertheless, whatever its faults, the southern romance that Simms had developed had helped to create some sense of regional distinctiveness, however overblown it was. Later and greater novelists would thus be enabled to situate their more probing work against a set of mythologies and habits of mind deeply embedded in the southern psyche. What would Quentin Compson at Harvard have been able to say to Shreve about his homeland were it not for the literary record that Simms and company produced? Their novels reflected the way southerners liked to think of themselves. Faulkner and his compatriots had a useful backdrop against which to propose their own sense of the real and false.

More important, Simms had proved that it was possible to be a professional writer in the South. Augusta Jane Evans, Caroline Hentz, and others, both men and women, would follow suit.[76] In a section of the country that held intellectuality in little esteem, that was no shabby achievement. But as a pioneer, like many of his backwoods heroes, Simms could not free himself from the restraints that the southern social order imposed. In fact, he and Cooke reveled in the projection of a southern Anglo-Saxon order of things that never was nor ever could be. Instead, they welcomed its embrace and never questioned the rightness of slavery and honor, the South's ancient tyrannies. Such acceptance doomed their art to an outworn mode of romantic expression. Even in his rare introspective moments, Simms failed to recognize the price he had paid for fidelity to the Cavalier South. Slavery as an institution did not shackle his inventiveness. Instead, the self-imposed censorship stemmed from imprisonment in a tightly controlling community of slaveholders that mistrusted any flights of imagination, no matter how true to the southern ethic their author was. Sadly, neither Simms nor any of the other romancers wanted it to be another, more hopeful, more democratic way.

75. Edward V. Valentine to Cooke, 7 September 1872, John Esten Cooke MSS, Duke University.

76. See Elizabeth Fox-Genovese, "Introduction," in Augusta Jane Evans, *Beulah* (Baton Rouge: Louisiana State University Press, 1992), xi–xxxvi.

4

The "English Malady" in Southern Poetry
1830–1880

> O Raven Days, dark Raven Days of sorrow,
> Will ever any warm light come again?
> Will ever the lit mountains of To-morrow
> Begin to gleam across the mournful plain?
> —Sidney Lanier

The children, when they die, are hardly noted by the world; and yet to many hearts, their deaths make a blank which long years will never fill up.
> —Elizabeth Gaskell

MUCH can be learned about southern masculine intellectuality from examining the lives and works of minor nineteenth-century poets. They, it might said, cast a different, unexpected light on the general intellectual landscape of that particular time and place. With one exception, most of the figures discussed here had limited or at least brief reputations even in their own day. By and large these figures, influenced by the general currents of a lyrical romanticism, have all but vanished from the scrutiny of nineteenth-century southern literary specialists. Who has heard of Thomas Holley Chivers, Mirabeau Lamar, Theodore O'Hara, or Abram Ryan? Henry Timrod and Sidney Lanier may still earn a brief nod of recognition. Yet the general reader may never have heard of either one. A special and intriguing case is the occasional verses of Abraham Lincoln, even though this unexpected figure in the literary pantheon of the unremembered and the easily forgettable obviously stands quite apart with regard to both fame and political ideology. Like the lesser lights, Lincoln transformed his moods of sorrow and worry into conventional verse. But he made these efforts into something grander than anything the others ever composed. Lincoln demonstrated what could be done with a fresh imagination and a rejection of southern conventionality. The poets in the land from which he had sprung, however, did not reach that standard of achievement.

After Poe, in fact, no major poet arose in the South to match the art of Herman Melville, Walt Whitman, and Emily Dickinson. Why was southern literary romanticism so thin? After all, many in the antebellum South had possessed the wealth to sustain lives of experimentation, self-examination, and creativity had they wished to pursue that career. Even that indomitable fire-eating southern nationalist Edmund Ruffin of Virginia deplored the mediocrity of contemporary southern letters. For poetry reading, Ruffin preferred Lord Byron far above Edgar Allan Poe. He felt that the latter's gothic tales and verses were quite "as monstrous & abominable as his morals, & as absurd as his course of life."[1] An admirer of the works of Hawthorne and Melville, he tried valiantly but failed to finish four Virginia novels that had received acclaim even in the North and in England. Sourly Ruffin remarked that it just "shows there is more bad taste there than here."[2]

The need for a sturdy defense of slavery cannot be cited as a deterrent to art, whether it be literature, painting, or sculpture. Southern defenders had immediately challenged that notion. Ruffin pointed out that ancient slaveholding Greece and Rome had managed pretty well in an artistic way. Likewise, over the same span of time, the czarist state produced Pushkin, Gogol, Turgenev, Dostoevsky, and Tolstoy, despite censors, secret police, and repressions of serfs and peasants. Russian artists rose above their provincial and anti-intellectual surroundings, whereas the southern contingent remained mired in a cultural backwash. The consequences of war, lost fortunes, and defeat did nothing, apparently, to shake off old ideas, venerated

1. Entry for 7 September 1857 in William Kauffman Scarborough, ed., *The Diary of Edmund Ruffin*, 3 vols. (Baton Rouge: Louisiana State University Press, 1972), 1:102; Betty L. Mitchell, *Edmund Ruffin: A Biography* (Bloomington: Indiana University Press, 1981), 133.

2. Mitchell, *Ruffin*, 133.

principles, and habits. Although Cassius Marcellus Clay, James Gillespie Birney, Angelina and Sarah Grimké, the Rev. John G. Fee, and a few others were driven out of the South for their antislavery convictions, southern white thinkers were rarely banished or lynched. The reason should be clear enough. Except for the handful mentioned, few, particularly in the nineteenth century, ever strayed far enough from the racial and social boundaries of the society to warrant extracurricular punishment. What we discover is an almost unchanging intellectual continuity spanning the nineteenth century—and going somewhat beyond.

The reasons for such stagnation—and that is what it amounted to—were closely related to the limited role that intellectuals played in the social order. They would like to have been more noticed, praised, and rewarded. But this treatment would have required a bold flouting of that very order of things. The ready retort of a southern apologist, though, would have been that published violations of the racial or ethical code would simply have gained no audience anyhow. Besides, writing to earn cash was the Yankees' approach. Since they pushed themselves harder than the intellectual southern gentleman, they were bound to excel. In 1859 travel-writer Charles Mackay observed how much more distinguished northern letters were over southern because of the prohibitions that slavery imposed. Reacting to the comment, Ruffin conceded that Yankees produced more and better "poetry & light literature." They did so, however, only for the "pay & support of the writer." In Ruffin's gentlemanly eyes, writing for profit was demeaning and low class.

In the lives and works of the second-rate or almost amateurish southern author we can tease out some of the factors that encouraged an intellectual timidity. But more important, the work of undistinguished writers throws fresh light on the relation of art, even bad art, to the moods and needs of the less-than-ingenious author, that is, the majority of nineteenth-century southern writers. Their productions might never even have commanded a column in a country newspaper. That was not the point. As Edmund Ruffin observed, "Writing for gain is a business not yet begun in the southern states."[3] Yet, the generation to follow—which would include Kate Chopin, Willa Cather, Ellen Glasgow, William Faulkner, Walker Percy, and other modernists—was reared within that culture and had to react against it to survive intellectually and perhaps emotionally.

First and foremost, the intellectual southerner worked out his experience

3. Entry for 27 August 1859, in *Ruffin Diary*, ed. Scarborough, 1: 335–36.

of depression less creatively than a Russian and even English counterpart. We must recall that serious emotional downturns have always been a source of artistic stimulation. During the eighteenth-century Enlightenment, melancholia was so pervasive in the most refined literary and fashionable circles of Great Britain that it came to be called "the English malady." George Cheyne, a popular Scottish physician in London, had so named his 1733 best-selling book on the subject. Samuel Johnson warned his friend James Boswell by all means to read Cheyne's *English Malady*, "but do not let him teach you a foolish notion that melancholy is proof of acuteness."[4] Despite Johnson's counsel, depression has seemed historically to bear some relation to acuteness of vision and creativity.

Whether gifted or not, the antebellum southern gentlemen of letters faced the imposing dilemma of how to conduct the life of the mind in a society that failed to honor it. The problem was partly a matter of appearances. How could anyone claiming virility write verse? That diversion belonged, gentlemen of leisure assumed, in the province of the opposite sex. Too cultivated a mind suggested effeminacy, as the southern male was well aware. Yet he could not admit that imputation even to himself. Instead, he was likely to lash out against the unthinking "worthless crowd / Whose breath is poison," as novelist and law professor Nathaniel Beverley Tucker versified in 1830. Many times William Gilmore Simms had lamented the lowly status accorded writers in his society: "A literary man is obnoxious . . . and were it not for the outrageous indecency of the thing they would legislate" against him as a public menace. If one were to raise a serious subject for intellectual discussion, ordinary Charlestonians would "slink off as if from a contagious distemper."[5] The southern poet reacted by composing; it served to firm up a sense of identity and fortify the spirit against hints of unmanliness.

At the same time that southern poets were giving vent to their frustrations and feelings in verse, however, they had to be wary of delving too deeply into their own minds and revealing matters that society would find

4. See Anita Guerrini, *Obesity and Depression in the Enlightenment: The Life and Times of George Cheyne* (Norman: University of Oklahoma Press, 2000).

5. Nathaniel Beverley Tucker quoted in Drew Gilpin Faust, *The Sacred Circle: The Dilemma of the Intellectual in the Old South, 1840–1860* (Baltimore: Johns Hopkins University Press, 1977), 20; William Gilmore Simms to James Lawson, 11 September 1830, in *The Letters of William Gilmore Simms,* ed. Mary C. Simms Oliphant, Alfred Taylor Odell, and T. C. Duncan Eaves, 6 vols. (Columbia, S.C.: University of South Carolina Press, 1952), 1:5; and Simms to Lawson, 1 November 1830, ibid., 8.

embarrassing, perverse, or mad. That worry also extended to artists in other parts of the Anglo-American world. Like Poe, the New Englander Nathaniel Hawthorne, for instance, was preoccupied with preserving "the inmost Me behind its veil."[6] The concept of literary privacy was well developed in the Victorian era, as Rochelle Gurstein has pointed out.[7] Nearly all southern writers of the early period skirted intimate matters of the mind and heart. Those inclined to verse, though, persuaded themselves that the stylized forms of addressing subjective issues fell within permissible and palatable limits. Therefore they could use that vehicle of self-expression more freely than they could prose. That conclusion seldom led to memorable verse but satisfied an inner need without loss of self-esteem.

Despite the relative ease with which poetry could be used to convey personal sentiments (albeit veiled), the verse of the nineteenth-century South continued to be fastidious and discreet. Perhaps its most revealing characteristic is its frequently dolorous tone. Most of its practitioners were enveloped in the misery of heavy depression. Certainly that was the case of the poet Mirabeau Bonaparte Lamar, the Georgia planter's son who became vice-president and later president of the Texas Republic. Melancholy made an appearance in the family's history. According to one source, too much intermarriage in the Lamar clan was responsible. It is quite feasible that this might compound a genetic predisposition. Lamar's brother, Lucius Quintus Cincinnatus Lamar, father of the famous Mississippi politician of the same name, committed suicide in 1834. Mirabeau Lamar also agonizingly suffered from periodic breakdowns.[8] (Apart from Mirabeau and his brother Lucius, however, it is not known how many others in the family suffered from the disorder.) Lamar's adventurous life on the Texas frontier, fighting for the Mexican province's independence, and his participation in the Mexican War had a touch of suicidal recklessness. In that respect he was very much like Shakespeare's Henry Lord Percy—Hotspur—in possessing both a high sense of honor and an abiding melancholy.[9] According to Lamar's

6. William Charvat, Harvey Pearce, and Claude M. Simpson, eds., *The Centenary Edition of the Works of Nathaniel Hawthorne*, 23 vols. (Columbus: Ohio State University Press, 1962–1997), 1:4.

7. Rochelle Gurstein, *The Repeal of Reticence: A History of America's Cultural and Legal Struggles over Free Speech, Obscenity, Sexual Liberation, and Modern Art* (New York: Hill & Wang, 1996).

8. Philip Graham, *The Life and Poems of Mirabeau B. Lamar* (Chapel Hill: University of North Carolina Press, 1938), 29, n29.

9. On Henry Lord Percy (Hotspur), see Geoffrey H. White and Lord Howard de Walden, *The Complete Peerage of England, Scotland, Ireland, and the United Kingdom*, 13 vols. (London: St. Catherine Press, 1945), 10:464 and "Sir Henry Percy," in Sir Leslie Stephen and Sir

biographer, "The quizzically up-turned corners of his mouth softened an expression otherwise stern, but could not hide a distinct tendency toward melancholia."[10]

The personal losses that Lamar endured also compounded the problem. In 1826, at twenty-eight, he married Tabitha Jordan, age seventeen. A carriage accident on the honeymoon, however, nearly killed her. She survived the facial and head wounds but in so weakened a state that she shortly contracted tuberculosis. Tabitha gave birth to a daughter, Rebecca Ann, and then in 1830 predictably succumbed to consumption. Mirabeau destroyed all his love poems to her and sank so low that his friends and parents feared he might do away with himself. Then Mirabeau's married sister died in 1833. His wealthy father of "unblemished honor" and "consistent virtue" passed away just a few weeks afterwards. His brother's self-inflicted death a year later affected Mirabeau as much as the loss of Tabitha. No doubt fearing his own possible fall into self-destructive madness, he could not utter Lucius's name for many years thereafter. Having already withdrawn from a U. S. senatorial race after his wife's death, he left in a state of grief for the revolution in Texas in 1835.

Lamar's poetry is decidedly not memorable. Yet it expressed feelings that he could not otherwise articulate. According to friends, he seldom revealed what was weighing most on his mind. He once declared that "the labor" of composition "steals the heart from woe," an outlet he sorely needed in the absence of any other restorative for the despairing. When suffering one of his periodic physical and mental breakdowns, he helped his recovery by writing about his show of outward cheeriness, which hid his gloom from an always prying southern public:

> There is a sorrow in my heart
>   The world may never know—
> A pang that never will depart,
>   Till Death shall lay me low;
> Yet light and cheerful still I seem—
>   No signs of sorrow see;
> I wear to all a cheerful mien,
>   That none may GRIEVE FOR ME.[11]

Sidney Lee, eds., *Dictionary of National Biography* [*DNB*], 24 vols. (rpr; London: Oxford University Press, 1921–22), 15:840–4.

10. Graham, *Mirabeau Lamar*, 9.

11. Quotation ibid., 209; "Grieve Not for Me," ibid., 208.

His verse is naively unstudied. He assessed his efforts as a light diversion that he, like most southerners, thought gentlemen should undertake for pleasure alone. He dismissed any thought of ambition for literary fame: "I never hoped in life to claim / A passport to exalted fame" for the lines set on paper. He dipped his pen, he wrote his daughter Rebecca Ann, simply because "there's joy in rhyme" and the hope of truthful thoughts of feeling in the verses.[12] He fashioned occasional rhymes without success—chiefly patriotic lines for the Texas cause and for state-rights partisan purposes. Singing of the immortal remembrance awaiting noble warriors and statesmen engaged none of his clearly limited powers. Yet for the most part the humorless Lamar, even more self-constrained than others of his day, took sorrow as his subject. That was the acceptable mode of the time—at least before Mark Twain satirized the matter with Emmeline Grangerford's funereal tunes. The language and themes of drear and death were so stylized that Lamar felt little self-consciousness in reaching the local papers.

"To My Daughter," one of his most poignant pieces, was addressed in 1843 to sprightly Rebecca Ann, then sixteen. She had been raised by two aunts in Georgia rather than by her wifeless soldier-politician father far away in Texas. She beseeched him to send her some verses. His touching response expressed his love for Tabitha, Rebecca Ann's mother:

> Oh, do not ask me now for rhyme,
>   For I am lonely-hearted;
> And lost are all the dear delights
>   The muses once imparted,
> I sigh no more for Hybla's dews,
>   Nor Helicon's bright water;
> I only crave a sable wave
>   Of Lethe's stream, my Daughter.
>
> . . . .
>
> Then name some other boon, my child;—
>   Thou know'st I can deny thee
> No gift thine innocence demands,
>   While thou are smiling by me;
> But should I dare to string the harp
>   By Chattahoochee's water,
> The bitter tears of other years
>   Would flow afresh, my Daughter.

12. "Apology for Verse," ibid., 216.

Later that same year, 1843, Thomas Lamar wrote his brother Mirabeau at his plantation in Fort Bend County, Texas: "God grant you strength to sustain the dreadful blow. Rebecca Ann has been taken from us—she is no longer of earth."[13] Mirabeau fell at once into another black gorge of despair. Although unable to share his feelings with others, even close kin, until his death just before the Civil War, Lamar found some release from pain in writing about a dead wife, a dead daughter. He was scarcely alone in this enterprise.

Although politically far removed from Lamar and his proslavery, honor-conscious convictions, Kentucky-born Abraham Lincoln was similarly affected. We tend to think of the future president as a northern, Illinois politician, but during his formative years he was deeply immersed in the culture of Virginia and Kentucky. It goes without saying that his poetic side was scarcely his most important creative outlet. Yet the amateur's writing of poetry was at that time a more serious undertaking than it is today, and in examining that means of expression we can see, however slightly, into the writer's personality, despite his cultivation of a prized taciturnity. Lincoln serves as well as any in exploring the phenomenon and how it might develop far beyond the capacities or imagination of such a casual practitioner as Mirabeau Lamar.

Like other men of mind of his region and era, Abraham Lincoln was not altogether comfortable in the anti-intellectual environment of the Southwest. Self-conscious about his differentness, he developed early a preoccupation with reading, whether by light of the mythological late evening hearth-fires or not. Reading materials were scarce in his younger days and he could not afford to be particular about the literature that came his way, but later, when books were more readily available to him, he developed a passion for the works of Shakespeare and other poets, which he preferred to novels and biographies and whose lines he often committed to memory.[14]

As historians have long pointed out, Lincoln, like the other thinkers in this study, suffered deeply from chronic despair. David Donald put it best: "He seemed to drip melancholy as he walked, but his fits of deep depression would alternate with gusty outbreaks of humor." Biographers point to the

13. "To My Daughter," ibid., 214, 215–6; letter quoted in Graham, *Mirabeau B. Lamar*, 66.

14. Charles B. Strozier, *Lincoln's Quest for Union: Public and Private Meanings* (New York: Basic Books, 1982), 15, 20–1.

many early losses over which he was obliged to grieve: the death of his
younger brother when he was three, and the demise of his mother, as well
as of his aunt and uncle, all victims of the "milk sick," when he was nine
years of age. Lincoln's father, Thomas, virtually abandoned him and his sister shortly after their mother's death and did not return to them, except
briefly, for a year and a quarter. His departure at that crucial juncture was
bound to have a most serious effect on young Abraham. The passing of his
elder sister, almost a surrogate mother, when he was eighteen, was yet another blow.[15]

In light of recent findings about the causes of depression, it is reasonable
to speculate that a genetic predisposition may also have been a factor in
Lincoln's frequently low spirits. We know little of the mental history of his
progenitors. Although Thomas Lincoln made light of his own motherless
youth, he had to have suffered grievously. On the Kentucky frontier in
1781, an Indian murdered his father, Abraham, before the six-year-old
boy's eyes. Orphaned and, owing to the prevailing rules of primogeniture,
disinherited, Thomas grew up discouraged by poverty and loneliness. (His
eldest brother Mordecai was the sole beneficiary.) Although outgoing and
garrulous, he never exerted himself in self-education—or at least his unsympathetic son so charged. "He grew up," Lincoln commented in 1859, "lit-
terally [sic] without education."[16] Despite this deficiency, however, Thomas
Lincoln was, according to more than one reminiscing neighbor, straight-
dealing, sober, and skilled at cabinet making and hunting, his favorite occu-
pations. Even so, Abraham's father was ill-equipped to deal with an intellectual virtuoso like his son. Perhaps his apparent lovelessness toward his
children had emotional roots, but it could also have been simply a difference
in temperament—the macho, thickly built, and aggressive father and the

15. David Donald, *Lincoln Reconsidered: Essays on the Civil War Era* (New York: Vintage, 1956), 40–1; Charles B. Strozier, "Lincoln's Quest for Union: Public and Private Meanings," in *The Historian's Lincoln: Pseudohistory, Psychohistory, and History*, ed. Gabor S.
Boritt and Norman O. Forness (Urbana: University of Illinois Press, 1996), 211–41; Alistair
Munro, "Parental Deprivation in Depressive Patients," *British Journal of Psychiatry* 112
(1966):443–57; Felix Brown, "Depression and Childhood Bereavement," *Journal of Mental
Science* 167 (1961):754; H. Barry Jr., and E. Lindemann, "Critical Ages for Maternal Bereavement in Psychoneuroses," *Psychosomatic Medicine* 22 (1960):166; M. J. Gay and W. L. Tonge,
"The Late Effects of Loss of Parents in Childhood," *British Journal of Psychiatry* 113
(1967):753–59.

16. Lincoln to J. W. Fell, 20 December 1859, in *Abraham Lincoln: His Speeches and Writings*, ed. Basler, 11.

stringy, reclusive son, whom he thought prissy and too tender-hearted. At age eight, Abraham shot a wild turkey. Never afterward had he "pulled a trigger" on other game. Was his repudiation of the hunting mentality a defiance of his father's near obsession with hunting or simply an expression of disgust and anguish over killing a vulnerable creature? According to a family friend, "Thos Lincoln never showed by his actions that he thought much of his son Abraham when a Boy. He treated him rather unkind than otherwise." Thomas preferred his second wife's son, John D. Johnston.[17] If, however, there were any element of depression in the father, that state of mind, in which the sole concern is one's own feelings of self-disdain, might well have prevented him from being the affectionate and sheltering protector of his young ones in their time of need.[18]

We know so little about Nancy Hanks Lincoln that speculation must be equally tentative. Biographer Stephen Oates, though, describes her as Abraham's "thin, dark-haired mother, her eyes like pools of sadness." She raised her children with "a melancholy affection." A Primitive Baptist, she inculcated the fatalism of that Calvinistic faith. "What is to be will be and we can do nothing about it," she used to say. A reason for her rueful outlook was perhaps her uncertain birth. The name of her father has never been ascertained. The possibility that she was illegitimate in a society intolerant of bastardy would help to account for her fatalistic perspective.[19] The mournfulness that so marked her son could, however, have had paternal more than maternal sources.

It must be noted that in his recent biography, David Donald offers a much more positive view of Thomas Lincoln than have many earlier writ-

17. "Short Autobiography Written for the Campaign of 1860, June [1?], 1860," in *Abraham Lincoln*, ed. Basler, 548; Dennis F. Hanks-Erastus Wright Interview, 8 June 1865, in *Herndon's Informants: Letters, Interviews, and Statements about Abraham Lincoln*, ed. Douglas L. Wilson and Rodney O. Davis (Urbana: University of Illinois Press, 1998), 27; A. H. Chapman to WWH, 28 September 1865, ibid., 134. Strozier sees in the telling of this story a child's sense of guilt over a mother's death because Lincoln placed it amidst references to Nancy Hanks's death and the arrival of his step-mother in his life. See Strozier, *Lincoln's Quest for Union*, 25–6.

18. Richard N. Current, *The Lincoln Nobody Knows* (New York: McGraw-Hill, 1958), 23–4; Hanks-Wright Interview, 8 June 1865, in *Herndon's Informants*, ed. Wilson and Davis, 27–8, Hanks to WHH, 13 June 1865, ibid., 37, 41; A. H. Chapman (written statement), ante 8 September 1865, ibid., 95–7.

19. Stephen B. Oates, *With Malice toward None: The Life of Abraham Lincoln* (New York: New American Library, 1977), 5.

ers.[20] Donald asserts that Abraham did not appreciate his father's relatively successful climb from manual laborer at three shillings a day to a freeholder with over three hundred acres. Lincoln's first biographer, William Herndon, deemed Thomas a crude, unloving, and insensitive parent for a lad with a very precocious mind and a preference for books over physical labor. Today the tendency of biographers is to dismiss entirely Herndon's hostile opinions about Thomas Lincoln. Nevertheless, tension between father and son was all too evident. Lincoln felt he had good reason to put a distance between himself and father Thomas. A. H. Chapman, an old neighbor, reported in 1865 that when Thomas Lincoln belatedly returned to the offspring he had abandoned, he was accompanied by his second wife, Sarah Bush Johnston. She was appalled to find the house in virtual ruin and the two children nearly starved and in rags. Implements for cooking and eating were all but absent. Sarah soon set matters to rights, no thanks to Thomas. Apparently she appreciated her stepson more than the father did.[21]

Benjamin Thomas, another biographer, staked out a position in the middle ground. He portrayed Thomas Lincoln as a hardworking, substantial farmer in his early years but claimed that gradually Thomas deteriorated mentally to the point that he could no longer remember how to write his own name.[22] Regardless of what interpretation seems most accurate, Abraham Lincoln's well-documented estrangement from his father might have been a son's bitterness over early parental neglect. It is also possible that he deeply resented what he and his father shared: an inclination to despair. In that instance, Herndon's portrayal of Thomas Lincoln's irresponsibility toward and neglect of his offspring must be given more credence than it has lately enjoyed. Thomas may have provided more sustenance and home life than Herndon contended, but that still left plenty of room for an emotional withdrawal from the boy. In any event, all biographers agree that Abraham reacted against his father's relative inconsequentiality and strove all his life to outperform his old man. Although ready to send money to help his parent in his old age, Lincoln made feeble excuses for not visiting him when Thomas was dying in 1851. Lincoln failed to attend the funeral or even to

20. David Donald, *Lincoln* (New York: Simon and Schuster, 1995), 22, 603 (Louis A. Warren, *Lincoln's Parentage and Childhood* [New York: Century Co., 1926] served as the basis for Donald's approach). See Strozier, *Lincoln's Quest for Union*, 10–5.

21. A. H. Chapman (written statement), ante 8 September 1865, in *Herndon's Informants*, ed. Wilson and Davis, 95–7.

22. Benjamin Thomas, *Abraham Lincoln: A Biography* (New York: Knopf, 1952), 5–6.

have a tombstone placed over the grave.[23] His inaction may have been a shrinking back from yet another familial loss. It could also have involved a withholding of affection for his parent. Certainly his decisions in dealing with his father's decline and death speak of strong feelings, perhaps brought on by the burden of personal loss or by depression-related inheritance—or possibly both.[24]

As if earlier losses had not been a sufficient wound, another blow was the death by typhoid fever of Lincoln's beloved Ann Rutledge. She had been so important in his life that he found it hard to cope with her death. Using the terminology of the day, he called his subsequent gloom "hypochondria" or the "hypo." Lincoln's courtship of Mary Owens, his next marital venture, was so ambiguous and filled with confessions of his gloominess that finally the engagement was broken. On one occasion in 1836 he wrote her, "This letter is so dry a[nd stupid] that I am ashamed to send it, but with my p[resent feel]ings I can not do better."[25]

Never one to romanticize his early beginnings into the rail-splitter image, he told a campaign biographer in 1860, with perhaps a touch of self-pity, "Why, Scripps, it is a great piece of folly to attempt to make anything out of my early life. It can all be condensed into a single sentence and that sentence you will find in Gray's Elegy—'The short and simple annals of the poor.'"[26] His bent for poetry extended far beyond a poem so familiar in Lincoln's day. His fascination with the art never flagged and gave his prose a special musicality.

Throughout his life, Lincoln's favorite poem remained "Mortality," by William Knox, the verses of which he copied and carried about until he had them memorized. In 1850 he recited the poem at a public memorial for Zachary Taylor, the deceased Whig president, and often quoted the quatrains to friends. A stanza of Knox's poem reads: "Oh! why should the spirit of mortal be proud? / Like a swift-fleeting meteor, a fast-flying cloud, / A flash of the lightning, a break of the wave, / He passeth from life to his rest in the grave." Even in his last years Lincoln remarked that Knox's poem was "my almost constant companion; indeed I may say it is continually present with

23. Abraham Lincoln to Thomas Lincoln, 24 December 1848, in *Abraham Lincoln*, ed. Basler, 250; Lincoln to John D. Johnston, 12 January 1851, ibid., 251.

24. Michael Burlingame, *The Inner World of Abraham Lincoln* (Urbana: University of Illinois Press, 1994), 94–5.

25. Abraham Lincoln to Mary Owens, 13 December 1836, in *Abraham Lincoln*, ed. Basler (New York: Grosset & Dunlap, 1946), 61–2.

26. Quoted in Thomas, *Abraham Lincoln*, 4.

me, as it crosses my mind whenever I have relief from anxiety." After visiting the grave of his mother and sister, he composed a poem, "My Childhood-Home I See Again." Clearly Knox had inspired it: "O memory! Thou midway world / Twixt earth and paradise / Where things decayed and loved one lost / In dreamy shadows rise." The last verse has a particularly mordant tone: "I range the fields with pensive tread, / And pace the hollow rooms; / And feel (companions of the dead) / I'm living in the tombs."[27]

No less interesting is Canto 3 of that poem. In it Lincoln ruminates about "poor Matthew" Gentry, a neighbor who had lost his mind. At age nineteen Matthew tried to maim himself, fought his father, and strove to kill his mother. Lincoln himself often spoke of fearing insanity, which, psychohistorian Howard Kushner suggests, was tied to his desperate dread of anonymity and failure to achieve the fame he needed to affirm his life. "Heroism shares with suicide a fantasy of remembrance," Kushner remarks. In "My Childhood-Home I See Again," Lincoln vividly describes Matthew Gentry's frantic struggles to free himself from his alarmed captors, and the narrator sympathizes with his plight. How strange that the insane youth was still alive but spiritually dead, a verse proposes, when others of sound mind and heart had been swept away into the oblivion of death. Bearing in mind the loss of loved ones, the poet appeals: "O death! Thou awe-inspiring prince, / That keepst the world in fear; / Why dost thou tear more blest ones hence, / And leave him ling'ring here?[28] The poem ends on a very poignant note, suggesting the universality and kinship of all human tragedies. The poet can no longer contemplate the predicament of the madman without emotional risk. Yet the memory leaves its trace as the narrator personalizes the situation, bringing him back to the site of his childhood home: "The very spot where grew the bread / That formed my bones, I see. / How strange, old field, on thee to tread / And feel I'm part of thee![29]

As yet Lincoln had not discovered Poe, but later he did read the "The

27. Abraham Lincoln to Andrew Johnston, 6 September 1846, in *Abraham Lincoln,* ed. Basler, 190–1; Robert V. Bruce, *Abraham Lincoln and the Riddle of Death* (Fort Wayne, Indiana: Fourth Annual Gerald McMurtry Lecture, 1981), 11. I am indebted to Howard I. Kushner, *Self-Destruction in the Promised Land: A Psychocultural Biology of American Suicide* (New Brunswick, N.J.: Rutgers University Press, 1989), 132–44, for his enlightening discussion and helpful references.

28. Lincoln to Andrew Johnston, 6 September 1846, in *Abraham Lincoln,* ed. Basler, 193; Kushner, *Self-Destruction in the Promised Land,* 143n.

29. Lincoln to Andrew Johnston, 6 September 1846, in *Abraham Lincoln,* ed. Basler, 191–3.

Raven" and memorized it.[30] To be sure, Lincoln never intended to be a professional writer of poetry, fiction, or any other literary form. Yet can it be doubted that an element of artistic creativity was connected with Lincoln's lifelong episodes of almost clinical mourning? In *Lincoln at Gettysburg,* Garry Wills denies such a conjoining of art and emotional experience and dismisses his early work as merely "fashionably mournful." As Roy Basler and Douglas Wilson recognize, however, the seeds of greatness were discernible in those overly maligned works.[31] Of course, Lincoln's prose style, with its simple elegance and depth of meaning, was his forte. Yet his two surviving poems show that he had an originality rising above the sentimental style of so many aspirants of that poetry-reading era. Most probably he wrote many more verses but did not save them. As he explained with regard to Knox's "Mortality," Lincoln found reading—and also crafting—poems a means to restore his equipoise against the imbalance of hopeless rumination.

Needless to say, many others have thoroughly explored the elegance and structure of his prose. Its relationship to his emotional life, though, bears further comment. It may seem almost absurd to suggest the Gettysburg Address as the best example of prose-poetry written by a southerner in the nineteenth century. Garry Wills has most perceptively unveiled its simplicity of language, discipline of authorial command, sonorous repetitions, and moving cadences.[32] In the Gettysburg Address the artist and statesman built his memorial upon his own emotional foundations within the character of the elegy. The death of his son Willie from typhoid in 1862 had recently exacerbated his mordancy. "Long after the burial the President repeatedly shut himself in a room so that he could weep alone," biographer David Donald writes. "At nights he had happy dreams of being with Willie, only to wake to the sad recognition of death."[33] Delivered in his high tenor voice with a distinctive Kentucky accent, the elegy honored the fallen and announced in memorable terms the purpose of American nationhood. Apart from its bearing on policy and politics, the 272 words united Lincoln's inti-

---

30. Lincoln to Andrew Johnston, 18 April 1846, ibid., 184, and see also 185n.

31. Garry Wills, *Lincoln at Gettysburg* (New York: Simon and Schuster, 1992), 75; Basler, ed., *Abraham Lincoln*, 1–49; Douglas L. Wilson, "Abraham Lincoln's Indiana and the Spirit of the Mortal," *Indiana Magazine of History* 87 (June 1991):155–71.

32. In *Lincoln at Gettysburg*, Wills places the Address in the genre of funeral oration rather than the elegy, but its brevity and its density of meaning suggest a more poetic form, the elegy.

33. Donald, *Lincoln*, 336.

mate acquaintance with grief, his personal appreciation of the human sacri-
fices that had brought those men to their fate, and his esteem for the elegy
itself, that genre of poetry that he had studied all his life. George William
Curtis of *Harper's Weekly* put it well: "The few words of the President were
from the heart to the heart."[34] These words, broken into lines, read in part:

> It is for us the living, rather, to be dedicated
> Here to the unfinished work which they who fought
> Here to thus far so nobly advanced.
> It is rather for us to be here dedicated to the great task
> Remaining before us—that from these honored dead we
> Take increased devotion to that cause for which they gave
> The last full measure of devotion that we here highly resolve that
> These dead shall not have died in vain—that this nation,
> Under God shall have a new birth of freedom—and that
> Government of the people, by the people, for the people,
> Shall not perish from the earth.[35]

The powerful repetitions of such words as "dedicated," "devotion," and
"people," and the strength that comes from the alliteration and the bilabial
stops—"p" of "people," "perish," and "b" of "birth"—and the addition of
the labiodental "f" of "freedom" creates an almost explosive catharsis. One
of Abraham Lincoln's favorite poems was Thomas Gray's "Elegy Written
in a Country Churchyard." In the last three lines, the eighteenth-century
Gray uses the same alliterative device—the labiodental "f" sound and the
alveolar "d" and "s":[36]

THE EPITAPH

Here rests his head upon the lap of Earth
A youth to Fortune and to Fame unknown,
Fair science frowned not on his humble birth,
And Melancholy marked him for her own.

34. Curtis quoted in Donald, *Lincoln,* 465.
35. Abraham Lincoln, "Address Delivered at the Dedication of the Cemetery at Gettysburg, November 19, 1863," in *Abraham Lincoln,* ed. Basler, 734.
36. Edward Callary, "Phonetics," in *Language: Introductory Readings,* ed. Virginia P.
Clark, Paul A. Escholz, and Alfred F. Rosa (New York: St. Martin's Press, 1994), 311.

Large was his bounty, and his soul sincere,
  Heaven did a recompense as largely send:
He gave to Misery all he had, a tear,
  He gained from Heaven ('twas all he wished) a friend.
No further seek his merits to disclose,
  Or draw his frailties from the dread abode
(There they alike in trembling hope repose),
  The bosom of his Father and his God.[37]

The comparison does not imply a direct link or borrowing but simply suggests that Lincoln possessed a poetic frame of mind. After all, poetry is a condensed, musical conveyor of the spoken—more than written—word. James M. McPherson discovers other poetic factors in the Gettysburg "elegy," as he fittingly calls it. While no metaphors appear, McPherson observes, there are "'concealed' or 'structural' ones—three parallel sets of three images each that are intricately interwoven: past, present, and future; continent, nation, battlefield; and birth, death, rebirth." With a logical symbolism devoid of overt metaphor, Lincoln proclaimed that the warriors to be honored had died to keep alive a nation and its mission. In addition, they helped to dispatch to the grave the old confederation, which, the President implied, had long sustained slavery and southern pretensions to chivalry. A rebirth of nationhood and freedom—in fact an entirely new beginning—could now emerge.[38]

Thus it could be said that the Gettysburg Address is a poem that came from the greatest nineteenth-century exemplar of southern melancholy in the evolution of that inspirational source. Did president Jefferson Davis, another southern depressive, ever match Lincoln's mixture of sorrow and renewal as it was spoken in 1863 on a field less than a score of miles north of the Mason-Dixon line?

To return to more unexceptional poetry of dark coloration, we move from the sublimity of Lincoln's oration to little known Theodore O'Hara. Like Lincoln, this soldier-poet of the Mexican conflict was concerned with the battlefield dead and briefly enjoyed considerable celebrity before the Civil War began. He well exemplified the romantic ethos of death, which had be-

---

37. Thomas Gray, "Elegy Written in a Country Churchyard," in *The Norton Anthology of Poetry Revised,* ed. Alexander Allison et al. (New York: Norton, 1970), 510.

38. James M. McPherson, *Abraham Lincoln and the Second American Revolution* (New York: Oxford University Press, 1991), 111.

come a preoccupation not simply because Poe had helped to popularize that theme but because it struck a chord in both England and America. However mediocre O'Hara's effort might now be evaluated, it outshone Mirabeau Lamar's war poetry even if it did not match Lamar's intensity of feeling. Certainly Theodore O'Hara's once-famous poem, "Bivouac of the Dead," touched the popular mood in a way that Lamar never did. Son of an Irish immigrant, O'Hara attended Catholic St. Joseph College in Kentucky. His poetic output was modest, to put it kindly. Yet the more prominent of only two poems received universal acclaim. It offered no challenge to the romantic, honor-drenched theme of soldiering and death. A recent critic has called it "surely one of the best-known elegies in American literature."[39] O'Hara, a commissioned volunteer in the Mexican War, won honors at the battle of Churubusco and afterwards wrote verses for his fallen comrades:

> On Fame's eternal camping ground
>   Their silent tents are spread,
> And Glory guards, with solemn round,
>   The bivouac of the dead.

Throughout the country, North and South, these lines in "Bivouac of the Dead" were later to grace the graves of both Confederate and Union casualties of a much bloodier war than the brief one in which O'Hara had fought. None of the stanzas voiced Christian sentiments about the Mexican or any other war. Instead, O'Hara stressed the ancient code of pagan martial honor:

> Rest on, embalmed and sainted dead,
>   Dear as the blood ye gave,
> No impious footstep here shall tread
>   The herbiage of your grave;
> Nor shall your glory be forgot
>   While Fame her record keeps,
> Or Honor points the hallowed spot
>   Where Valor proudly sleeps.

Likewise, O'Hara's well-received poem "The Old Pioneer," which commemorates Daniel Boone, had a melancholy, death-haunted character. Eter-

---

39. Rayburn S. Moore, "Antebellum Poetry," in *The History of Southern Literature,* ed. Louis D. Rubin Jr. (Baton Rouge: Louisiana State University Press, 1985), 120.

nal remembrance of the frontier hero's mettle serves as the rich postmortem reward:

> A dirge for the brave old pioneer!
>   The patriarch of his tribe!
> He sleeps, no pompous pile marks where,
>   No lines his deeds describe;
> They raised no stone above him here,
>   Nor carved his deathless name—
> An empire is his sepulchre,
>   His epitaph is Fame.[40]

As early as his teenage years, O'Hara had lingered for hours in the State Cemetery of Frankfort, Kentucky. His Irish heritage and the moody preoccupations of poets in the Romantic era seemed to encourage countless visits to such a site. A friend later remarked, "Always inclined to Celtic meditation tinged with sadness, he loved to walk here amid the solitudes and to allow his imagination free flight."[41] Yet, the origins of his melancholy spirit—usually hidden from view by his back-slapping conviviality—are not known. He did not suffer early familial losses as Lincoln did. Kean O'Hara, his school-teaching father, died in 1851 when Theodore was thirty-one, and his mother outlived him.

Nonetheless, some form of depression dogged him, for all his struggles to find release in wild adventures. A dedicated proslavery ideologue, O'Hara joined Narciso López's abortive filibuster against Cuba in 1850. But within minutes of landing at Cárdenas, he received severe leg wounds and was quickly evacuated.[42] Under the on-and-off leadership of former Mississippi governor John A. Quitman, he plotted several times with other self-proclaimed liberators to free Cuba. Later, in 1859, he briefly fell in with the equally disastrous schemes of William Walker against Nicaragua but did not accompany that leader on his last and fatal filibuster. Despite outward signs of high spirits and easy male comradeship, there can be no question

---

40. Poems quoted in Nathaniel Cheairs Hughes Jr. and Thomas Clayton Ware, *Theodore O'Hara: Poet-Soldier of the Old South* (Knoxville: University of Tennessee Press, 1998), 58, 59, 71.

41. Ibid., 16.

42. George H. Genzmer, "Theodore O'Hara," *Dictionary of American Biography,* 22 vols. New York, Charles Scribner's Sons, 1928–58), 14:4–5; Edgar Erskine Hume, "Colonel Theodore O'Hara and Cuban Independence," *Bulletin of the Pan American Union* 71 (May 1937):363–7.

about his early and late alcoholism, an illness that often makes alliance with serious depression. During Captain O'Hara's brief antebellum U.S. Army career (1854–56), Colonel Robert E. Lee had to bring against him charges of "Drunkenness on Duty" while in pursuit of marauding Comanches in Texas. As a result, Colonel Albert Sidney Johnston, Lee's superior, demanded that O'Hara resign or face the ignominy of a court-martial. Humiliated, he obeyed.

After O'Hara had left the army and swiftly squandered a substantial inheritance from his slaveholding, successful father, he continued on a self-destructive path. His biographer remarks that, in the mid-1850s, "like a vagabond" he wandered "from home to home, city to city, job to job," allowing "chances for distinction" to pass through his "hands like water."[43] Then, in 1861, with the outbreak of war in America itself, his military ambitions revived once more. Ill-luck as well as allegiance to patrons with insufficient sway cramped his chances for heroic service. A bureaucratic mixup led to his demotion from colonel of the Twelfth Alabama to second in command. O'Hara felt misused, and, resigning his commission, wrote in fury to the War Department to that effect.[44] Further discourtesies developed after his re-enlistment, so that finally, after eighteen months and a demotion to the still lower rank of captain without sufficient explanation, O'Hara complained, "I have good reason to feel humiliated and degraded by this state of things."[45] The moment of vindication seemed to have arrived when O'Hara's close friend John C. Breckinridge became Jefferson Davis's last secretary of war in January 1865. But it was too late for appointment to brigadier. The Rebel cause was almost dead. Accompanying his patron Breckinridge, O'Hara fled Richmond and had reached Georgia when the war came to an end. In 1867 he had still not found adequate employment and died 7 June, probably from cirrhosis of the liver. How curious it was that this minor poetic figure, who yearned for Confederate laurels above all else, should be solely remembered for some fugitive verses over Union soldiers' graveyards, among them Vicksburg, Cave Hill, Kentucky, Shiloh, Petersburg, Stone's River, and Fredericksburg.[46]

An orator of local renown, O'Hara's eulogy over the grave of Major William Barry, a Mexican War veteran, was famous enough to have had a

43. Hughes and Ware, *Theodore O'Hara*, 95.
44. Ibid., 111.
45. Ibid., 118.
46. Ibid., 145.

minor influence on Lincoln as he prepared the Gettysburg Address. Like Lincoln, O'Hara repeated for emphasis that the dedication was to be rendered "here"—at the State Cemetery, Frankfort. The commemoration closes: "We are here . . . to execute upon these remains . . . that consecrating judgment of ancient Egypt, which, upon a severe trial of the greatest worthies after death, and a cold scrutiny of their whole lives, admitted those of spotless fame and of the loftiest worth to the sublime repose of her everlasting pyramids." Although Lincoln may have read O'Hara's widely reproduced address, he felicitously took his theme in a direction different from O'Hara's, which so resembled Poe's "the glory that was Greece and the grandeur that was Rome."[47] The classical Egyptian cliché and outworn oratorical flourishes place O'Hara far from the simple majesty of Lincoln's effort. Yet, there is a final irony. Thanks to the inspiration and direction of Union Quartermaster Montgomery Meigs, O'Hara's lines "On fame's eternal camping-ground, / Their silent tents are spread, / And glory with solemn round / the bivouac of the dead" embellish, on a prominent plaque, the cemetery that Lincoln so memorably dedicated.[48]

Though much more dedicated to his art than O'Hara, Thomas Holley Chivers, a Georgian, recognized better than his contemporary Poe the futility of composing poetry for profit. In 1830 Chivers took a degree in medicine at Transylvania University in Lexington, Kentucky, but he demonstrated less ambition to practice medicine than to pursue the lyric muse. For his first artistic experiments, published in 1829–30, he chose laments and self-justifications for the failure of his first marriage. Chivers's bride, Frances Elizabeth Chivers, was only sixteen when they wed, and he had barely reached the age of nineteen. Sharing his last name, she was his first cousin, daughter of Thomas's paternal uncle Joel. In *The Path of Sorrow* (1832) and *Songs of Sorrow; or, Cantilodes of Rosemary Gathered from the Grave of Joy* (1837), Chivers sprinkled small details about the marital breakup. His wife had given birth to a daughter not long after her departure in utter fury, accusing her husband of gross monstrosity, which in his autobiographical poems remained unspecified. Chivers never once saw the infant. His wife lived, he declared in one poem, "Away from him—forlorn in weeds of wo! / And would not let him see his only child, / Then born unto his name—nor ever did!"[49]

47. Speech quoted ibid., 18–9; Edgar Allan Poe, "To Helen," in *Complete Tales and Poems of Edgar Allan Poe* (New York: Vintage, 1975), 1017.

48. Hughes and Ware, *Theodore O'Hara*, 69.

49. Charles Henry Watts II, *Thomas Holley Chivers: His Literary Career and His Poetry* (Athens: University of Georgia Press, 1956), 5–7, quotation 7.

Byron, Coleridge, Keats, Shelley, and Kant were Chivers's early guides. Most especially important was Lord Byron, whose theme of the poet as victim of wanderlust, what he called "the blue devils," and social rejection, caught the imagination of so many Anglo-American romantics. But Chivers's derivativeness as an inexperienced apprentice understandably won him little critical acclaim.[50] "Have at you," a contemporary critic mocked, challenging "[all you] mystifiers and double-mystifiers" to bring out "your fog-volumes" to find "a passage equal" to Chivers's absurdities. His first play, *Conrad and Eudora* (1834), dramatized the notorious Sharp-Beauchamp love triangle and murder. In the romantic fashion of the day, he changed the setting of the Kentucky Tragedy, as it was often billed, to Venice, with the customary fittings of Doge's Palace, dark canals, and latticed balconies. The real-life affair had ended in the hanging of Jeroboam O. Beauchamp for killing his wife Ann's alleged seducer, Solomon P. Sharp, a Kentucky politician. William Gilmore Simms's *Beauchampe* (1842), Poe's unfinished play *Politian* (also set in Italy, c. 1835), and Robert Penn Warren's *World Enough and Time* (1950) made use of the well-publicized case.[51] Chivers was an old friend of Beauchamp's defense attorney and incorporated details gleaned from his conversations with the lawyer. But the choice of subject was no doubt related to his continuing obsession over his own aborted marriage. In fact, his whole purpose in writing poetry, he declared, was to sing only of grief as his own misfortune had prompted him to tune "heart strings to music again."[52]

The actual causes for that domestic disaster cannot be known, though both husband and wife shared a tendency to depression—or at least so he characterized his wife's moods. Chivers blamed an interfering relative, his wife's aunt, for the hymeneal wreck. He spoke of her as "a fiend, cursed fiend," but surely the aunt was not wholly responsible for the immature couple's difficulties. A more significant component may have been Chivers's singular devotion to his mother, against whom he constantly and unfavorably compared his new wife. In a poem, he rhapsodized, "Oh, mother! art

50. Ibid., 112–32.

51. Entry for 7 November 1825 in *The Poe Log: A Documentary Life of Edgar Allan Poe, 1809–1849*, ed. Dwight Thomas and David K. Jackson (New York: G. K. Hall, 1987), 65; also, entry for 15 December 1836, ibid., 184; "Scenes from 'Poilitian:' An Unpublished Drama," in *Complete Tales and Poems*, 977–91. The scene is Rome, and the play opens with these words: "**Alessandra.** Thou art sad; **Castiglione.** Castiglione. Sad—not I."

52. Watts, *Chivers*, 211.

thou not that precious light / Which shuts out chaos from my soul?"[53] Refusing to pay alimony or child support, Chivers escaped to a life of wandering about the country until, after several abortive tries, finally obtaining a divorce. At last Georgia law enabled him to win his suit because Frances Elizabeth had absented herself from his hearth for over five years.

With all its twists and turns, the scandal dogged Chivers's reputation and left him in a state of anguish for over a decade. "Have I not been a mock for hell and all / Her clan?" he moaned. In a letter to Alexander H. Stephens in 1838, he poured out his many cares. (Stephens, his attorney and friend, later became a Georgia senator and vice-president of the Confederacy.) "Oh! It is pitiful indeed!" Chivers sighed. "If you could only conceive, for one moment, of the sorrow that I have seen, day and night, for ten years past, you would seek some solitude, as Shelley did for Keats, and brood over my miseries until you lay down in the final sleep of rest where misfortunes are all forgotten!" Stephens, a lifelong bachelor subject to fits of deep gloom himself, probably was not up to the task that Chivers set him to perform. Chivers, though, took the full burden of commiseration on himself, so much so that he claimed to stand as ready as any suicide "to topple headlong in the eddying and pitchy gulf of despair beneath him!" He translated the thought to poetry in the lines "Oh! Would it not be joy to lie / Beneath some green arcade and die."[54]

In addition to these familial woes, Chivers had to meet the sneers and anti-intellectuality of his neighbors in Macon, Georgia. He loved his native land "better than" any other "on the face of the earth." Yet "a certain set of biped Asses," he burst out to his friend Edgar Allan Poe, filled him "with unutterable disgust" over their "miserable carpings," the accumulation of which had forced him into monastic seclusion for nearly a decade. No wonder, he continued, that northerners look with such contempt upon southern culture, "when a man cannot write a decent Editorial for a News Paper without being deafened by the obstreperous cachinnations of thirty thou-

53. Thomas Holley Chivers, "To My Mother," quoted in *The Complete Works of Thomas Holley Chivers, Volume 1, The Correspondence of Thomas Holley Chivers, 1838–1858*, ed. Emma Lester Chase and Lois Ferry Parks (Providence, R.I.: Brown University Press, 1957), 6; Watts, *Chivers*, 113, 267. He wrote five elegies to his mother, but only one poem ever referred to his father.

54. Thomas Holley Chivers to Alexander Hamilton Stephens, 19 September 1838, in Emma Lester Chase and Lois Ferry Parks, eds., *The Complete Works of Thomas Holley Chivers, Volume 1, The Correspondence of Thomas Holley Chivers, 1838–1858* (Providence, R.I.: Brown University Press, 1957) *Chivers*, ed. Chase and Parks, 3–4, 6n16; Watts, *Chivers*, 116.

sand Asses who can neither read nor write." Still worse was the unrelenting boredom that anyone seeking to advance the "honour of his native State" had to endure when dealing with such "ignorant wretches."[55]

No doubt the absence of local admirers as well as distant ones was very vexing. Yet Chivers's art was constricted by his own provincialism, a problem he shared with most other southern writers of that era. They all lacked the rebelliousness, the searching mentality and venturesomeness that came with experiences abroad and in more intellectually receptive surroundings. Chivers's plays were turgid, stilted, full of confusions and laughably illogical sequences. How many plays had he actually ever seen well performed? Happily none of his was ever put on the stage.[56] Remarking on Chivers as a versifier, his friend Poe criticized him in 1842 as "one of the best and one of the worst poets in America. His productions affect one as a wild dream— strange, incongruous, full of images of more than arabesque monstrosity, and snatches of sweet unsustained song." His worst lines were "horrible," his meanings were muddled, his metaphors "mad," and his grammar nonexistent. Other critics were even less charitable. They could not understand his unconventionality, his failure to use the acceptable tropes and similes so often employed, while those of his own making seemed indiscriminately to hit or miss.

Chivers's threnodies on unrequited or betrayed love, loss of children, and other sorrows were scarcely uncommon in the Romantic Age. One of his many books of poems, *The Lost Pleiad* (1845), consists entirely of variations on the subject of death and sorrow. The poems feature shrouds, tombs, angels, graves, spiritual reconnections with the dead, and similar trappings. He was not, however, simply indulging himself in a fashionable poetic mode. For him grievous loss was a matter of sad reality. By then four of his children by his second wife had been swept away by disease. Yet even though his emotions were not as well controlled as Keats's were, he was willing to explore their depths with the accepted Victorian formulae.

The poetic exercise in mourning, in which Chivers engaged himself, was so common in that era, both in America and England, that we might deem it merely sentimental gush on the level of the deaths of Little Nell Trent in Charles Dickens's *The Old Curiosity Shop* or Little Eva in Harriet Beecher Stowe's *Uncle Tom's Cabin*. Although these examples were thoroughly ridi-

55. Chivers to Poe, 1 November 1845, in *Chivers,* ed. Chase and Parks, 62.

56. See Charles M. Lombard, ed., *The Unpublished Plays of Thomas Holley Chivers* (Delmar, N.Y.: Scholars' Facsimiles, 1980).

culed as lugubrious nonsense, even in the Victorian period, many a reader was thoroughly touched by the fictional accounts. After all, child deaths occurred then twenty-five times more often than they occur today. Victorian mothers and fathers—whether English or American, northern or southern—felt the anguish with no less intensity than modern parents would, despite the greater number of offspring that most nineteenth-century families produced. In the epigraph to this chapter, the contemporary English novelist Elizabeth Gaskell points out an important insight. That the deeply felt loss of a child, wife, mother, did not attract the world's notice made the death seem especially rueful. A permanent gap had opened in the lives of those who survived the loved one, and the passage of time would never close it. The creation of a poem served as a memorial that came from the poet's heart, no matter how trite the expression, how overused the metaphor.

Unlike Poe, Chivers did not seek solace in alcohol or other substances. Nonetheless, in their melancholy the pair for a time became soulmates of sorts. Chivers wrote up his reminiscences of his companion after Poe's death and displayed an adoration for the poet's genius and for his inspiring eloquence in conversation. Yet Chivers did not overlook Poe's irresponsible behavior, petty and even vicious quarreling, overdrinking, and mad depressions. Poe's "home," the memoirist declared in his overwrought style, "was a Dream Land, peopled with Ghosts, Ghouls, Vampyres, and the spirits of the unapproachable dead—for whose eternal communion he moaned with an irrepressible groaning as uncommon as the night-long vigils of the Moon in Heaven."[57]

Perhaps somewhat cynically, Poe played to Chivers's vanity, in the hope that the wealthy Georgia doctor would provide the wherewithal to advance his literary ambitions when funds to start a journal were hard to raise.[58] Chivers, however, cagily evaded Poe's investment suggestions. He always kept a close eye on his purse. In his unstimulating solitariness, he did, however, invite Poe to live with him indefinitely in Macon, "although, if ever there was a perfect mystery on earth, you are one—and one of the most *mysterious*."[59] Poe had better sense than to accept the halfhearted offer.

Chivers was more influential on Poe's conception of poetry than Poe ever wished to acknowledge. According to Edmund Wilson, the physician-poet

57. Richard Beale Davis, ed., *Chivers' Life of Poe: From the Manuscripts in the Henry E. Huntington Library, San Marino, California* (New York: Dutton, 1952), 64.
58. Edgar Allan Poe to Chivers, 6 July 1842, in *Chivers*, ed. Chase and Parks, 11–2.
59. Chivers to Poe, 9 September 1845, ibid., 51–5, and Chivers to Poe, 21 February 1847, ibid., 69; see also ibid., 74n5.

had penned lines that Poe adopted as his own but markedly improved upon, particularly in "The Raven" and "Annabel Lee." The use of onomatopoeic sounds to convey a sensuousness and authenticity were hallmarks of Chivers's work. Poe followed suit.[60] Chivers had written these lines:

> While the world lay round me sleeping,
>   I, alone, for Isadore,
> Patient Vigils lonely keeping—
>   Someone said to me while weeping,
> "Why this grief forever more?"
>   And I answered, "I am weeping
> For my blessed ISADORE!"[61]

The obvious resemblance to "The Raven" would not seem so offensive a case of plagiarism when one recalls that Chivers haplessly served other Victorian poets, Gabriel Rossetti and Algernon Swinburne in particular, who took similar liberties with his conceits and style.

Like Poe, Chivers believed poetry had to spring from the heart, not the brain, and that heart was often allegedly broken. A second marriage, to Harriette Hunt, who came from a wealthy New York family, raised his spirits considerably. His second bride was no first cousin, but, like the first, Harriette had yet to reach her seventeenth birthday. Chivers's release from emotional anguish did not last long. When a few years later he lost his laughing, three-year-old daughter Allegra, in a two-day illness, he wrote Poe, "My God! There is a darkness gathering round [my] soul of the deepest sorrow, which the light of no future joy can illumine."[62] She had died on her own birthday, which happened to be Chivers's as well. Apparently he kept the child's body immersed in alcohol until the burial. In 1842 he published "To Allegra Florence in Heaven" to honor her memory but also to demonstrate the connection of art to life—and death.[63]

Chivers fell ill with heart disease in 1858 and died on 18 December—two years before the beginning of the South's great calamity. Recognition of his

60. Edmund Wilson, *Patriotic Gore: Studies in the Literature of the American Civil War* (New York: Oxford University Press, 1962), 498–9.

61. Watts, *Chivers*, 135.

62. Thomas Holley Chivers to Edgar Allan Poe, 7 December 1842, in *Poe Log*, ed. Thomas and Jackson, 388. Also see Chase and Parks, eds., *Chivers*, 19–23.

63. Kenneth Silverman, *Edgar A. Poe: Mournful and Never-Ending Remembrance* (New York: Harper, 1991), 189–90; Chase and Parks, eds., *Chivers*, 21n8.

many books of verses and plays did not come during his lifetime, nor has his work aroused much literary interest since. Yet he was another link connecting despondency and the southern imagination, and therefore deserves a concluding evaluation.

One of Chivers's overlooked achievements, as one critic notes, was his interest in African American speech patterns and rhythms as well as the messages conveyed in song. Poe had taken no interest at all in black folklore or life, but Chivers, though a traditionally minded slaveholder, did. In fact, he championed the integrity of blacks' speech, gift for metaphor, hypnotic use of rhythm, and the rich musicality of their songs. Northerners, Chivers complained, ridiculed black speech out of total ignorance. One of his poems concerned a slave who takes pride in his vigor but looks for heavenly reward in his addressing a friend:

> Doane yoo heer dis Nigur hollur,
>   Old Georgy Joe?
> Sowner dan a silbur dollur
>   Ole Georgy Joe?
>
> . . . .
>
> May de Chay-yot of Alyjur
>   Ole Georgy Joe!
> Kum fum Heben abobe to blidge you
>   Ole Georgy Joe![64]

He meant no slur on rural slave dialect but sought by the misspellings to imitate with unusual sensitivity the sounds he had heard. Chivers had nothing but contempt for the northern minstrel shows with their meanspirited distortions for purposes of mockery. To be sure, Chivers despised the Yankee abolitionist but also the evil-hearted slaveholder. In fact, he had an unusual humanitarian bent, opposing capital punishment when few southerners of his day would have countenanced such radicalism. In 1837 he penned verses that promised a severe but just punishment after death for cruel planters: "The stripes that on [slaves'] backs were laid / Shall heal before their eyes; / And they shall see their servants made / Their masters in the skies." He called it "The Silent Voice." The poem never found a publisher but lies buried in the Duke University archives.[65]

In this regard, Chivers showed considerable sympathy for other human

64. Quoted in Lombard, *Chivers*, 119.
65. I am indebted to Lombard, *Chivers*, 114–27, for these remarks.

creatures beyond or on the margins of respectability. Most notable was his willingness to separate his friend Poe's personal weakness from his artistry, a distinction few other early biographers and contemporaries were willing to make. While he seldom lent or gave Poe a desperately needed penny, he was unstinting in his praise for his friend's creativity and literary discipline. Having made so many enemies, Poe, to the end of his life, was grateful for the steadfastness of Chivers's faith in his art.[66]

A much more accomplished poet, Sidney Lanier, who also came from the upper social ranks of Macon, Georgia, wrote poetry that somewhat resembled Chivers's in tone and style. He also showed marked signs of alienation, though to a much lesser degree than Chivers. Lanier's tendency to depression was not inborn as it was in O'Hara's case nor as sharp and obsessive as Chivers's. Outwardly at least, Lanier's home life seemed so effusively loving that his expressions of love for parents, siblings, wife, and children even exceeded the taste for familial sentimentality that prevailed in Victorian America. His most critical modern biographer suggests that a note of insincerity marked Lanier's letters. He gushed to fiancee, to brother Clifford, or whoever else with whom he corresponded. After three years of marriage he still wrote in this vein: "And so, Most Rare Comrade, I got me to my lonely room, in the night, and sat me down by my lonely fire, and fell a-musing of thee."[67] In this case, more reticence might have been welcome, then and now.[68]

Lanier's gloom—episodic and related to understandable circumstances—reflected the drastic situation in the post–Civil War South, a state of affairs that Chivers had not lived to face. In that respect, Lanier can represent the increased sense of hopelessness that beset those intellectuals who felt the pressures of a lost war, a ruined economy, and a new materialistic spirit of trade and industrial exploitation. Artistically, however, the most serious result was a reinforcement of the provincial conservatism that already had limited the possibilities of a fully vibrant literature. A nostalgic retreat into the past offered no space for experimentation.

Born in 1842, Lanier, like Chivers, had achieved a degree of wealth that might have permitted a kind of artistic development that Lanier actually

66. See Richard Beale Davis, "Introduction," in *Chivers' Life of Poe,* ed. Davis, 9–13.
67. Quoted in Wilson, *Patriotic Gore,* 454.
68. Aubrey Harrison Starke, *Sidney Lanier: A Biographical and Critical Study* (New York: Russell and Russell, 1964), 11–2.

was not to have. His several flourishing plantations would have at least provided him a happy future but for the onset of war. His Huguenot ancestry included musicians at the Renaissance Court of the Tudor-Stuart monarchs. A romantic who loved the poetic mode of "thee's," "thou's" and "methinks" enough to bedeck his correspondence with them to men and women alike, Lanier thoroughly enjoyed his early war years in the Confederate Signal Corps, which was a contrast to war veteran O'Hara's discontent. Stationed at the mouth of the Chesapeake, he spent happy months strumming a guitar, playing the flute, writing poems, riding fine horses, courting plantation belles, and, he wrote, making "plenty of hair-breadth 'scapes from the roving bands of Federals who were continually visiting that Debateable [sic] Land." It had been so "delicious," he later sighed. Up to this point, the young Lanier's experience conformed with the myths that white southerners even today like to think was typical of those chivalrous days.[69]

Then suddenly his life took a disastrous turn. Captured on a blockade-runner in late 1864, he spent the brief remainder of the war at Fort Lookout, Maryland, a camp of some notoriety. His imprisonment lasted only four months but left him a permanent invalid, spitting blood from tuberculosis between extended remissions. Vanished were wealth, slaves, and even hope. The disastrous economic conditions of the postwar era reinforced a point of view shared by all too many antebellum "gentlemen of leisure," as the phrase went—the southerner's customary suspicion of cultural and intellectual matters. Thus Lanier and his brother Clifford considered themselves exiles in their own country. Back in Georgia, the veteran pair found that all the local newspapers had shut down, and subscribing to northern ones was beyond their means. Like Chivers before the war, they could locate no one among their neighbors to sympathize "enough to warrant showing him our little productions." Life in the rural Deep South had never been as busy as a comparable district in the North, but things had come to a standstill. Lanier reported, "I don't think there's a man in town who could be induced to go into his neighbor's store and ask how's trade: for he would have to atone for such an insult with his life. Everything is dreamy, and drowsy, and drone-y." Even nature, from the trees "standing like statues" to the now songless mockingbirds, conspired to imitate human misery. "Our whole world here, yawns in a vast and sultry spell of laziness," he wrote. Lanier mourned that up North business and intellectual activity were thriving, but, he confided to a friend, "you know that with us of the younger

69. Wilson, *Patriotic Gore*, 456–66 (quotation, 456–7).

generation in the South since the War, pretty much the whole of life has been merely not-dying."[70] If Lanier found any comfort at all, it was in nostalgia for the slave world lost. "Trade killed Chivalry," the poet complained, "and now sits in the throne." But at least in the South, he continued, streams "wimpled down the burn" to make nature "beautiful" but not to "make money by turning mill-wheels."[71]

Lanier had little interest in party partisanship, but this southern white dutifully failed to question any of the racial and political conventions of his day. His poem "The Raven Days," which introduces this chapter, was as close to a statement on Republican Reconstruction as he was ever to make. At the time he wrote it, he was a penurious school teacher at manufacturer Daniel Pratt's village of Prattville, Autauga County, Alabama.[72] The verses had a gloomy, fruitless tone that Lanier had pursued before. His brother Clifford described his earliest verses as "*Byronesque,* if not *Wertheresque,* at least tinged with gloominess." Like Chivers's early verses, Lanier's were immature experiments that revealed the influence of Poe. The poet did not preserve most of them.[73]

Lanier's depression did not stem, however, from an inherent and permanent despair. In fact, he was remarkably resilient. Nonetheless his social, financial, and medical problems were sufficient to beat down the most sanguine of spirits. "A happy family life," a biographer notes, was "the only thing that saved him from succumbing to depression," but, it should added, his enduring love of music also helped to raise his flagging spirits.[74] Often ill from a hemorrhaging of the lungs, desperately poor with a wife and brood to care for, Lanier seldom could afford the luxury of writing. The result was frustration and sometimes bitterness. His self-taught flute-playing and enthusiasm for classical works, however, won him appointment at the Peabody Institute in Baltimore in 1873. Later he held an appointment at the newly established Johns Hopkins University. Although at first unable to move his family from Macon because of the low salary, he entered his period of greatest creativity in the mid-1870s there.

    70. Sidney Lanier to W. H. Ward, 7 August 1875, *Letters of Sidney Lanier: Selections from His Correspondence, 1866–1881,* ed. Henry W. Lanier (New York: Charles Scribner's Sons, 1911), 121.

    71. Wilson, *Patriotic Gore,* 459, 460, 461.

    72. Charles R. Anderson, *Sidney Lanier: Poems and Letters* (Baltimore: Johns Hopkins University Press, 1969), 68–9, 87.

    73. Quoted in Starke, *Sidney Lanier,* 37.

    74. Jane S. Gabin, *A Living Minstrelsy: The Poetry and Music of Sidney Lanier* (Macon, Ga.: Mercer University Press, 1985), 17.

Despite his talent, Lanier never quite found himself for reasons that were probably more circumstantial than purely psychological. The war diverted his career in a way that proved detrimental to his art. In 1861 his well-to-do family had planned to send him to Germany for study. Without a war, he would have been open to educational, intellectual, and social maturation—study abroad and perhaps New York and Boston. The opportunity was lost, though, by the disappearance of wealth and of physical health. As a result, his best poems are few, but they do have a musicality and sometimes a radiance that matched his own disposition when playing the flute or listening to an opera by Wagner, a composer whom he most enjoyed. Even his most sympathetic critic, Aubrey Starke, admits that his early verses were "smooth and easy in versification." His post–Civil War poetry was "rarely simple and lyrical" but rather overloaded with theory. Painfully, says Starke, "we are reminded inevitably of the apologetic literature that came from the pens of southern political and military leaders during this same period." In the final throes of consumption, Lanier died at thirty-nine in 1881. He had seldom shown signs of melancholy in his poetry or in his life. All the same, however, his verse is tinged with sadness—with the might-have-beens. One of his poems aptly reflects that struggle to envision the brighter side: "I am strong with the strength of my lord the Sun: / How dark, how dark soever the race that must needs be run, / I am lit with the Sun."[75]

Sidney Lanier drowned in the conventionality and narrow provincialism that characterized the postbellum South. He was simply one among many others less talented than he. Two examples will suffice to illustrate the point.

Happily, Lanier did not participate in the lugubrious work of memorializing the heroes of the late conflict. That task, though, was certainly not neglected, particularly by those much more afflicted by melancholy than was Lanier. The most lachrymose example came from the Confederate poet laureate Father Abram J. Ryan:

> Furl that banner, for 'tis weary;
>   Round its staff 'tis drooping dreary;
> Furl it, fold it, it is best;
>   For there's not a man to wave it,
> And there's not a sword to save it,
>   And there's not one left to lave it

75. Starke, *Sidney Lanier,* 432 (poem quoted), 448.

In the blood which heroes gave it;
   And its foes now scorn and brave it;
   Furl it, hide it—let it rest![76]

Father Abram Ryan's Poe-like elegy on the Rebel cause, composed in April 1865, will never appear in the *Norton's Anthology of American Literature*.[77] Nonetheless, we might consider Ryan's verses representative of the simplest form of elegy—the mourning of the dead, particularly those who died in war—a ritual expression as old as warfare and consciousness of death itself. The Lost Cause with which Ryan so closely identified himself lent itself to the traditional elegiac theme—the mourning of lost heroes, spotless in their purity and dedication to family, community, and country. He was for the Confederate dead what O'Hara ironically had become for the Union fallen.[78]

Father Ryan's woeful verses had their analog in his temperament. Charles Regan Wilson describes him as "a melancholy, morose figure" both in habit and apparel, as he draped himself in a faded black coat that reached to his feet. His poetry not only extolled the idea that "There's grandeur in graves, / There's glory in gloom" but also dwelled on dead mothers and brothers, lost childhoods, unfulfilled loves, and similar themes.[79]

76. Abram J. Ryan, *Poems: Patriotic, Religious, Miscellaneous* (Baltimore: Baltimore Publishing Company, 1885), 185.

77. I will not forget having those lines read by my father to me at age six or seven in the mid-1930s. When growing up in Harrisburg, Pennsylvania, I remember feeling belligerently anti-Yankee when the Rt. Rev. Wyatt Brown, as my Episcopalian father was then known, recited for the family's general benefit the lines of the Catholic priest from Mobile, where my father had begun his ministerial career in the early twentieth century. I do not know if he ever met Father Ryan. Maybe the poetic recitation was an incantation against our Pennsylvania Dutch surroundings. The Browns of Alabama were among the only Democrats on the state capital's Front Street. The governor's mansion, a few doors away, usually housed a Hoover-style Republican.

78. Lewis P. Simpson, *The Dispossessed Garden: Pastoral and History in Southern Literature* (1975; reprint, Baton Rouge: Louisiana State University Press, 1983), 35–100. See also "The Southern Writer and the Great Literary Secession," in Lewis P. Simpson, *The Man of Letters in New England and the South: Essays in the History of Literary Vocation in America* (Baton Rouge: Louisiana State University Press, 1973), 230–5.

79. Charles Reagan Wilson, *Baptized in Blood: The Religion of the Lost Cause, 1865–1920* (Athens: University of Georgia Press, 1980), 58, 59 (quotation), 60–1; Charles C. Boldrick, "Father Abram Ryan: The Poet-Priest of the Confederacy," *Filson Historical Quarterly* 46 (July 1972):201–17; Oscar H. Lipscomb, "Some Unpublished Poems of Abram J. Ryan," *Alabama Review* 25 (July 1972):164–72; Oscar J. Lipscomb, "When and Where Father Ryan Died," *Confederate Veteran* 1 (September 1893):262; F. V. N. Painter, *Poets of the South: A*

Somewhat less pessimistic and personally more agreeable than Father Ryan was Henry Timrod of Charleston, a poet with a degree of genuine talent and literary taste. Like fellow Charlestonian William J. Grayson, Timrod at ten years old lost his father, a victim of tuberculosis. That ubiquitous scourge also killed Timrod, when he was only thirty-eight—as it had Lanier at thirty-nine. "What a sad life!" exclaimed the Yankee poet and short-story writer Constance Fenimore Woolson. She found Timrod's poems very close in ideas to her own. "We fell upon the same train of thought, it seems." In contrast to Grayson and others, Timrod recognized that a chasm had widened between the feelings that an artist experienced and the modes for their expression. The "stilted diction and obligatory high-mindedness" of the Romantic Age stifled the creative impulse.[80] A stanza from "Why Silent" speaks to the matter: "For, I know not why, when I tell my thought, / It seems as though I fling it away; / And the charm wherewith a fancy is fraught, / When secret, died with the fleeting lay / Into which it was wrought."[81]

In the prewar years, Timrod had complained that the southern writer, faced with a limited and indifferent audience, earned the title, "Pariah of Modern Literature."[82] He allowed public rejection to reinforce his own sense of futility and "flat dull waste of dreary pain."[83]

Once the Confederacy was launched, Timrod adopted a new, public voice of cheer and zeal. His contribution to slave-state patriotism won him a popularity that ironically signaled his unpoetic submission to the ideological banalities of the day. But privately, as Louis Rubin has wisely observed, he sounded a different note: "I know not why, but all this weary day, / Suggested by no definite grief or pain, / Sad fancies have been flitting through

---

Series of Biographical and Critical Studies with Typical Poems, Annotated (New York: American Book Co., 1903), 104–09; Kate White, "Father Ryan—the Poet-Priest of the South," *South Atlantic Quarterly* 18 (January 1919):69–74.

80. Constance Fenimore Woolson to Paul Hamilton Hayne, 1 May 1875, in "Some New Letters of Constance Fenimore Woolson," ed. Jay B. Hubbell, *New England Quarterly* 14 (December 1941):723; Louis D. Rubin Jr., "The Poet Laureate of the Confederacy," in Louis D. Rubin Jr., *The Edge of the Swamp: A Study in the Literature and Society of the Old South* (Baton Rouge: Louisiana State University Press, 1989), 192 (quotation).

81. Henry Timrod, "Why Silent," in *The Collected Poems of Henry Timrod: A Variorum Edition,* ed. Edd Winfield Parks and Aileen Wells Parks (Athens: University of Georgia Press, 1965), 91–2.

82. Henry Timrod, "Literature in the South," in *The Essays of Henry Timrod,* ed. Edd Winfield Parks (Athens: University of Georgia Press, 1942), 83.

83. Rubin, *Edge of the Swamp,* 204.

my brain."[84] Timrod's friend Paul Hayne observed how the poem "expresses that numbness of heart" and that "numbness of the hopes, which does not subdue the fancies, but endows them with shapes of doubt, and dread, and terror." Hayne knew whereof he spoke. His northern correspondent, the poet and writer Constance Fenimore Woolson, had tried to cheer him up during one of his cycles of gloom. She urged him to "fight against 'Depression,' that evil spirit that haunts all creative minds. Do not let him conquer you."[85]

Timrod's moodiness had become evident as early as the victory of First Manassas. He wrote of "meadows beaten into bloody clay," flags "drooping in the rain," and of "whispers round the body of the dead!"—not at all martial or inspiring.[86] Rubin eloquently chronicles how Timrod's poetry grew ever more spare and precise as the war made conventional rhetoric seem inappropriate to him. Such an approach of genuinely grim realism never occurred to Lanier or Father Ryan.

Peace, however, brought neither Timrod nor most others in the South much joy. Burdened with wife and child, the poet, then unemployed, nearly starved to death, though it was consumption that took his life in 1867. He had been forced to sell almost all the family's household furnishings. His artistic friends, poor themselves, could do little to help.[87] Considering these circumstances, Timrod's last poem has a touching simplicity.

> In a dim and murky chamber,
>   I am breathing my life away;
> Some one draws a curtain softly
>   And I watch the broadening day.
> As it purples in the zenith,
>   As it brightens on the lawn,
> There's a hush of death about me,
>   And a whisper, "He is gone!"

The lines are flawed. We are not discovering a southern threnody to equal Emily Dickinson's on dying. But that is perhaps the point. Writers from a

84. Parks and Wells, eds., *Collected Poems,* 100.
85. Jay B. Hubbell, ed., *The Last Years of Henry Timrod, 1864–1867* (1941; New York: AMS Press, 1966), 163; Constance Fenimore Woolson to Paul Hamilton Hayne, "All Saints' Day," 1875[?], in "Some New Letters of Constance Fenimore Woolson," 728.
86. Rubin, *Edge of the Swamp,* 205.
87. Hubbell, ed., *Last Years of Henry Timrod,* 77–96.

region of conservative ideals and equally conservative habits of language lacked the sureness to overcome a self-restraint that was conformed to prevailing social conventions and an ethic that privileged the appearance over the substance of things. Some scholars today have boldly suggested that the nineteenth-century South had fashioned a literary culture as rich as that of the contemporary North. Certainly the archeological work of Eugene Genovese, Michael O'Brien, and others might have unearthed a gem or two in the ruins of a defeated slavocracy. But the alienated southern writer had not yet found the means or audience for deeper probing of himself—with the exception of the rebellious and erratic Edgar Allan Poe. He helped to provide a new romantic syntax and an artistic realm of magical gloom, but how quickly these devices had become a convention, even a bulwark against facing the realities of a former nation defeated and forlorn. Their use in the hands of such poets as Father Ryan, for instance, showed that practitioners of gothic imagery and sentimental forms possessed little intellectual confidence.

For this state of affairs, neither slavery nor even racist assumptions should be blamed. At fault, rather, was the kind of culture that the Old South developed, slavery, or race subordination, being part of a larger whole. The collapse of the honor code as a literary assumption and its erosion as a foundation of southern culture could have freed the writer to transform personal pain and trial into art and to gain a new audience. But who had the boldness to do so? Certainly none of the postbellum writers treated here met that challenge.

In the post–Civil War South, as we have seen, faith in "progress" had limits. After the military, political, racial, and economic disaster, a sense of regional humiliation persisted and found little outlet in print. Yet rather than explore the depths of despair that war, penury, and shame might entail, Thomas Nelson Page, and even the more discerning George Washington Cable, kept to the traditional romantic and sentimental conventions. Their prose depicted a conflict they had not experienced and an "Old South" that they knew only through the haze of their elders' nostalgia. Even if the late-nineteenth-century male writers had wished to break from tradition, their editors would not have acquiesced.[88] Basil Gildersleeve, a classicist at the University of Virginia, romantically likened the southern war against northern aggression, as many thought of it, to the Peloponnesian conflict between

88. Fred Hobson, *Tell about the South: The Southern Rage to Explain* (Baton Rouge: Louisiana State University Press, 1983), 134–43; Wilson, *Patriotic Gore*, 579.

Sparta and wealthy Athens. In the analogy, Athens represented Yankee arrogance and Sparta righteous nobility and dedication to principle.[89]

Vigilant guardians of the Confederate shrine held the public true to the Lost Cause. Memories of Stonewall Jackson's calamitous death and Lee's celebrated nobility, annual veteran parades, and other Rebel paraphernalia reminded the upcoming generation about former glories. The old ethic of honor, though diminished, had survived the bloodletting and continued to magnify the gray-clad heroes, still alive or dead. As in all honor cultures, the past was seen as grander and morally worthier than anything in the present. The credo of the young, lamented the aging head-shakers, was rank acquisition and a rule of every man for himself (but, of course, not woman for herself).

Until the last quarter of the nineteenth century, writers in the American North and South for the most part had only restricted devices of literary expression. Anglo-American letters had not furnished them with the means to express antipathy to the unexamined pieties and shallow values that seemed to mark the Victorian era. Only the most ingenious professionals, Hawthorne, Melville, and Henry James among them—all of whom lived in the cosmopolitan Northeast—could surmount conventional literary devices. With the exception of Lincoln, the poets treated in this chapter, for instance, were mostly engaged in translating their personal misery—whatever its psychological antecedents might have been—into romantic lines. Their work memorialized their long-embraced causes and their beloved wives, children, comrades at arms, all deceased. The less-than-burdensome task required little self-exploration. Empathy for those outside the selected orbit had negligible place. Seldom did they reach out to discover wider contexts.

The tenor of the times began to change, however, as American belletrists heeded the warnings of William Dean Howells, Richard Watson Gilder, Roger Burlingame, and other prominent literary figures who tightly held the reins of power. They embraced a literature devoted to "the more smiling aspects of life." Such sentiments were truly "American," Howells insisted, in contrast to Old World decadence and perversity.[90] As the age identified with the English queen waned, intellectuals responded to the ambivalences in life which had yet to be treated seriously. The new questioning found its way southward as the century drew to a close. A bright sun of

89. See Hobson, *Tell about the South*, 130–1.
90. William Dean Howells, *Criticism and Fiction* (New York: Hill and Wang, 1967), 128, 153–4, 159.

experimentation was rising. Indeed, scholars have long recognized the role of modernist thought in transforming the cultural life of early-twentieth-century America. In noting the intellectual rebellion against the restraints of convention, Peter Gay rejoiced in "its bursting" of intellectual "boundaries." This movement did not succumb to "depression; its profound exploration of unreason was not a celebration of irrationality." Yet even Gay recognized that the dominant force at work in this period was a "confluence of anti-rationalism, experimentation, and alienation." Its practitioners sought "a deeper, more penetrating and more expressive radical subjectivity which would give access to the causes of conduct, the springs of imagination, the grounds of being."[91] The fissures in personality—the insubstantiality of human identity—received creative recognition in late Impressionist and Cubist paintings of grim, uncompleted, tormented shapes.[92] Literature would follow suit. The English novelist Virginia Woolf offered her contemporaries the following advice in her essay "Mr. [Arnold] Bennett and Mrs. Brown": "Tolerate the spasmodic, the obscure, the fragmentary, the failure."[93]

91. Peter Gay, *Freud, Jews, and Other Germans: Masters and Victims in Modernist Culture* (New York: Oxford University Press,1978), 23, 26.

92. See T. J. Clark, *Farewell to an Idea: Episodes from a History of Modernism* (New Haven: Yale University Press, 1999).

93. Virginia Woolf, *The Captain's Death Bed and Other Essays* (New York: Harcourt Brace Jovanovich, 1950), 119.

III

SUBVERSIVE HUMOR, MELANCHOLY DUALITIES

5

The Little Shop Girl's Sad Knight
O. Henry

And be it said, amid his pranks so odd
With something nigh to chivalry he trod—
And oft the drear and driven would defend—
The little shop girl's knight, unto the end.
—Nicholas Vachel Lindsay on O. Henry

ANY analysis of southern writing after the Civil War must include the embittered and highly complex satirist Mark Twain, southern to the core but alienated from what white southerners practiced and believed. Though much less celebrated than Twain, two other southern-born humorists of equally melancholy disposition deserve ample discussion. In their own ways, Joel Chandler Harris of Georgia and William Sydney Porter of North Carolina, Texas, and later New York, exploited, like Twain, the genre of subversive humor. While much more circumspect than Twain in the employment of wit, the pair still questioned set beliefs of nineteenth-century southern life. They did so without intending to ignite outrage or disturb the romantic underpinnings of popular literary expectation. More restless, more driven, Twain took bolder steps.[1] Whatever their degrees of dissent

1. See Wayne Mixon, "Humor, Romance, and Realism at the Turn of the Century," in *The History of Southern Literature*, ed. Louis D. Rubin Jr. et al. (Baton Rouge: Louisiana State University Press, 1985), 246–57.

from literary, moral, and social convention, all three authors adopted the mask of comedy to hide deepest feelings from their fragmented selves—and also from the public. The doubleness of their art and their lives was reflected in each assuming a pen name: Samuel Clemens wrote as Mark Twain; Joel Chandler Harris as Uncle Remus; William Sydney Porter as O. Henry. While admittedly the argument is purely speculative, could it be that of these figures' two "selves," one was perilously manic, the other almost fatally despairing, and that by so dividing the states of mind—and dividing their personal from their professional identities—they hoped to lessen the ill effects of both conditions?

In any event, Porter, to whom this chapter is devoted, is the least studied and therefore is treated here with more attention than the other two, who are discussed in the chapter that follows. So much has been written on Twain, most especially, and on Harris as well, that it is hard to say anything new about them. But with regard to psychological configurations and their relation to art and regional culture, some fresh perspectives about all three are possible. Neither Porter nor Harris had the requisite temerity to disclose their alienation and personal feelings. Only through the agency of their stories did they unknowingly reveal more than they ever acknowledged. Harris, for instance, once declared, "Honestly speaking, I have tried to keep Joel Chandler Harris as much out of my works as possible." Yet Louis Rubin comments that "there were depths to Harris' view of the Negro, which I suspect he secretly realized, that carried implications ultimately contradictory to the way his stories were received during the years of their greatest popularity."[2] Likewise, when Porter was not turning out boilerplate tales with trick endings, he could betray a very dark side, as I will shortly discuss. Like Porter, Twain usually hid his disaffection in humor, but of a more sardonic, biting kind. Although he managed to hold securely his Victorian audience, he struggled to express a desperation within while retaining his command over his reading public. Only in his late work, some of which was published posthumously, did he drop the social mask and reveal the full depths of his despondency and nihilistic pessimism. The similarities and differences of outlook and personality that marked the lives and writings of the three professionals illuminates the effect of southern culture upon their

2. Quoted in Joseph M. Griska Jr., "Instead of a 'Gift of Gab': Some New Perspectives on Joel Chandler Harris Biography," in *Critical Essays on Joel Chandler Harris,* ed. R. Bruce Bickley (Boston: G. K. Hall, 1981), 210; Louis D. Rubin Jr., "Uncle Remus and the Ubiquitous Rabbit," in *William Elliott Shoots a Bear: Essays of the Southern Literary Imagination* (Baton Rouge: Louisiana State University Press, 1975), 83.

careers: We see it in their choices of fictional subjects, attitudes about race, and literary inhibitions. Porter and Twain, exiles to the North, may have felt less tied to the South than Harris did. Though his family and boyhood community were deeply southern, Twain grew up in the border state of Missouri before heading west in the late 1850s. Porter, too, left his home state, North Carolina, as a young man and settled in Texas. Harris lived his entire life in Georgia and seldom ventured beyond the state limits. As they grew up, all three were enveloped in traditional southern values, white supremacy, honor, and familial loyalism.

Despite an immersion in the precepts of regional life in their early years, the trio, all of whom were both journalists and fiction writers, showed unmistakable signs of disillusionment with their native land, even as they sometimes extolled its virtues. A major reason was that each one felt that he had been the victim of a malevolent fate that had shattered his family status and substance. In the rank-conscious South such a sense of declension might have engendered a greater degree of shame than it would have elsewhere. Twain exaggerated his family's plight after his father's early death. Taking a different tack, Porter and Harris hardly admitted their humiliation. Curiously, all three presented themselves before the world as having enjoyed happy childhoods—fictions that veiled the bleak truth. Twain's autobiography, for instance, gives the impression of a youngster more or less like the mischievous Tom Sawyer, without a care in the world. William Sydney Porter told interviewers practically nothing about his early years except for the sunnier times. More than the other two, however, Porter sought a literal dualism for special reasons that neither Twain nor Harris had to accommodate. His past required a degree of prevarication, as I will later explain. All three shared these elements: the use of deception, satire (gentle or harsh), artifice, prankish trickery, jocularity, and extraordinary artistic invention.

Ambition for popularity and profit in Porter's case inhibited any painful dissection of the southern soul—or indeed the inner life of anyone else. Like Twain, he understood his market and sought to please the reader with the usual fare of quirky but harmless stereotyping of characters and a happy or ironic twist at the story's close. In contrast to many of his characters, Porter himself underwent experiences in life harrowing enough to try anyone's mental stability. Seldom, though, did he allow stark reality to interfere with the simple object of entertaining. But for his reticence, dread of dishonor, and loyal adherence to the old shibboleths of southern culture, he might have been a superb novelist whose work grew ever more mature and richer as he developed self-confidence. That trajectory, however, was not to be. Nonetheless, his best work did rise above the ordinary. Throughout the first half of the twentieth century, O. Henry stories were the staple fare of young readers. Who does not know the "The Gift of the Magi"? As Vachel Lindsay put it in his doggerel, quoted in the chapter's epigraph, Porter was, in his own day, "the little shop girl's knight, unto the end."

Born in 1862, Porter grew up to receive the customary inculcation into the rituals and ideology of the Lost Cause. After the war, his place of birth, Greensboro, North Carolina, was a center for the state's Reconstruction experiment, under the stern but honest rule of novelist, judge, and Republican carpetbagger Albion Tourgée. Algernon Sidney Porter, M.D., William's father, was christened with a name distinguished in the annals of British liberty. He had, however, become a hopeless drunk who supplemented his fiery diet with drugs. Nowadays, we might attribute Dr. Porter's troubles to post-traumatic stress, or to shell shock or battle fatigue as the condition was called in World Wars I and II, respectively. Algernon Porter had been a Confederate surgeon at a military hospital, where he had amputated limbs to prevent gangrene. The chaos, blood, appendages tossed aside, and screaming and blank-staring patients might have been too much to witness. After the war, Dr. Porter kept a shed out back of the house as a hideout. He would lock the door and pretend to be at work on marvelous inventions. Among them were a flying machine, a steam-run carriage, a mechanical cotton-picker, and a perpetual-motion contraption. (One is reminded that Twain also expected great things from such experiments—and lost thousands of dollars in their pursuit.) Much of the time, though, the senior Porter was holding communion with a bottle or a potion of laudanum. His practice dwindled away. Money for the family was always short.[3] Making matters worse, William Sydney Porter's mother, Mary Jane Virginia Swaim, died from consumption when he was four.[4]

With Porter's father seldom on the premises, household management fell to the doctor's mother, a formidable old lady, and also to his unmarried sister, Evelina. The latter ruled with the proverbial iron fist. In frequent fits of anger, Aunt Lina, swore like a besotted sailor. She ran a private elemen-

3. E. Hudson Long, *O. Henry: The Man and His Work* (Philadelphia: University of Pennsylvania Press, 1949), 11; Richard O'Connor, *O. Henry: The Legendary Life of William S. Porter* (New York: Doubleday, 1970), 6–7.

4. Robert H. Davis and Arthur B. Maurice, *The Caliph of Bagdad: Being Arabian Nights Flashes of the Life, Letters, and Work of O. Henry* (New York: D. Appleton & Co., 1931), 3–9. This work states that she died when he was only three. Other accounts differ.

tary school next to the house. Once, when a student was fleeing hysterically from her fury, she halted his exit with a carefully aimed brick. She kept a bundle of switches near her desk. They were often in flaying use.[5]

Under the circumstances, young William survived his aunt's harsh regime rather well. In 1898, as an adult, he altered the spelling of his middle name both to add English distinction and to distance himself from a past that he did not care to remember. He also claimed a birth date of 1867, five years later than the actual one. By that means he sought further to hide his identity and wipe out memories of a later difficult period in his life. But Porter's childhood was not all gloom. Aunt Lina was a fervent reader of literature. She insisted that her charges should delight in the practice as much as she did. Of course, the canonical list was thoroughly southern. Among her selections were the poems of Father Abram Ryan, John Esten Cooke's early fiction, and the obligatory Scottish novels by Sir Walter Scott. In addition, though, she introduced her youngsters to *One Thousand and One Arabian Nights* and Robert Burton's *Anatomy of Melancholy.* Her nephew read and reread the *Anatomy* with gusto, and also Dickens's *Bleak House,* another favorite.[6]

Aunt Lina shared her nephew's love of cats and with a twinkle named his newborn barn pets Dink, Dank, Dunk, Link, Lank, Lunk, Spink, Spank, and Spunk. No doubt she was being whimsical about Latin conjugating. For games in the yard, Porter and his friends joyfully played Ku Klux Klan. It was especially thrilling to don the makeshift costumes and masks that a neighboring boy's mother made for them. By local reputation, Judge Tourgée, who lived nearby, was the resident monster, even though the townspeople grudgingly admitted his courage and integrity. Almost certainly he did not find games of racial terrorizing a very amusing pastime.[7]

In March 1882, at age twenty, Porter left his job at the local pharmacy. He set out to make his fortune in Texas, which was then afflicted with murderous struggles between cattle ranchers and horse thieves. Such a hotbed of contention offered opportunities for the young writer. Porter considered journalism his prime occupation. Nevertheless, he had to take on other jobs to survive in Austin, the state capital. He fell in with one of the local heroes—Captain Lee Hall, rancher and trigger-ready foe of the cattle robbers and often the target of their threats.

5. Ethel Stephens Arnett, *O. Henry from Polecat Creek* (Greensboro, N.C.: Piedmont Press, 1963), 19; Davis and Maurice, *Caliph of Bagdad,* 9–13, 19.

6. Long, *O. Henry,* 16–7; Davis and Maurice, *Caliph of Bagdad,* 15.

7. Arnett, *O. Henry from Polecat Creek,* 37; O'Connor, *O. Henry,* 9–10.

In 1887, thirty-five-year-old Porter eloped with seventeen-year-old Athol
Estes Roach. Two years later, his child bride gave birth to Margaret Worth.
He and a partner then began publishing a small magazine called *The Rolling
Stone.* Unfortunately, its wit and originality won few subscribers. Porter
was then serving as a teller at the First National Bank of Austin. Abruptly
he resigned to work full time to rescue *The Rolling Stone.* His sudden departure caused suspicion. He was charged with embezzlement, but his guilt or
innocence is still a mystery. Hyder E. Rollins, an Austin, Texas, compatriot
and noted Renaissance scholar, recalled years later, "The affairs of the bank
were managed so loosely that Porter's predecessor was driven to retirement,
his successor to attempted suicide."[8] (Financial wizardry in free-wheeling
Texas seems to have a long history in banking circles.) Even though a grand
jury threw out the indictment for lack of sufficient evidence, not long afterward a second grand jury reopened the case. Apparently Porter had altered
the books to cover his purloining cash to play the cotton futures—an effort
that gained him little but dire trouble. One biographer summed up his evaluation of Porter's dubious decisionmaking: "His reaction to financial temptation, as to marital stress, had been less that of a responsible adult than
that of the overprotected child."[9] In fact, all his life, Porter was unable to
manage money. He was constantly short and in acute need of loans from
friends and publishers.

Porter was served with a subpoena in Houston, where he was working
for a newspaper. The law required him to return to Austin, but on the appointed day, he struck out in the opposite direction, taking a train to New
Orleans and leaving his wife and child behind. At some point, months later,
the fugitive slipped off to Central America. As he came to recognize, the
decision to flee was the height of foolhardiness. Later, after reading Joseph
Conrad's *Lord Jim,* he mourned that he had much in common with the
tragic figure: "I am like Lord Jim, because we both made one fateful mistake
at the supreme crisis of our lives, a mistake from which we could not re-
cover."[10]

8. Quoted in C. Alphonso Smith, *O. Henry Biography* (New York: Doubleday,
1916), 137.

9. Gerald Langford, quoted in Eugene Current-Garcia, *O. Henry (William Sydney Porter): A Study of the Short Fiction* (New York: Twayne Publishers, 1965), 33.

10. Long, *O. Henry,* 47–81; Karen Chairmaine Blansfield, *Cheap Rooms and Restless
Hearts: A Study of Formula in the Urban Tales of William Sydney Porter* (Bowling Green,
Ohio: Bowling Green State University Popular Press, 1988), 15–7; Smith, *O. Henry Biography,*
145 (quotation).

While on the run, Porter secretly kept in touch with his family and his rancher friend Lee Hall. As a result, he learned the tragic news that his wife was dying of tuberculosis, the cause of his mother's death. The couple had already lost their second child, making daughter Margaret their only offspring. Porter came back from Honduras, devastated by the disorder he had caused and by his wife's impending death. For her few remaining months he nursed her as best he could while consulting his lawyers about his coming ordeal before the bench. He tried to comfort his daughter, then eight years old. Margaret recalled in 1923 that "the early days were untinged with the quite natural reserve of maturity. Uncle Remus was a strong bond between us. These stories were read and reread until he would find himself prompted for the slightest variation from the text."

After Athol's death in July 1897, Porter had to face the inevitable. The trial jury found him guilty of embezzlement. His sentence was to serve five years in a federal prison (he had worked at a national bank). When Porter was removed by guards after the trial, Margaret's grandmother and step-grandfather, the Roaches of Austin, became her surrogate parents. The authorities shipped Porter to the Ohio State Penitentiary in Columbus, a huge, grim medieval fortress that apparently housed felons convicted under federal laws. The effect of incarceration on his formerly gregarious personality was almost immediate. He exercised considerable self-control and became extremely tight-lipped as a prisoner. In later years, Margaret explained that his extreme reserve was not shyness but a "passionate desire to be wholly and only himself. Against the intrusion of more aggressive personalities an invisible barrier was erected." He used words, Margaret wrote, as a "barrage of sound protecting the innermost silences of self." Once, when asked what he thought of the hereafter, he replied lightly: "I had a little dog and his name was Rover, / And when he died he died all over."[11]

Porter kept in touch with his in-laws and daughter and indeed keenly longed to reestablish his connection with Margaret as soon as that would be possible. He wrote her charming letters from the penitentiary. One of them began, "Hello, Margaret: Do you remember me? I'm a Brownie, and my name is Aldibirontiphornikophokos." It closed, "Well, Goodbye. I've got to take a ride on a grasshopper." Vainly Porter anticipated a pardon. Not until she was thirty did Margaret learn what had befallen her father during her early years.[12]

11. Davis and Maurice, *Caliph of Bagdad*, 121, 122.
12. Ibid., 119, 120–3 (quotation 123).

Feeling the disgrace as only an honor-conscious southerner might, Porter often expressed in letters to others his desire for a quick and even self-inflicted death.[13] Yet, life behind bars was neither as unwholesome nor as uncomfortable for him as it could have been. Indeed, by the prison standards of the day, Porter, prisoner number 30664, suffered an enviable tenure. He had decent fare, a room without bars, and association with the more enlightened guards and officials. His duties as the prison hospital's night pharmacist for the 2,500 prisoners kept him free from the violence of the regular cells. Yet that privilege and the time it allowed for quiet, uninterrupted writing in the late hours did not assuage his resentment and sense of shame. Dr. John M. Thomas, his boss as prison physician, recalled that in handling over ten thousand inmates in his eight years of tenure, he had "never known a man who was so deeply humiliated by his prison experience as O. Henry."[14]

Indeed, what Porter saw and experienced there at first nearly drove him to take his own life. He wrote his dead wife's mother in 1898 how the prisoners were "regarded as animals without soul or feeling." The majority faced "slow death" from overwork, but many took a different option. Suicides were "as common as picnics." Denied freedom and dignity, inmates "cut their throats and hang themselves and stop up their cells and turn the gas on." Understandably, Porter was powerfully affected by these common horrors as well as by his own plight: "I often get as blue as any one can get and I feel as thoroughly miserable as it is possible to feel."[15] However loathsome conditions were, Porter observed but remained stoically silent. One prisoner, an Indian presumed dead, had been thrown into a trench for burial. Somehow he revived and found the strength to crawl out before the earth had completely covered the pit. Knowing of such matters, Porter might have protested the inhumanity of the authorities, then or later. He had seen other scenes of degradation, which, in that pre-muckraking, Victorian period, he was constrained never to write up or even to mention. Reading behind his remarks about degenerate behavior, though, one detects hints of male rape. When later importuned to expose the horrors and perversities of prison life, he exclaimed, "I shall never mention the name of prison. I shall never speak of crime and punishments. I tell you I will not attempt to bring a remedy to the diseased soul of society. I will forget I ever breathed

13. Smith, O. Henry Biography, 143.

14. Davis and Maurice, Caliph of Bagdad, 140; Current-Garcia, O. Henry, 34.

15. William Sydney Porter to Mrs. C. P. Roach, 5 June 1898, in Davis and Maurice, Caliph of Bagdad, 153–4.

behind these walls."[16] It was the reaction of an emotionally bruised, conservative southerner, not that of a Yankee journalistic reformer.

While in the penitentiary, Porter assumed the facade of the model prisoner. He never complained, never spoke out, and he made few close associates. Harry Peyton Steger knew Porter both before and after his incarceration. In recollection he declared, "In his twenties and later in New York, he was the same lone wolf." Porter did, however, befriend a seventeen-year-old boy, nicknamed Kid, whose swimming companion had accidentally drowned in the Scioto River. On the slimmest of evidence, the simple, possibly retarded teenager was charged with murder, sentenced, and scheduled for electrocution. Porter and his only friend, Al Jennings, witnessed the fatal scene. The warden approached the boy as he sat quivering in the chair, the electrodes sticking to his shaved head and bare legs. "Confess, Kid," yelled the warden. It took some time for the frightened victim to understand, but at last he said quietly, "I ain't guilty. I never killed him." The warden threw the lever, and the body jumped, wriggled, fell back "like a piece of barbed wire vibrates out when it is suddenly cut from a fence."[17] Porter was deeply moved. He burned with indignation that a jury could convict an innocent boy and have him put to death. Yet he did not use such prison experiences as this in his fiction. Comedy, not sad reflection or representations of hideous realities, would be his literary aim. But what a burden of memory to suppress.

By the use of his humorous side, by a studied conscientiousness and honesty as a pharmacist, and by his repression of emotions, Porter stayed out of trouble and reduced his time in prison to a little over three years. He returned to freedom in 1901.

Porter had every reason to draw an impenetrable veil over his prison experience and never to speak of it in any venue that might reach the public. Settling in New York in 1902, he found he could be as anonymous as he could hope for. There he presented himself to the public and to strangers as O. Henry, a guise that prevented people from learning about his past. Most of Porter's life after prison was spent in New York. The majority of his work concerned life in the urban North. All the same, he remained at heart a southerner in exile. Curiously, he never lost his southern accent.

In his fiction, as we shall soon see, he observed a world of pain and sorrow but colored it all in palatable, risible surprise. Deliberately Porter re-

16. Al Jennings, *Through the Shadows with O. Henry* (New York: H. K. Fly, 1921), 222.

17. Smith, *O. Henry Biography*, 116; Jennings, *Through the Shadows*, 243–4.

pressed his shattered idealism and fled in imagination any serious questioning about the human condition. He played the part of the sympathetic observer. He was never a moralizer like the pious George Washington Cable, who championed the cause of the freed people, a position that led to his exile to the North. The role of indignant reformer was something that Twain, often superficially and unoriginally, adopted, but Porter never did.

One of Porter's earliest and funniest accounts concerns southern life. Written in Texas long before his indictment and incarceration, it is called "Vereton Villa: A Tale of the South." Indeed, his other Texas stories are very much in the southwestern style of humor and exaggeration and form a separate part of his oeuvre. The narrator of "Vereton Villa" is a Boston schoolmarm visiting the South. Penelope Cook smugly claims an intimate knowledge of southern culture and habits from reading those notable experts, Harriet Beecher Stowe and Albion Tourgée, the latter being Porter's hometown judge and author of the popular Reconstruction novel A Fool's Errand.Playing it straight, O. Henry declares in a brief prefatory note, "Everyone living in the South will recognize the accurate portraits of Southern types of character."[18] In "Vereton Villa," Penelope leaves the Houston station, driven by an old freedman who suddenly bursts into tears. A broken trace chain reminds him of "Massa Linkum what am in heb'n." Piously the abolitionist Bostonian replies, "Pete . . . do not weep. In the mansions blessed above, your god-like liberator awaits you." Overtaken by her soothing kindness, he sobs into her lap. Penelope is obliged to drive the pair of desiccated mules up to the plantation. They arrive just as another mule is shooed out the front door with a broom. The disciplinary instrument is in the hands of the aristocratic Mrs. DeVere, whose diamond-bedecked bosom, "Grecian features, snowy white hair, and black satin dress" identify her as the allegedly typical southern matron. While the mule takes its ease on the veranda, the dignified old lady receives the newcomer with customary southern hospitality but warns her to stay clear of "that dam mule. I can't keep him out of the house." The interior is well appointed, but signs of decay and sloth soon become evident. A wheelbarrow with long-dried mortar occupies a place in the parlor, while some chickens roost on the piano. Somebody's pants hang from the central chandelier.

In the sketch, Aubrey DeVere, the young and handsome son and heir, a

18. "Vereton Villa: A Tale of the South," in O. Henry Encore: Stories and Illustrations by O. Henry, Usually Under the Name The Post Man, ed. Mary Sunlocks Harrell (New York: Doubleday, 1939), 119.

mere seven feet tall, graciously steps forward in an expensive suit in the latest fashion: "His eyes were immense, dark, and filled with haunting sadness, and his pale, patrician features and air of *haut monde* stamped him at once as the descendant of a long line of aristocrats." But his savoir faire is somewhat tarnished by the absence of shoes. Underneath the fancy dress coat he displays his underwear, offset by "an enormous scintillating diamond tied with a piece of twine." Tobacco juice streaks down the side of his face. When the naive Penelope says something unpleasant about Jefferson Davis, Aubrey flies into a rage. He seizes a clucking chicken, unfortunate enough to be strutting by, and wrings its neck. It flops about headless, spilling blood all over "the delicate Brussels carpet." Aubrey cries out, "That is the South, the bleeding and dying South after Gettysburg." Furious, he pitches the chicken's head into the schoolteacher's face. Then, in immediate remorse, he falls to one knee before her, lugubriously begging forgiveness. Aubrey explains that twenty-eight years earlier his daddy had died during the battle of Shiloh. At dinner, the main course is the hapless chicken. Once again Aubrey erupts in savage rage. He drives the carving knife into the breast of Pete, the black servant. The freedman has spilled a spot of gravy on the damask tablecloth. Penelope rushes to her carriage driver's side and hears his dying whisper, "Good-bye, missie . . . I hear de angels singing and I sees de bressed Mars Abraham Linkum smilin' at me from near de great white th'one."

Later on, Aubrey's anger flares up once again when Penelope refuses his grotesque advances. He hurls her through a window, following up with an avalanche of parlor furniture, including the piano. She faints and awakens in her own bed with the once more repentant Aubrey nursing her. Shortly afterwards, Cyrus, her fiancee from Boston, arrives, but the household is greeted by a party of masked men. They rush in to lynch "a damned Yankee," who, they have heard, has been skulking about. Aubrey seizes a table leg, wrenches it free, and kills all the intruders. Thus he shields the family honor, upholding his duty as a host by protecting his guests. At the train station, where Cyrus and Penelope await the train for Boston, Aubrey settles himself on a keg of blasting powder and blows himself to smithereens. His big toe lands in Penelope's lap as the train pulls out. The appendage becomes a poignant memento of her sojourn in the overly impulsive, slothful South. We are told that thereafter she holds it as a keepsake in a bottle of alcohol next to her bed.[19]

19. Ibid., 120–9.

Much of Porter's humor follows a similar pattern—unexpected distortions of probability, pratfalls, malapropisms, plays of language and dialect, southwestern tall-tale exaggeration, and an irony that seldom was as acerbic as Twain's. His satire is generally evenhanded, as we see in "Vereton Villa." Porter's intent in the story is not simply to mock one side of the sectional conflict and pit it against the other. "Vereton Villa" may be read not merely as a spoof of northern misconceptions about southern life but also as a critique of the South with its myths of wealth, ease, impeccable manners, and defensive Lost Cause preoccupations. So much attention is devoted to the violent whims of Aubrey DeVere that Penelope, the abolitionist storyteller, becomes more observer than object of derision. In fact, her plight at Vereton Villa arouses some sympathy.

Such stories as "The Duplicity of Hargraves" belong in the same southern Cavalier tradition. Planters had always loved to laugh at such pretensions even as they upheld the heroic ideal. Written in the Ohio prison, June 1900, "Hargraves" appeared in New York's *Munsey's Magazine*. It was among the first stories bearing the pen name O. Henry. ("Hargraves" earned the unknown author the meager sum of $60.00.)[20] Showing a greater acuteness and maturity than he did in his Texas parody, Porter in this story introduces the character of the trickster, which Twain and Harris also utilized to great effect. Porter also shared with Harris the employment of another, less-flattering character "type"—that of the old-time black cap-doffer who feels nostalgic about old slavery days. Though as is often the case with O. Henry, he gives his creation a twist.

Briefly recapped, "The Duplicity of Hargraves" gently lampoons Major Pendleton Talbot of Mobile, Alabama. In his worn-out frock coat and "little black string tie," Major Talbot, a stiff, honor-obsessed, veteran of the late war, and his daughter Lydia, reside in a Washington, D.C., boardinghouse on very slim resources. While writing his memoirs, the major regales another lodger, a young vaudeville actor named Henry Hopkins Hargraves, with endless stories of bench, bar, and battle. Hargraves seems most respectful and attentive to every detail, which endears him to the major. Finding his funds all but exhausted, the major nonetheless scorns reality and buys two tickets for the vaudeville theater. He and Lydia attend, only to discover that Hargraves has reproduced the major's "queer clothes," his antique mannerisms, and his stories of former wealth and glory to perfection. The performance wins hearty applause from the audience and rave newspaper

20. Davis and Maurice, *Caliph of Bagdad*, 191–2, 239, 262.

reviews. Major Talbot, though, is thoroughly humiliated. In a confrontation with the actor, he resentfully denounces his doppelgänger. Claiming that no disrespect was intended, Hargraves offers him three hundred dollars. The actor explains that he knows all about the unsound state of the Talbots' finances. Peremptorily the major spurns the offered compensation. After Hargraves has moved away, an old and slavishly deferential freedman asks to see the decrepit veteran at the lodgings. Identifying himself as Uncle Mose, the visitor explains that he had worked for the Talbots many years before and has come to repay an old debt. After emancipation, Talbot's grandfather had generously lent him some mules. Mose has prospered so well that he now owns his own land in "Nebrasky" and seeks to make good the longstanding obligation. Touched by the simple honesty of a former and grateful slave, whom he could not actually remember, Talbot graciously accepts the sum of three hundred dollars. A short time afterward, Lydia receives a note from Hargraves, boasting of his success in New York and inquiring, "How did I play Uncle Mose?"[21]

Slight though the story is, the actor Hargraves belongs in the venerable and almost universal literary tradition of the trickster. He is a subversive imposter who deceives the major, not once but twice, with his acting ability. Like some amoral tricksters in other stories, Hargraves is rather unscrupulous in pursuing his own ends—in this case the acclaim of audiences. It suits his purpose to treat the source of his theatrical success to a second display of his talents. Even though the object is also to repay the old Rebel for Hargraves's first deception, the ultimate cruelty is the actor's hubris in informing the major's daughter of his trick, which not only diminishes the generosity of his gesture but also places a burden on Lydia, who must thereafter bear the secret, and the shame, alone. One wonders how Porter expected the reader to perceive the second deception. Did he want the reader to see it as unfeeling, as if Hargraves were saying to Lydia, "I can manipulate you. See how clever I am?" To be sure, Hargraves is not entirely without principle. He has benefitted father and daughter with money he apparently can easily spare. Nonetheless, Hargraves's character, and hence the story, seems partially unrealized. Porter's own cleverness allowed for a certain detachment that kept him from investing in fully credible, rounded figures. In his understanding of the writing craft, plot usually trumped character development.

21. "The Duplicity of Hargraves," in *The Complete Works of O. Henry* (New York: Garden City Publishers, 1937), 850–9.

Porter often took up the theme of deception, occasionally with a more biting and pessimistic tone, suggesting that he had the innate resources for richer work than what he produced. "The Furnished Room" tersely relates the story of two callous Irish landladies who gossip downstairs while the newly arrived young lodger carries out his suicide in a room where the prior occupant had done the same. This powerful sketch and the still grimmer "The Enchanted Kiss" were among Porter's more realistic, astringent stories. "The Furnished Room" was more appreciated abroad than in this country. Stephen Leacock, another short-story professional, declared that in it O. Henry had surpassed Maupassant.[22]

In contrast to the life Porter led and the lives in the streets he observed, his fiction made few claims to realism. In this respect he was true to his romantic heritage. His object was light entertainment. Porter may have fretted that writing anything more serious would lead to probings into depths that he would rather leave untouched. At least in part, however, the romantic bent in his fiction can be attributed to his long immersion in the southern literary style. The author, despite his brilliance of mind, had no wish to free himself altogether from his regional past. He could be sentimental about the South he knew as an apprentice pharmacist at the Greensboro store. There, old-timers, including his bibulous father, sat around a pot-bellied stove and whiled away the lazy hours.

A cynical streak sometimes appeared in his less sentimental stories. In "The Plutonian Fire," for instance, Porter has a young aspiring writer from Alabama try his fortune in the brisk, cut-throat world of journalism in New York City. He had enjoyed literary success in home newspapers, largely because he was "the son of 'the gallant' Major Pettingill Pettit, our former County Attorney General and hero of the battle of Lookout Mountain."[23] The young writer tries his hand at lengthy, Scott-like medieval love novels, set in Picardy, 1239. At night, though, he discovers New York's bars and beans—only ten cents. Inspired by an encounter with a gorgeous New York girl, he scribbles down a story titled "Suffering Sappho!" Pettit's narrator-friend judges it "sentimental drivel, full of whimpering softheartedness and gushing egotism." When the girl jilts him, Pettit moans of prussic acid, the

22. "The Furnished Room," ibid., 96–101; "The Enchanted Kiss,"ibid., 466–76; see also "The Cabellero's Way," ibid., 197–206; Davis and Maurice, *Caliph of Bagdad,* 375. On the trickster motif, see "Introduction," in *O. Henry's Texas Stories,* ed. Marian McClintock and Michael Simms (Dallas, Tex.: Still Point Press, 1986), xxi–xxvii. I am indebted to these editors for their insights.

23. Porter, "The Plutonian Fire," *Complete Works,* 1265.

grave, or banishment to South America. An evening of whiskey swings him around, and he writes with a new fervor. Another young woman falls in love with him, but he rejects her, and she nearly commits suicide. His latest effort wins an editor's highest praise and promises of contracts and good pay. Yet Pettit tears up his masterpiece and bitterly rejoins, "I see the game now. You can't write with ink, and you can't write with your own heart's blood, but you can write with the heart's blood of someone else. You have to be a cad before you can be an artist." He goes to his Alabama home "to sell ploughs for father." Porter may well have felt that way about his own career, which was then coming to a close.[24]

In Porter's last three years, he grew aware of his declining health and worried about his creative legacy. His fame was then at its height. Yet spendthrift habits and poor remuneration for his stories kept him close to insolvency. Behind that downcast attitude about the meager monetary value of his work lay Porter's devaluation of his stories' literary worth. In 1909 he exclaimed, "My Stories? No, they don't satisfy me. It depresses me to have people point out or introduce me as a 'celebrated author.' It seems such a big label for such picayune goods."[25]

Yet Porter was a dazzling storyteller. He drew his material from his own sense of alienation. He spent his time away from pen and desk "bumming" through the sleazier parts of New York, or indeed wherever he happened to be. Dr. D. Daniels, an acquaintance from Porter's Austin days, recalled how the writer had never "cared for the so-called 'higher classes.'" Instead, he roamed the bars, casinos, brothels, and downtown streets where the homeless and the poor prowled about. "I've seen the most ragged specimen of a bum hold up Porter, who would always do anything he could for the man," Daniels reported.[26] No doubt Porter's time in prison further helped to shape his contrasting attitudes toward the rich and poor. Yet even as he despised the seedy post–Civil War southern aristocracy, such as it was, and the Yankee moneybags, he could not shake off the culture in which he was raised. Despite his extraordinary verbal and literary skills, he never slipped away from the gentlemanly code to pass along a dirty joke. In his stories he seldom exposed the full extent of misery, morbid cruelties, and penury in the lives of the lower classes with whom he consorted in real life.

Toward the end of O. Henry's brief life, he turned from depictions of

24. Ibid., 1267–9.
25. Current-Garcia, O. Henry, 140.
26. See Smith, O. Henry Biography, 117.

northern urban society to settings in his homeland. He talked about writing a novel centered in a backwater, his place of birth. Only thirty of his six hundred stories had been set in the South. Yet while planning this excursion into uncharted memories, Porter may have known that his life was ebbing away. Increasingly he felt desperate, nostalgic, and confused—all at the same time. "I always have the feeling," he confided to a *New York Times* reporter, "that I want to get back from somewhere, but I just don't know where it is." The place he vaguely sought lay in the somnolent town of Greensboro, but he said "back from," not "back to somewhere." Among other characters in the tale, he planned to depict the "professional Southerner," quick to blame all his troubles on the late war and defeat. The main character, though, would forswear that role, he promised himself. The unnamed character would undergo various adventures in the criminal underworld but always retain a vigorous integrity. On some level this hero (Porter himself) was to be no facetious cynic, no silent observer of the degradation surrounding him. "I want this man to be a man of natural intelligence . . . absolutely open and broad-minded; and show how the Creator of the earth has got him in a rat trap . . . and then I want to show what he does about it. There is always the eternal question from the Primal Source—'What are you going to do about it?'" In fiction, if not in real life, Porter, the author, alcoholic, ex-convict, in this second self would do something grand, humane, and heroic. His outline won him an advance and contract from *Collier's Weekly.* But a curious inability to carry through on the autobiographical project led him to accept instead sums for other work that he could not begin, much less finish. In one instance, against wise advice, he sold for $250 a story, "A Retrieved Reformation," to George Tyler, a New York theater producer, rather than work on the script himself. The original version was based on incidents picked up from his Ohio Prison days. Although he had sentimentalized the narrative, Porter developed the main character, a safe-cracker, into a rather vivid figure. Hastily rewritten by Paul Armstrong, a noted playwright, the subsequent production became a standing-room-only stage hit. Under the title *Alias Jimmy Valentine,* Porter's work earned Armstrong over $100,000.[27] Meantime, the southern novel still was on his mind—without, however, any sign of its completion.

Partly responsible for his late-flowering interest in things southern was his marriage in 1907 to Sara Coleman, then thirty-seven to his forty-six. He

27. O'Connor, *O. Henry,* 195 (first quotation), 197 (second quotation), 213–15; Current-Garcia, *O. Henry,* 3.

had known Sara back in Greensboro so many years before. By wedding her, he sought to recapture his youth and, above all, to gain renewed respectability—not the most promising reasons for wedlock. As Porter noted to his friend Al Jennings, Sara was "a high-bred woman," with all the gentility that a southern lady from North Carolina could represent.[28] Jennings thought Porter very ill-suited for such a union—or any marriage, given his nighttime habits and moodiness. Even Porter later admitted that he had "brought all my troubles upon her. Was it right?" Her ladylike manners made his New York journalist chums uncomfortable. In truth, Sara's husband actually preferred their company to hers. Porter's declining health and tensions arising from Sara's trouble handling Margaret did not make for a tranquil home. For her part, teenage step-daughter Margaret had long since learned that the outwardly casual fellow with the smiling countenance and twinkling eyes was only one part that her father played. When his melancholia seized him, it was like a descending shadow. She wrote, "he would be plunged into silence, black silences, the portent of which he alone could know; for, although there is understanding, it is not humanly possible to accompany one of those dark journeyings." Margaret herself felt left in the cold. Her father always called her Bill, Jim, or Pete, as if she were one of his drinking cronies. He seldom could convey his love for her in her presence. On their very last meeting before his death, he awkwardly mumbled something of his feelings. Finally, to override his embarrassment, she told him, "I have seen . . . and understood." The effect of her words was immediately evident: "There flashed across his face an expression of inestimable relief and one of his rare smiles."[29]

Never exactly sure of who he was or how he felt, Porter fooled his friends and himself about his health toward the close of his life. A local sawbones, he claimed, found no physical ailments at all, only "neurasthenia," at that time a common name for depression and its accompanying symptoms of sleeplessness and headaches. Porter dismissed the gloomier diagnoses of his New York physicians.[30] Nonetheless, he had to confess a lack of progress to

28. Long, *O. Henry*, 126; O'Connor, *O. Henry*, 186.

29. Margaret Porter quoted in Davis and Maurice, *Caliph of Bagdad*, 133; O'Connor, *O. Henry*, 201. Margaret was herself a writer, but tuberculosis overtook her and she died at thirty-eight in the arms of Guy Sartin, her English lover, who married her just before she expired. She insisted on the ceremony so that he could inherit her estate, consisting of royalty contracts for her father's works. See Davis and Maurice, *Caliph of Bagdad*, 134–6.

30. William Sydney Porter to Harry Peyton Steger, 5 November 1909, William Sydney Porter Papers, Perkins Library, Duke University.

his waiting publishers. Admitting to a raging hangover, he wrote an editor at Doubleday, "I was so much under the weather today that I didn't get up to my work shop 'til now."[31]

There is no question that deep despair was speeding Porter toward the grave. In January 1910 he wrote his friend George Tyler that he was suffering from "cirrhosis of the liver, fatty degeneration of the heart, and neurasthenia." The maladies, he joked, made him "about as nervous and reflaxactionary as the hind leg of a frog."[32] Chief among Porter's medical problems was his acute alcoholism. His friend Robert H. Davis thought it amazing that the author of so vast a volume of fiction could put away as much liquor as he did. Yet toward the close of his life, Porter's productivity declined dramatically. Davis speculated that "the recollection of the dark hours in his earlier life took toll of his resistance."[33] After he had died, nine empty whiskey bottles were found in his room at the Caledonia.

In early 1910, Charles Russell Hancock, Porter's last New York doctor, hastened him to the Polyclinic Hospital on East 38th Street. Porter was perilously ill, yet so discomfitted by his vulnerability that he insisted on signing the registry as "Dennis." Then he changed his mind and wanted to be called "Will S. Parker" to retain his initials. Even on the edge of death, he scrambled his identity. Emptying his pockets on the reception counter, he muttered, "Here I am going to die and only worth twenty-three cents."[34] In a sense this underground man, like Dostoevsky's, considered himself worth little more. The only remedy the author O. Henry had found for his profound melancholy—as had so many other writers, southern and otherwise—was the feat of imaginative creation.

Porter died in the Polyclinic on 5 June 1910. During the evening before, a nurse had come in to prepare the room for the night. He whispered to her, "Turn up the lights. I don't want to go home in the dark." He died early the following morning. At the very end he was quite alert and knew that death was upon him. His friend Dr. Charles R. Hancock recalled, "I never saw a man pluckier in facing it or in bearing pain. Nothing appeared to worry him at the last." By that time Porter realized that he need no longer bear the

31. William S. Porter to H. W. Lanier, n.d. [1909], ibid. See also Porter to Lanier, 1 January, 13 February, 16 March, 6, 9 April 1909, ibid.

32. William S. Porter to George Tyler, [?] January 1910, in Davis and Maurice, *Caliph of Bagdad,* 389.

33. Ibid., 362.

34. Smith, *O. Henry,* 249–50; O'Connor, *O. Henry,* 228–9; Davis and Maurice, *Caliph of Bagdad,* 361–2, 397.

shame that had dogged him so long. On 7 June at the Episcopal Church of the Transfiguration, the site of so many weddings and funerals of theater people and newsmen, the pallbearers included Richard Harding Davis, Walter Hines Page, the Virginian author who later served Woodrow Wilson as ambassador to London, and other notables in the journalistic world. He knew none of them well. Porter would have been much more comfortable if his barkeeping friends and policemen on the Bowery beat had borne him to his grave.[35]

As one of the more inventive of the nineteenth-century practitioners of the short story, Porter was to have an annual prize for that fictional form presented in the name of O. Henry. Curiously, most of the nineteenth-century short-story giants died at relatively young ages; Porter was only forty-eight. Edgar Allan Poe (forty), Guy de Maupassant (forty-three), Robert Louis Stevenson (forty-four), Stephen Crane (twenty-nine), and Jack London (forty) also died early, and the emotionally crippled Bret Harte, who died at sixty-six, burned out at fifty and wrote no more. To greater or lesser degree, each of these figures suffered from a sometimes disabling emotional distress—or worse. De Maupassant and Poe died insane; Crane lived far beyond his means, perhaps to fend off a fear of death from tuberculosis. Porter, Harte, and London drowned their depression in alcohol. Ambrose Bierce lived to seventy-three but suffered severely from depression. In 1913 he disappeared during the Mexican Revolution.[36] All of these writers were alienated from their roots, and most lived elsewhere—Porter and Poe in New York, Crane and Harte in England. As a journalist, Bierce was often away from San Francisco. Wracked with tuberculosis, Stevenson resided in the South Pacific, far from his homeland. Like Mark Twain, these inveterate souls were spiritual as well as physical exiles. Because southerners generally turned an indifferent and even hostile eye upon the solitary, artistic impulse, they added an extra burden to intellectuals native to the region, whether they resided there or elsewhere.

Although his end was not untypical of alcoholic sufferers, O. Henry's death brought a sad conclusion to the life of an artist who thought little of his accomplishments. He knew that he had not achieved the sort of literary greatness that a less inhibited soul might have reached. In his story "The

35. O'Connor, *O. Henry*, 229 (quotation), 230.
36. Bierce's life was tragic. A son committed suicide when only sixteen. Another died from heavy drinking at age thirty. A daughter obtained a divorce in 1904, a legal action seldom taken and often leading to social declension.

Roads We Take," he produced the character Bob Tidball, a bandit soon to be murdered after a train robbery out West. Tidball remarks, "It ain't the roads we take; it's what's inside of us that makes us turn out the way we do."[37] The sentiment fit Porter as well. He had passionately loved New York but somehow was constantly drawn southward—in his second marriage and in his late attempts to record in fiction some of his southern experiences.

Porter's heart, his habits, his crippling sense of propriety, and his unrealized hope for respectability belonged to Dixie. Although he seldom articulated his mixed feelings about his native culture, his portrayals of the city-dwelling working classes arose not from a loyalty to but in opposition to the agrarian South. He identified with the lowly, the forlorn, with felons, prostitutes, bar men, and hard-fisted landladies in the urban North. For the most part he sentimentalized their stories. After all, he wrote during the era of genteel traditionalism. That dominant construction rewarded expressions of the reigning pieties. Porter was no iconoclast. Still, the land of his birth had helped to mold his career and provide a source of inspiration. At the same time, southern reticence and propensity to romanticize had held him in a suffocating embrace.

Quite aware of public expectations, Porter strove in fiction for a hopeful rather than a cynical or brutal close. His art, he believed, should not represent the life he had known. It should provide instead a means to escape from a chronically untrustworthy and unresponsive social order. Unfortunately, Porter used the romantic-sentimental tradition—even if ironically—to avoid more serious psychological probing. He would have scoffed at any attempt to over-intellectualize what he had done. Nonetheless, that superficiality, even if strictly designed to market his fiction, indicated a certain emotional fragility, a reluctance to delve for fear of unearthing troubling matters. While it is easy to understand such fears in light of Porter's unhappy experiences and lifelong struggle with the shadow of melancholy, his preference for the clever turn over psychological depth is lamentable, particularly in an author who might have risen to greater literary heights.

37. "The Roads We Take," *Complete Works,* 1145.

William Sydney Porter
Courtesy Austin History Center,
Austin Public Library

Porter's daughter, Margaret
Worth Sartain
Courtesy Austin History Center,
Austin Public Library

Joel Chandler Harris
Courtesy Special Collections
Department, Robert W.
Woodruff Library,
Emory University

Mark Twain
Courtesy Library of
Congress

Constance Fenimore Woolson
Courtesy Department of College
Archives. Special Collection &
Records Management, Rollins
College, Winter Park, Fla.

Kate Chopin
Courtesy Missouri Historical Society

Willa Cather
*Courtesy Nebraska State
Historical Society*

Ellen Glasgow
Courtesy Virginia Historical Society

6

The Trickster Motif and Disillusion
Uncle Remus and Mark Twain

In the South, the war is what A.D. is elsewhere; they date from it. All day long you hear things "placed" as having happened since the waw; or du'in' the waw; or befo' the waw; or right aftah the waw; or 'bout two yeahs or five yeahs or ten yeahs befo' the waw or aftah the waw.
—Mark Twain

Well I tell you dis, ef deze yer tales wuz just fun, fun, fun, en giggle, giggle, giggle, I let you know I'd a-done drapt um long ago.
—Uncle Remus

LIKE William Sydney Porter, Joel Chandler Harris led an unhappy but highly productive life in which creativity overmastered his depressive state of mind. His innovations in fiction, like Twain's, were not unrelated to his melancholy disposition. Louis D. Rubin Jr. points out that the plantation legend was never the same again after Harris had published his Uncle Remus tales and other narratives. He showed high regard for the unlettered but shrewd folk whose culture had generated the tales. He was as ardent a believer in sectional reunion as Porter, but his own sense of alienation led him to treat with artistic seriousness the lives and values of the underclasses of both races. We may recall that Thomas Holley Chivers had found inspiration in the African American dialect, and his work might be said to have served as a precursor of Harris's more extensive and sustained interest in black speech and speech acts. In the 1880s, when many southern whites gave the freed people little respect, Harris lent a modicum of dignity to the race. "He was showing black characters as suffering, because mistreated, misjudged, misunderstood—during an era when" so many were "deprived of all human dignity and joy by cruel or thoughtless whites," Rubin avers.[1]

Despite his writerly attention to African Americans, however, Harris's racism, like that of Chivers, conformed to the prejudices of his countrymen. Moreover, it grew increasingly pronounced during the escalating racial tensions of the 1890s. Yet in his fiction Harris promoted a racial paternalism and concern for the helpless that ironically recognized the self-respect, resilience, and honor of African Americans. If Uncle Remus became a stereotype used to justify white supremacy and black inferiority, Harris was not to blame. As African American literary critic Julius Lester observes, Harris conflated three former slaves from whom he, as a child, had heard many tales into the memorable storyteller, and Harris's composite reveals no distortions. The figure did become "a symbol of slavery and a retrospective justification for it," Lester continues, but that consequence only mirrored "the times in which the Uncle Remus tales appeared."[2]

Harris's dualism as an artist was reflected in his utilization of African American lore. That sense of fragmentation had its origins in childhood. In his memoir, *On the Plantation,* Harris omits any hint of the emotional difficulty he experienced as a youth during the Civil War. Autobiographies are notoriously unreliable. In the case of Twain and Harris, reticence and pleasant half-truths predominate. Nonetheless, they could not fully hide the central problem of identity. For all three authors—Twain, Porter, and Harris—conformity often conflicted with feeling, which led to their sense of being two people. All three used pseudonyms to delineate these other selves as if they were separate individuals—Twain and Clemens, O. Henry and Porter, Uncle Remus and Harris. In these artists' work, this doubleness was almost necessary. Writers may "become" or may think of themselves not as single personalities but as two distinct beings. By that strategy, they can

1. Louis D. Rubin Jr., "Uncle Remus and the Ubiquitous Rabbit," in *William Elliott Shoots a Bear: Essays of the Southern Literary Imagination* (Baton Rouge: Louisiana State University Press, 1975), 100.

2. Julius Lester, "Introduction," in Joel Chandler Harris, *Uncle Remus: The Complete Tales As Told by Julius Lester* (New York: Penguin, 1994), xiv. I should add that Lester by no means condones or excuses the language, sycophancy, and use of anti-black pejoratives, but, truth be told, the freed people of that era were not as self-conscious about such matters as we might expect them to have been.

more easily generate a variety of characters. Some, like Porter, Harris, and Twain, may choose another ego or identity to represent the whole of that imaginative life which stands apart from ordinary routine and living. The authors slip into these fictional skins, as it were, and often they imagine that the figures created have an independent existence and direct the thoughts of their creator. Harris, for instance, declared that his other self was "a creature hard to understand, but, so far as I can understand him, he's a very sour, surly fellow until I give him an opportunity to guide my pen in subjects congenial to him."[3]

Harris was articulate about this dual role. He explained to his daughters that when he sat down to write, "the 'other fellow' takes charge. You know all of us have two entities, or personalities." Harris claimed frequently to quiz his alter ego about "where he gets his information, and how he can remember, in the nick of time, things I have forgotten long ago; but he never satisfies my curiosity." When Harris was scribbling out an editorial under a deadline, the "other fellow" had no part in the procedure, but when creating imaginative scenes and characters, Uncle Remus (more often than not) was holding the pen.[4] Twain's fascination with the possibility of near cloning—as found in the biracial novel of twinship, Pudd'nhead Wilson—has long stimulated critical interest. Haunted by his own adoption of a pseudonym, Twain on his deathbed allegedly muttered incoherently some words about "Jekyll and Hyde and dual personality."[5]

More than once Harris referred to the "other fellow" inside him who produced the imaginative work. Yet he thought of this somewhat mysterious being as much more violent, unpleasant, and suspicious than the one who routinely went to the office and in the evenings played with children at home. In fact, in his letters to his little ones, when telling stories, jokes, or posing puzzles, Harris often adopted several personae of both sexes, in a remarkably complex but caring way.[6]

---

3. Joel Chandler Harris to his daughter "Tommie" Harris, 19 March 1898, in Julia Collier Harris, The Life and Letters of Joel Chandler Harris (Boston: Houghton Mifflin, 1918), 385. It would seem that he expected the whole family to read these generally lighthearted letters.

4. Ibid., 384–5.

5. Leslie Fiedler, "As Free as Any Cretur . . ." in Mark Twain: A Collection of Critical Essays, ed. Henry Nash Smith (Englewood Cliffs, N.J.: Prentice-Hall, 1963), 130–9; Susan Gillman, Dark Twins: Imposture and Identity in Mark Twain's America (Chicago: University of Chicago Press, 1989), 2 (quotations) and 53–95.

6. See R. Bruce Bickley Jr., "Foreword" in Dearest Chums and Partners: Joel Chandler Harris's Letters to his Children: A Domestic Biography, ed. Hugh T. Kennan (Athens: University of Georgia Press, 1993), x.

Harris's description of the way that writing takes on a life of its own is scarcely unusual. E. M. Forster, the early-twentieth-century English novelist, described the phenomenon in 1927 with his customary drollness. The writer of fiction, he wrote, "prefers to tell his story about human beings" and not rely simply upon a "rattling good" plot. The more arresting and vibrant "characters arrive when evoked full of the spirit of mutiny. For they have these numerous parallels with people like ourselves, they try to live their own lives and are consequently engaged in treason against the main scheme of the book. They 'run away,' they 'get out of hand'; they are creations inside a creation, and often inharmonious towards it." Given an opportunity, he continued, such characters stand ready "to kick the book to pieces, and if they are kept too sternly in check they revenge themselves by dying, and destroy it by intestinal decay."[7]

One could carry Forster's insight further in the case of both Harris and Twain. They both created fictional beings who subvert the conventions of fiction and the expectations of the reader in chiefly subtle, indirect ways. Since the characters are, of course, the products of the novelist's imagination, they represent the repressed rebelliousness and the alienation of the writer himself, whether consciously or not. In Harris's case, and probably in that of most other writers of this dual nature, the creator of Uncle Remus distanced himself from that underside of his own work by treating the characters—especially the protagonist—as if they led independent lives.

For Harris, that "other fellow" could sometimes be so subversive as to overcome the racial barrier.[8] His tragic story of "Free Joe and the Rest of the World" (1884) shows a depth of sympathy quite extraordinary for that time and place. I have little doubt that this literary bifurcation—the conformist and the alternate identity who resented white hierarchy—was connected with Harris's profound dismay about the society he lived in but steadfastly refused publicly to denounce.[9]

Like Porter, Harris could not free himself from the chains of southern convention. To do so would in a sense blow his cover and expose him to the condemnation of the reading public and political forces of racism. He well knew that was the case. In an essay published in 1879, Harris remarked that the English novelist William Makepeace Thackeray "took liberties with the

7. E. M. Forster, *Aspects of the Novel and Other Writings* (1927; London: Edward Arnold, 1974), 46.

8. See Bickley, "Foreword" in *Dearest Chums and Partners*, ed. Kennan, x.

9. See Albert Rothenberg, *Creativity and Madness: New Findings and Old Stereotypes* (Baltimore: Johns Hopkins University Press, 1990).

people of his own blood and time that would have led him hurriedly in the direction of bodily discomfort if he had lived in the South." In the current climate, he added, the southern author was not allowed to "draw an impartial picture of Southern civilization, its lights and shadows." In 1881, he confessed, however, that the problems were internal as well: The southern writer had to overcome his own sectional prejudices, addiction to romantic claptrap, and a degree of inhibiting self-consciousness.[10] Yet Harris, who seldom ventured outside the South and turned down lucrative offers from New York publishing firms, may not have felt free-spirited enough to become a physical exile. He would remain an internal one, hiding his skepticism and even bitterness from his most conscious self and from his readers.

The origins of Harris's mistrust of the world began in his most unhappy childhood. That period shaped his life thereafter and affected his writing interests enormously. He grew up fatherless in Eatonton, a small town in middle Georgia's plantation belt. "My history," Harris wrote in 1870, in a rare moment of self-revelation, "is a peculiarly sad and unfortunate one."[11] Born in 1848, Harris had the misfortune to be illegitimate. Such a stigma indelibly marked him as different from all others in the little community. The Harris clan consisted of prominent citizens in Newton County. Despite the admonitions of her relatives, his mother, Mary, when in her early thirties, fell madly in love with an Irish day-laborer, perhaps out of spinsterish desperation. She was a habitual reader—an intellectual. That predilection placed her outside the marriageable set. The couple fled from the disapproving kinfolk and settled in Eatonton, Putnam County. They did not wed, however, even though matrimony would have afforded Mary a measure of respectability. Shortly after the birth of their son, the father absconded, leaving Mary and her infant to the mercy of their neighbors. Her mother eventually came to live with her. The other family members, including her sister, felt outrageously disgraced and rejected their kinswoman.

Fortunately, the community was not as unkind as one might expect. A leading townsman, Andrew Reid, provided the pair with a tiny cottage behind his own mansion. Mary became the local seamstress. The work was sufficient to provide her and her son with a means to survive. When Joel, or "Joe" as he was called, reached school age, Reid paid the tuition at the boy's

10. Quoted in Jay Martin, *Harvests of Change: American Literature, 1865–1914* (Englewood Cliffs, N.J.: Prentice-Hall, 1967), 100, and also in Jay B. Hubbell, *The South in American Literature 1607–1900* (Durham, N.C.: Duke University Press, 1954), 791.

11. Joel Chandler Harris to Mrs. Georgia Stake, 9 December 1870, in Harris, *Life and Letters of Joel Chandler Harris,* 78.

co-educational school. Young Joe was too shy with the girls to flourish there. His chronic stutter was so pronounced that under stress he could not speak at all, a problem that haunted him throughout his life. He had flaming-red Irish hair and a slight frame that could well have made him the object of schoolyard ridicule. Later in the same year, at the Eatonton Academy (solely for boys), he managed to acquire some self-possession. Nevertheless, all his life Harris was pathologically afraid of public notice, preferring to move in the shadows. Mark Twain wrote of that aspect in his *Autobiography:* "He was the bashfulest grown person I have ever met. When there were people about he stayed silent and seemed to suffer until they left." As a boy, Harris compensated for his unsociable demeanor by arranging elaborate practical jokes out of sight—a pastime for which he became locally notorious. Humor was the shy boy's way to hide his own confusion.[12]

In March 1862, at a time when the war was fully underway, lucky circumstances placed Harris on Turnwold, an unusual plantation near Eatonton where he could develop his literary bent. He became a printer's apprentice for planter Joseph Addison Turner, a devout whiskey-lover, poet of the southern romantic school, avid reader, and proprietor of *The Countryman,* a weekly. Unlike most other southerners, who stressed such matters as states rights, Turner, a prewar Unionist, supported the Confederacy but with a difference. He had no illusions about why the South had seceded. It sought independence, he wrote, solely "to perpetuate the institution of slavery," the basis of "our social and industrial system, and the source of our prosperity."[13] Though scarcely antislavery, Turner permitted his slaves plots to plant their own cotton, corn, or other vegetables to sell at market. Certainly young Joe Harris's understanding of slavery was affected by the relatively benevolent regime he witnessed—even though constant indebtedness made it hard for Turner to sustain his paternalism, especially as the war continued. In November 1864 William Tecumseh Sherman's Federal troops invaded middle Georgia. For the first time, Harris had brought home to him the humiliation of Confederate reverses and the depredations of war. The Yankees seized Turnwold's livestock and food supplies. The slaves disappeared. Turner's paper announced on 9 May 1865 that the South no longer

12. Mark Twain, *Autobiography,* ed. Charles Neider (New York: Harper & Brothers, 1959), 47; Paul M. Cousins, *Joel Chandler Harris: A Biography* (Baton Rouge: Louisiana State University Press, 1968), 19–26; Harris, *Life and Letters of Joel Chandler Harris,* 12–22, 57–8.

13. Harris, *Life and Letters of Joel Chandler Harris,* 26; quotation in Cousins, *Harris,* 39.

had a country. "Our people, it seems to me, are ready to bow their necks to take the yoke."[14]

The experience of the disastrous war helped to shape Harris's deeply embedded sense of hopelessness and vulnerability. In 1870 he wrote, "I am morbidly sensitive." He condemned his tendency to react against "the slightest rebuff." Often, he continued, "I wished a thousand times that I was dead and buried out of sight." He found himself appalled at his own misery, compounding the trouble. The torture of self-doubt, he said, was "*worse* than *death* itself. It is horrible." Unlovable and ugly (or so he thought), he recognized that townspeople saw him as the offspring of an unwed mother. No less demeaning was the added stigma of being a low Irish immigrant's son.[15]

Despite or perhaps because of this problematic status, Harris found his professional calling early—in the life of the mind and literary composition. Under Turner's severe but constructive criticisms, the teenager learned how to write simply, concisely, and pungently. In 1866, however, *The Countryman* closed its pages "in a land filled with desolation and despair," as Harris later recalled.[16] After several years with various Georgia newspapers, he joined the Atlanta *Constitution*, having attained a statewide reputation for his humor and insight. He held the post until 1900, when he resigned, at age thirty-eight, to start his own magazine.

Unlike Porter's, Harris's home life was remarkably normal, thanks to the heedfulness of his wife, Esther LaRose, who had to deal with his unpredictable moods. The marvel was that she found beneath his morbid outpourings and his intractable shyness a worthy lover and husband. The couple had nine children. When Evan Harris, less than two years old, died from the measles in 1878, Harris went to pieces. He blamed himself for catching the disease and passing it on to his son. His mother-in-law sternly warned him, for the sake of family stability and the quality of his writing, that he had to quit drinking altogether. The admonition worked for a while. But one suspects he became thereafter a closet drinker who refused to admit a problem with alcohol.[17]

14. Harris, *Life and Letters of Joel Chandler Harris*, 49–52, quotation, 52; Cousins, *Harris*, 46–9.

15. Walter M. Brasch, *Brer Rabbit, Uncle Remus, and the "Cornfield Journalist": The Tale of Joel Chandler Harris* (Macon, Ga.: Mercer University Press, 2000), 4–5 (quotation 5).

16. Quoted in Harris, *Life and Letters of Joel Chandler Harris*, 52.

17. Brasch, *Brer Rabbit*, 49–50.

When another child, Linton Harris, a boy of seven, died of diphtheria, Harris surprisingly did not fall into one of his morbid spells and thought as much about the effect on Linton's brothers and sisters as he did about the death itself. He proved a very caring father at less trying times, too. His assiduousness in avoiding the role of paternal tyrant showed that he found equipoise as a parent. His letters to his children were most endearing. Taking a humorous turn, Harris wrote two of his young daughters about their mother's need to keep a fruit cake moist with whiskey. Apparently the cake required, he wrote, no less than a dram a week, "and it drinks so heartily you can almost hear it hiccough. It may happen that we have to send the cake to the Keeley Institute, the place where they reform poets and other geniuses." (The Faulkner family was later to know that hospice well.)[18]

Despite the support that his wife and lively youngsters gave him, Harris could not forget the sadness, uncertainties, and sense of humiliation of those early years. Even at the height of his fame, Harris avoided appearances in crowds with pathological determination. Even when he did appear, his bashfulness was evident. In 1882, for instance, he was invited to speak at the Tile Club in New York. He refused to offer a single word if he would have to speak on his feet. Allowed to remain seated, he enjoyed the evening. But while he was walking with some of the guests up Fifth Avenue to his hotel, one of them chided him gently for not entertaining the gathering with a story or persiflage. Harris responded, "What! Make a speech before all those brilliant fellows! No, sir! All I can do is to tell you *good-night*!" With that parting shot, he ran full speed to his hotel and was not seen by the group again. In fact, upon receiving another dinner invitation at the Century Club, he felt the need to escape, packed his bags, and left New York for home. Learning of his unannounced departure, Mark Twain scolded Harris, who replied, "I thought it would be better to come home and commit suicide rather than murder a number of worthy gentlemen by making an ass of myself."[19] His overreaction on this and many other occasions had much to do with his stutter, about which he felt acute shame.

For all the literary reputation he acquired with his 263 Uncle Remus tales in eight volumes, Harris gained little gratification or confidence. Like Porter, he rejected praise as mere puffery. As his daughter Julia put it, he was "almost morbidly doubtful of the merit of his work, easily discouraged" and

18. Harris, *Life and Letters of Joel Chandler Harris*, 273–4; Harris to Mildred and Lillian Harris, [?] November 1897, in ibid., 377.

19. Ibid., 189–91 (quotation, Harris to Twain, 12 September 1882, p. 191).

requiring constant reassurance from his publishers and friends.[20] Always the perfectionist, he sometimes destroyed perfectly good material in one of his downturns of mood. To Mark Twain in 1881, he admitted, "I am perfectly well aware that my book has no basis of literary art to stand upon . . . my relations toward Uncle Remus are similar to those that exist between an almanac-maker and the calendar." Responding to Twain's enthusiasm for his African American tales, Harris wrote as if Uncle Remus were the authentic author of the stories: "You cannot escape my gratitude for your kindness to Uncle Remus."[21] Indeed, he often referred to Remus in this vein. Rather than seeing himself as one of the anonymous little white boys listening to the tales, Harris most likely identified with Uncle Remus himself. Fearful of public appearances, he sought safety in being as humble as his black character, as self-deprecating as the most obsequious of the Sambo stereotypes.

Of course, there was some truth in what Harris implied about the provenance of the tales. After all, they were the work of African Americans, and Harris was in a sense their amanuensis, albeit an artful one. Uncle Remus, he told an interviewer, "was not an invention of my own, but a human syndicate, I might say, of three or four old darkies whom I had known. I just walloped them together."[22] But being the first and one of the most prolific collectors of black folklore, Harris went about his work with the meticulousness of a professional ethnologist. That title, however, he would quickly have rejected as self-inflating.

The stories suited his temperament to perfection. The slave tales were themselves studies in alienation, hostility, and darker moods—more so than might first appear—all of which were carefully hidden behind the surprises, the humor, and seeming simplicity of the fictional doings of rabbits, wolves, foxes, possums, lions, and other creatures. Just as Harris understood himself as two separate entities—the artist and the "cornfield journalist," as he styled himself, so too were the stories often a doubling. It was not just that the small animals were really slaves and the big ones the masters, but the plots unfolded in two forms. The outward thrust was, of course, meant to be humorous, but another level dealt with a darker, violent resistance against oppression. The American Negro, as W. E. B. DuBois famously observed, "ever feels his two-ness—an American, a Negro; two souls, two thoughts, two unreconciled strivings; two warring ideals in one dark body

20. Ibid., 202.
21. Harris to Samuel Clemens, 4 August 1881, ibid., 168–9.
22. Quoted ibid., 146.

whose dogged strength alone keeps it from being torn asunder." Is it beyond all possibility that Harris grasped something of that character in his early trickster talks of rabbits and wolves? As Louis Rubin observes, the animals, in their self-assertiveness and drive, exhibit very non-Victorian ethics. As in trickster narratives worldwide, Harris's creatures act as human beings might in reality, not as they should. As a result, they display a range of cruelty and betrayal, selfishness, malice, foolishness, and vengefulness. There is also an implied egalitarianism in this view of humanity, which Harris articulated at a time when few other southern whites recognized the humanness—and intelligence—of the freed people of the South.

For all his typically southern racial assumptions, Harris at first defended the authenticity of his Uncle Remus fables from racially prejudiced ethnological critics. He declared that the significance of the tales lay solely in "the unadulterated human nature that might be found in them." As the historian Lawrence Levine asserts, Harris's animals were too humanized to be content with mere survival. Their needs included the prizes males crave and strive for: wealth, success, prestige, honor, sexual prowess.[23]

Later in life, Harris found the burden of dancing between the races too taxing. Admitting the integrity of the black race was all very well, but he had a reputation in the South to uphold. His editorials in the *Constitution* buttressed his standing with the Democratic party and its white supremacist policies. For nearly a decade in the 1890s he withheld any further Uncle Remus stories from an eager public. He claimed that it was time for the old storyteller to join "the affable Ghosts that throng the ample corridors of the Temple of Dreams."[24] Finally, he succumbed to publishing pressures. Yet the last two sets of stories did not have foreboding interpretive or philosophical undertones about the human condition, slavery and mastery, survival and vulnerability. Instead Brer Rabbit becomes a cartoon-like trickster—superhumanly cunning and full of mischief for its own sake. The rabbit resembles the creatures in the animated shows like *Road Runner* or *Tom and Jerry*. As critic Kathleen Light points out, in the mid-1890s, when the position of the black in America reached its nadir, Harris no longer championed the under-race, however obliquely. Nor did he defend his stories any longer

23. Rubin, "Uncle Remus," 82–106.

24. See Julia Collier Harris, *Joel Chandler Harris: Editor and Essayist: Miscellaneous Literary, Political, and Social Writings* (Chapel Hill: University of North Carolina Press, 1931); quotation, Joel Chandler Harris, *Uncle Remus and His Friends: Old Plantation Stories, Songs, and Ballads with Sketches of Negro Character* (New York: Houghton Mifflin, 1893), x–xi.

against the racist ethnologists, who claimed that the folk narratives proved the inferiority of an allegedly simpleminded, primitive, immoral race.[25]

Despite Harris's backsliding or failure of nerve, the best of the stories—"Tar Baby" being too well known to revisit here—should receive their due. A typical short piece is about how Brer Rabbit and Brer Fox collaborate out of their mutual, ravenous hunger, an all too common problem in the slave quarters. Brer Fox confesses that his stomach is "having a long conversation with his backbone." Mr. (white) Man comes along the road with a big piece of meat. Catching up with him, the animals insist that it stinks and is so rotten that Mr. Man better restore it to an edible state. How can I do that? asks the simpleton. The answer: Why, just take a string and haul it through the dirt—a procedure to which he acquiesces. The animals supply a long vine to serve the purpose. While Mr. Man trudges ahead, they replace the meat with a heavy stone and quickly vanish into the woods with the prize. Both enjoy some of their loot, but Brer Rabbit is no loyal collaborator. He fools Brer Fox by sending him off to find water. Meanwhile, he buries the meat and cuts himself a switch. Upon Brer Fox's return from his fruitless errand, the rabbit, hiding in the bushes, hits a tree, howls in distress, and loudly begs Mr. Man not to strike him any more. Even the dimmest wit in the white community could have recognized what that lashing represented. Brer Fox is delighted that his comrade has met with his comeuppance. Brer Rabbit then shouts a warning—"Run, Brer Fox! Run! Mr. Man say he coming looking for you now!" The fox hastily takes to the road. At once, Brer Rabbit retrieves the meat and enjoys it all by himself.[26]

In making the story comic, Harris was, with a degree of naiveté or perhaps unconscious deliberateness, drawing the reader into his tale of simple entertainment. Nonetheless, the characters symbolized gnawing hunger, the possibilities of betrayal, and the desire to dominate. The fooling of the dull-witted white master, the competitive struggle between the animals/slaves for survival, the motives of revenge, and the pleasure taken in witnessing another's distress were not the qualities that middle-class white southern folks sanctioned. Yet through humor and clever use of animal representation, Harris made his stories palatable to the very group that was the target of his wit.

Thus Harris became a trickster, too. Subterfuge, disciplined control of

25. Kathleen Light, "Uncle Remus and the Folklorists," in *Critical Essays on American Literature,* comp. R. Bruce Bickley Jr. (Boston: G. K. Hall, 1981), 146–57.

26. Harris, *Uncle Remus As Told by Julius Lester,* 57–60 (quotations 57, 60).

the material, and submergence of the grimmer aspects enabled him to laugh at the animals' antics and beckon his readers to do likewise. How else could an embittered, depressed artist at the close of the nineteenth century deal with his own melancholy bile? As a youngster, Harris, fatherless, poor, and, along with his mother, dependent upon the largesse of richer folk, was drawn to the lower orders of middle Georgia and mingled with them in the way that Porter did with the unwashed of the city. In one of his school compositions Harris wrote bitterly, "Which is most respectable, poor folks or niggers?" Anger and resentment mingled with humor and nostalgia in his published work. In reference to Brer Rabbit and the other tricksters in the Uncle Remus tales, Harris observed their essential indifference to middle-class white morality: "It is not *virtue* that triumphs, but *helplessness;* it is not *malice,* but *mischievousness.*"[27] Like the black underclass, Harris understood the "helplessness" of those vulnerably outside the social circle. But a stronger term than "mischievousness"embodies his real feelings. Vengeance for wrongs, retaliation against power, recompense for betrayals—that is what Harris recognized in his deepest reaches. Unfortunately, he never articulated that connection between his own psyche and those of the animal tricksters. Yet by remaining in the shadows, he mastered his literary art.

Harris's peculiar reticence in the midst of company actually was a factor in his remarkable rapport with the freedmen from whom he obtained the trickster tales. An example is his account of a session at the Atlanta railway yards deep in the night. He came upon a group of black workmen passing a bottle, laughing, and exchanging jokes. He joined them, emboldened by the anonymity the darkness engendered, and no doubt partaking of some of the liquor. Soon he told the story of the mosquitoes and Brer Rabbit. The others then contributed their stories of a similar sort. When Harris returned home, he wrote down what he had heard in the dialect the men had used.[28] Such mutuality in white and black relations was possible when social and racial barriers were masked by nighttime, masculine interests. Hunting and fishing expeditions might take on something of that character, although a tacit understanding of who was who customarily lingered.

In his early years, Harris showed unusual forethought in his respect for the humble folk whom he owed so much. He recommended his methods to

27. First quotation from Michael Flusche, "Underlying Despair in the Fiction of Joel Chandler Harris," in *Critical Essays,* comp. Bickley, 175; second quotation in Harris, *Life and Letters of Joel Chandler Harris,* 158–9.

28. See Florence E. Baer, "Joel Chandler Harris: An 'Accidental Folklorist,'" in *Critical Essays,* comp. Bickley, 188–9.

others: "The only way to get at these stories is for the person seeking them to obtain a footing by telling one or two on his own hook—beginning, for instance, with the tar baby." He was very aware that the stories were not English in origin—an idea that was not fully accepted until the 1970s. He marveled that philologists and folklorists from around the world wrote him to note the similarities of the trickster tales and the lore of their own country folk. "All I know," he once remarked, "is that every old plantation mammy in the South is full of these stories. One thing is certain—the negroes [*sic*] did not get them from the whites; probably they are of remote African origin."[29]

In his later years, like Porter, Harris became ever more secretive and reclusive, spending as much time away from home as possible. His hideaway, situated some miles outside Atlanta, was called Snap Bean Farm. There Harris nursed his ill-health alone. Even his wife seldom accompanied him. Although ostensibly the purpose of his retreat was to enjoy the peace and quiet of country life, there was another reason for his withdrawal: He discovered toward the end of his career that he could no longer work effectively. Rumors among the blacks on the place held that he was drinking hard. Yet his biographers are as silent on the subject as Harris was himself. In May 1908, to ease the strain placed upon him by his business interests, he merged his highly popular *Uncle Remus's Magazine* with another family journal, the *Home Magazine*. But his health was rapidly deteriorating. The physicians detected nephritis and cirrhosis of the liver, also Porter's ailment. Uremic poisoning finally killed Harris on 3 July 1908.[30]

Just as Porter ultimately fell short in his literary achievements, so Harris did not attain the kind of permanent place in southern literature that his

29. Joel Chandler Harris to R. W. Grubb, 3 February 1883, in Harris, *Life and Letters of Joel Chandler Harris*, 193, quotation 162; also Baer, "Harris," in *Critical Essays*, comp. Bickley, 190–3; Henry Louis Gates Jr., *The Signifying Monkey: A Theory of Afro-American Literary Criticism* (New York: Oxford University Press, 1988), 238. See also William J. Hynes and William G. Doty, *Mythical Trickster Figures: Contours, Contexts, and Criticisms* (Tuscaloosa: University of Alabama Press, 1993); Lawrence W. Levine, "'Some Go Up and Some Go Down': The Meaning of the Slave Trickster," in *The Hofstadter Aegis: A Memorial 1916–1970*, ed. Stanley M. Elkins and Eric McKitrick (New York: Knopf, 1974), 94–124; Charles Joyner, *Shared Traditions: Southern History and Folk Culture* (Urbana: University of Illinois Press, 1999), 98–102; idem, *Down by the Riverside: A South Carolina Slave Community* (Urbana: University of Illinois Press, 1984), 191–5.

30. Baer, "Harris," in *Critical Essays*, comp. Bickley, 192; R. Bruce Bickley Jr., *Joel Chandler Harris* (Boston: Twayne, 1978), 62; Kennan, ed., *Dearest Chums and Partners*, xxvi; Brasch, *Brer Rabbit*, 255.

talents might have promised. As a pioneer folklorist and creator of memorable work that children most especially enjoy, he will be remembered. Moreover, he did advance the southern white literary tradition by recognizing African American aesthetics and narrative drive and treating blacks' lives and concerns with seriousness. But he was another victim of an inhibiting and racially exclusive culture and could not overcome the impediments that southerners imposed on their nineteenth-century writers.

Unsurprisingly, of the three journalists discussed in this section, the most gifted, most moralistic, and most acerbic in denouncing the nineteenth-century South was Mark Twain. Any analysis of southern writing after the Civil War must include Mark Twain. Few others of his time were so quick to recognize the catastrophic effect of the unimaginable bloodletting and then the defeat of war on the white southern spirit. He was especially hard on the continued romanticism of southern letters in the postwar period. Clearly the sappy nostalgia of the Lost Cause and the perpetual harkening to memories of the Ole Plan'ation repelled him. In this respect, he was among the first southern writers to turn a truly critical eye upon his people and region. (There were others, too, of course, including most notably George Washington Cable.) Twain found the tastes, values, social pretensions, and provincialisms of the antebellum elite abhorrent. In *Life on the Mississippi,* his tone is humorous on the surface, but underneath bitterness finds a voice. Yet rather than assail the midcentury romancers—William Gilmore Simms, Thomas Nelson Page, or John Esten Cooke—he ridicules Sir Walter Scott as the progenitor of the South's ethical and stylistic deficiencies. He even offers Scott as an excuse for southern slavishness to the old and outworn. But for the Scott disease, the character of the southerner—or Southron, in Sir Walter's starchier way of phrasing it—would be wholly modern, and the South would be fully a generation farther advanced. Of course, he intends his assessment to be taken as satire. Yet even in his anger he refrains from attacking those southern reactionaries responsible for perpetuating the myth.

Twain's critique of regional failings was as close to a Menckenian position as one might expect from a nineteenth-century inside observer. Asserting, half-facetiously, that the "waw" might not have erupted except for Scott's baleful influence, Twain explains that the romantic impulse was much stronger in the South than in the North. In literary terms, the northern reading public had abandoned that old inflated style. Many southern readers still preferred the constricted, obsolete forms that Page, Augusta Evans, and others kept alive and dismissed those few regional authors like Joel

Chandler Harris, Kate Chopin, and Cable, who ventured away from southern romanticism.[31]

Twain's disenchantment with the southern way prompted Lewis Simpson, as mentioned earlier, to identify him as not only the pre-Faulknerian
founder of the modern sensibility in the region but of the southern "culture
of failure," as he puts it.[32] I suggest that the process began much earlier. In
any event, it reached something of a climax in the work of Mark Twain.

Like most all the others discussed in these pages, Samuel Clemens (hereafter referred to solely as Mark Twain) was a man who had painfully felt
the iron rod of sorrow. Born prematurely, the boy Twain was sickly and
barely survived his first two years of life. Short and slender, he was highly
conscious that he did not match the muscular ideal of the rural South.
Moreover, his unprepossessing appearance forced him, like Harris, to find
refuge in his imagination while ever demanding unstinting love and solicitousness.[33]

Belonging to an old, once-aristocratic Virginia family, Twain's father followed the principles of southern patriarchal authority. John Marshall Clemens was reportedly so cold and solemn that family members shook hands
and never kissed when retiring for the night. A county justice of the peace
of great rectitude but little business sense, Clemens aroused feelings of resentment and awe in his children, most especially young Samuel. Like so
many other boys, Twain could not help resenting his father's power over
him. He grew ever more unhappy that the economically feckless parent
could not get his feet on the ground. Clemens dreamt of riches from some
Tennessee landholdings but always stood poised on the edge of insolvency.

In 1847, at the vulnerable age of eleven and a half, young Twain witnessed his father's death. Clemens had come down with pneumonia after an
exhausting return to Hannibal, Missouri, amid a rainstorm. After so brief
an illness, his death was a terrible shock. An autopsy followed. Through a
keyhole, young Twain watched as the attending physician reduced his formidable parent to a collection of body parts. As one biographer notes, the
sight made the father more powerful in his son's imagination. Late on the
night of the autopsy, Jane Clemens, his mother, saw the boy enter her bed-

31. Twain, *Life on the Mississippi*, 267.
32. Lewis Simpson, *The Fable of the Southern Writer* (Baton Rouge: Louisiana State University Press, 1994), 12, 72.
33. Justin Kaplan, *Mr. Clemens and Mark Twain: A Biography* (New York: Simon and
Schuster, 1966), 18.

room, ghostlike, wrapped in a sheet—sound asleep.[34] A sensitive and highly
gifted child like young Twain was bound never to forget that experience,
just as Poe never lost memories of his mother's death. Like Poe's, Twain's
imagination would find articulation in the angry violence of his fiction.

Twain's recollections of this period are not to be trusted. He claimed that
the disaster drastically altered the family's style of life, writing, "We were
about to be comfortable once more after several years of grinding poverty."
When Clemens died, the family fell suddenly to "the depths of poverty
again."[35] However true the first part of the statement may have been, the
plunge into penury was not. The justice of the peace had been a heavy user
of addictive drugs, on which he spent what few resources he had. He took
a concoction called Cook's pills, which included aloe, calomel, rhubarb, and
a narcotic that was most likely laudanum, a derivative of opium.[36] In his
last years, his health had been fragile, and he had suffered from frequent
migraine headaches. His widow, much more practical-minded and disciplined than her husband, kept the household financially afloat. Jane Clemens's son continued attending school uninterrupted for another two years.
Twain insisted that he had had to forgo further education almost as soon as
the burial took place in order to enter a printer's shop as an apprentice. But
poverty is a relative term. Young Mark Twain was disturbed by the inevitable decline in social status that the loss of his father represented. Certainly
the promise of success that his father's appointment to the bench signified
had not materialized. For the two years following Clemens's demise, young
Samuel did engage in Tom Sawyer–like mischief-making that his mother
could not control. He and friends, for instance, dislodged an enormous
boulder that completely demolished a shop downhill.[37]

To disguise anger at a parent's death beneath a wild, fun-loving demeanor might be common enough, but Twain found that boyish adventure
could turn into horror. One cold winter evening he and his companion Tom
Nash, the postmaster's son, defied their elders by playing on the ice far out
on the Mississippi River. As the cracking and grinding and crashing of the
floes signaled danger, they hurried toward shore. After an hour's struggle

34. Andrew Hoffman, *Inventing Mark Twain: The Lives of Samuel Langhorne Clemens*
(New York: William Morrow, 1997), 20–1.
35. Charles Neider, ed., *The Autobiography of Mark Twain, Including Chapters Now
Published for the First Time* (New York: Harper & Brothers, 1959), 1, 87–8; Kenneth S. Lynn,
Mark Twain and Southwestern Humor (Boston: Little, Brown, 1959), 210.
36. Hoffman, *Inventing Mark Twain*, 19.
37. Ibid., 22.

they had nearly reached the bank when Tom Nash fell into the icy slush. The pair made it home, but for Tom Nash, a succession of diseases ensued over the next few weeks. Contracting scarlet fever in his weakness, he lost all his hearing. Also, his speech was permanently impaired. Mark Twain never forgot the terror of that experience. He recalled many local tragedies, some of which were later incorporated into his fiction: "There was a slave man who was struck down with a chunk of slag for some small offense; I saw him die."[38]

There were signs of Twain's insecurity and melancholy early in his life. Even before his father's death, Twain was acutely fearful of parental desertion. He once reminisced that he had been forgotten in the haste of the family's departure from their residence in Florida, Missouri. The only problem with the story is that the incident did not occur to him. His brother Orion was the one who had been accidentally left behind. Such was Twain's terror of abandonment that he imagined himself in his brother's place. His father's demise only intensified his anxiety. A panic of being locked away haunted him, as it had gripped Edgar Allan Poe. In *Tom Sawyer, Huckleberry Finn,* and other works, a dungeon-like cave, a locked-up cabin, a floating coffin-barrel within which is Dick Albright's murdered baby, and similar confinements signify the deathly perils of the night.[39]

Later tragedies also drove home to him the transiency of life. In 1858 his brother Henry, then nineteen, was blown out of his bed over the boilers of the steamboat *Pennsylvania* when they exploded. Twain's nursing was unavailing. Henry's lungs were fatally damaged from his having helplessly breathed in scalding steam. Distraught, Twain wrote Mollie Clemens, his sister-in-law, "O, God! This is hard to bear. Hardened, hopeless—aye—lost—lost—lost and ruined sinner as I am." Twain also blamed himself for the death of his frail toddler, Langdon, whom he had not properly cared for on a long, freezing carriage ride.[40] Dreams of doom assailed him. As late as 1882, he observed, "My nightmares, to this day, take the form of running into an overshadowing bluff, with a steamboat—showing that my earliest dread made the strongest impress on me." The connection between the nightmares and his fiction is evident in the description in chapter 16 of

38. Twain, *Autobiography,* 41.

39. See Lynn, *Twain and Southwestern Humor,* 210–11; Mark Twain, *Adventures of Huckleberry Finn* (New York: Random House, 1996).

40. Samuel Langhorne Clemens to Mollie Clemens, 18 June 1858, in *The Selected Letters of Mark Twain,* ed. Charles Neider (New York: Harper & Row, 1982), 22; Kaplan, *Mr. Clemens and Mark Twain,* 119.

Huckleberry Finn, when Huck and Jim's raft is split by a huge oncoming steamboat.

As his biographer Justin Kaplan points out, Twain's life in antebellum years in far west California were not as happy as his autobiography and his memoir, *Roughing It,* would indicate. Twain had been "melancholy and restless, alternately idle and desperately industrious. His jokes and hoaxes were often strident and brassy, betraying raw nerve endings whipped by guilt about his family and by an oppressive sense of obligation to them." He had become the chief breadwinner for the whole family. A widowed mother as well as a sister, and a brother, Orion, who was often at the edge of bankruptcy and foreclosure, caused constant financial worry.[41]

A further source of anguish was Twain's relationship to his native South. Like Poe's, it was a mixture of fascination and disgust. Although in *Adventures of Huckleberry Finn* Twain scourged a pretentious and proslavery chivalry in some of the scenes, he could not forget the privileged position he and his family had once enjoyed, and the humiliation and social declension his father's death had caused.[42] Above all in that classic, Twain explored a theme that would become a permanent trope in southern male writers' fiction: the search of a lonely boy for the love and guidance of a worthy father. As Leslie Fiedler argues, the quest would often pair a white youth and a surrogate parent, like Huck's black companion Jim—anyone different from the natural father, who is usually missing or as dangerous as Huck's Pap. Being both a slave and African American, Jim, though, is more complex than a mere "substitute father," Fiedler insists. To Huck, he is a servant, even a child, but also the exploited victim of his alleged liberators, Tom Sawyer and Huck himself. Beneath most if not all of these issues of emerging youth, racial confusion, and the changing moral positions of each of the characters lies the psychic pain as well as the imaginative brilliance of the author himself.[43]

That connection between Twain's inner life and the novel emerges from the record of melancholy in Huck Finn's mind: "I felt so lonesome I most wished I was dead. The stars were shining, and the leaves rustled in the woods ever so mournful. And I heard an owl, away off, who-whooing about

41. Kaplan, *Mr. Clemens and Mark Twain,* 15.

42. See Louis D. Rubin Jr., *The Writer in the South: Studies in a Literary Community* (Athens, Ga.: University of Georgia Press, 1972), 54–5; Kaplan, *Mr. Clemens and Mark Twain,* 380–3.

43. Leslie A. Fiedler, *Love and Death in the American Novel* (Cleveland: World Publishing Co., 1962), 268–72, 348–9.

somebody who was dead . . . I got so down-hearted and scared, I did wish I had some company."[44] The last line undercuts the ending of the book. For all his bragging about being free and lighting out for the territory, Huck Finn yearns for a father who would actually love him, and barring that at least "some company." The trauma of murder and violence with which the novel is much concerned scarcely leads Huck to peace of mind. To the contrary. When the boy witnesses the deathly battle between the Grangerfords and Sheppersons, he is rendered almost speechless: "It made me so sick I most fell out of the tree. I ain't agoing to tell *all* that happened—it would make me sick again if I was to do that. I wished I hadn't ever come ashore that night, to see such things. I ain't ever going to get shut of them—lots of times I dream about them."[45] Toward the close of Huck Finn, while heading for the Phelps's small, isolated plantation, the hero again remarks on the absence of cheering company: "There was them kind of faint dronings of bugs and flies in the air that makes it seem so lonesome and everybody's dead, and gone . . . it makes you feel mournful, because you feel like it's spirits whispering—spirits that's been dead ever so many years—and you always think they're talking about you. As a general thing it makes a body wish *he* was dead, too, and done with it all."[46] It takes little imagination to detect an autobiographical tone in the passage—Twain's long-dead father and the guilt that a child feels about that loss, as well as the fear of a dead person's reading his thoughts of filial resentment.

Like Harris and Porter, Twain saw the uses of the trickster motif. In the author's hands, Huck, like other tricksters, survives by deception, disguise, and evasion of conventional rule. The immorality of his aiding a fugitive slave—as Huck understands his civic obligation in a slave society—causes him only a twinge of guilt. The boy belongs to the lowest order of whites, rendering his successful defiance of southern racist precepts and proslavery law an act of class subversion as well as the triumph of the weak over the powerful. Deceived by con men and forced to utilize imposturing to free Jim from their clutches, Huck seems to develop two identities—like the author himself. Also like his creator, Huck is no muscular, athletic lad but slim, small, as a creature dependent on wits and wiliness might well be. Huck wears a dress and becomes a girl in one (unsuccessful) role. He adopts various aliases, providing plausible biographies. As in other trickster stories,

44. Twain, *Huckleberry Finn*, 5.
45. Ibid., 97–8.
46. Ibid., 183.

though, he himself is easily duped and falls for the outlandish deceptions of "Royal Nonesuch"—"King" and "Duke"—for whom he adopts, as their servant, yet another disguise.

In the closing section of *Huckleberry Finn,* Tom Sawyer's trickster-like activities mock the Cavalier tradition of heroism, but this part of the story also has a more perplexing side. Huck's friend knows all along that Jim has been freed but pursues his own joke in a heedless way by compelling Jim to continue as a fugitive slave. This surely is a racist and thoughtless violation of trust, risible though Twain meant it to be. The deviation from Twain's sense of justice is almost out of character. In choosing his charities, the author did much for the uplift of the black race. He publicly denounced the increasingly frequent practice of lynching and dramatized his ridicule of it in the Sherburn-Boggs incident in *Huckleberry Finn.* Nonetheless, he was a southerner and could not escape his race prejudice in Tom Sawyer's conscienceless tease of the long-suffering Jim. Tom's behavior serves to undercut the moral centrality of Huck's more compassionate treatment.

Contemporary critics, newspaper editors, and such guardians of the genteel tradition as Louisa May Alcott, disapproved of *Huckleberry Finn.* Abolitionists though some of the critics were, they frowned not because of the novel's racist overtones. At first, the book was greeted with an astonished silence. Then the Library Committee in Concord, Massachusetts, announced an official ban. Alcott, among others, publicly worried about "our pure-minded lads and lasses." There was fear that younger readers would be corrupted by the novel's ungrammatical dialects, the rule-breaking, and the rebelliousness of the two white boys. Recognizing the value of the negative response for sales, Twain crowed that the Concord officials "have given us a rattling tip-top puff. . . . They have expelled Huck from their library as 'trash and suitable only for the slums.'" The publicity, he estimated, would be worth thousands of sold copies. But beneath his facade of delight, he was actually devastated and somewhat mystified. His most perceptive biographer discloses that he looked back upon the novel "with mingled pride, pain, and puzzlement."[47] Although soon highly popular, but earning the censure of the well-placed guardians of propriety, *Huckleberry Finn* cost his creator much peace of mind. According to Kaplan, Twain fumed, "Why banish Huck from the family circle but let in not only the Bible but also a paper like the New York *World,* which carried tidings of adultery?"[48] Nei-

47. Kaplan, *Mr. Clemens and Mark Twain,* 268–70.
48. Ibid., 269.

ther Harris nor Porter had overstepped the social and moral boundaries as boldly as Twain had done. Huck's shameless indifference to the rules of tradition, grammar, and law could not be tolerated in some of the more respectable parlors and parish halls.

Despite his success with such works as *Roughing It* (1872), *The Adventures of Tom Sawyer* (1876), *The Prince and the Pauper* (1881), *Life on the Mississippi* (1883), *Adventures of Huckleberry Finn* (1885), *A Connecticut Yankee at King Arthur's Court* (1889), and his brilliant guidance and promotion of Ulysses S. Grant's *Memoirs,* Twain could not long rejoice in his well-deserved success. Instead, throughout his career, he rose to heights of mania and fell into periods of depression and remorse. Part of the problem may have stemmed from familial sources, on his father John Marshall Clemens's side. Clemens's long absences from home, his drinking and possible drug habit, along with his manic dreams of riches suggest that he suffered from a similar disorder. Indeed, money to be quickly seized was all too suited to his obsessive style. As an adult, Twain pursued wealth with the same lack of realism that his father had. His famous and feverish quest of various patented machineries cost him thousands and brought him close to bankruptcy at times. Then, while Twain was away on a world lecture tour organized to repay his enormous debts, his favorite and eldest daughter, Olivia Susan—Susy—died of meningitis back in Hartford. In 1887, still in London, he learned the news from his wife, Livy, and his daughter Clara, who had hastened home on news of Susy's fast decline. Her physical as well as mental health had always been fragile and a great worry to her parents, though both doted on her, calling her "our wonder and our worship."[49] Having been at family gravesides many times already, Twain was himself surprised by how deeply he felt the loss. Yet death still had its remorseless sting. He mourned in a letter to Livy, "I eat—because you wish it. I go on living—because you wish it; I play billiards, and billiards, & billiards, till I am ready to drop—to keep from going mad with grief & with resentful feelings." Not since his brother Henry's death had he felt so empty and guilty. Twain remarked: "I have hated life before—from the time I was 18—but I was not indifferent to it." To make matters worse, Livy began a slide into permanent invalidism, even as Twain's own health was deteriorating.[50]

49. Twain, *Autobiography,* 324.
50. Samuel Clemens to Henry C. Robinson, 28 September 1896 in *Selected Letters,* ed. Neider, 240, also 235–8; Hoffman, *Inventing Mark Twain,* 413–4; Kaplan, *Mr. Clemens and Mark Twain,* 335–6.

Twain transferred his sense of guilt, anguish, and even complete worth-lessness into his writing. Bernard De Voto found *What Is Man?* the most despairing, perhaps, of all his work: "It is not only a treatise on man's insta-bility, weakness, cowardice, cruelty, and degradation," it is also, the critic writes, an "assault" on the universal convictions of free will, ordinary cour-tesy, dignity, and the other virtues that make civilization possible. But above all, "it is a plea for pardon." So much a whim of fortune is the human crea-ture, Twain argues, that he is not responsible for his own defects. The point is driven home so "wearisomely," De Voto asserts, that the reader feels "the terrible force of an inner cry: Do not blame me, for it was not my fault."[51]

Susy's death had prompted these mordant reflections. Livy Clemens thought the book unprintable and protested its appearance. To change his mood, the pair decided to move in 1898 to Vienna.[52] In a way, the political situation in the capital of the Austro-Hungarian empire did raise Twain's spirits. Moving in liberal circles, he relished his friendship with Jewish lead-ers and intellectuals, as well as the spirited, sometimes violent clash of ethnic and religious forces. Others did not share the openness of his views. He sneeringly became known as *"der Jude Mark Twain."* Anti-Semitism won a great victory when Carl Lueger became the elected mayor of the city.[53]

These occurrences were serious enough, but Twain treated them not as simply tragic events but as mortal blows to his own equipoise. To make mat-ters worse, it seemed as if the kind of financial mess that had dogged his father had reappeared. His last years were spent in almost frenetic writing, as if any break would signal artistic failure. In 1904 the death of his beloved Livy left him in a state of mind that the title of his unfinished, surrealistic novel *The Great Dark* seemed to epitomize. Yet Twain had almost never adopted a very optimistic view. In 1883, when he was as happy as ever he would be, he nonetheless questioned Victorian faith in progress. Twain doubted that the world had any cosmic meaning. He wrote in his notebook, "I think we are only the microscopic trichina concealed in the blood of some vast creature's veins, and it is that vast creature whom God concerns Him-self about and not us."[54] *A Connecticut Yankee at King Arthur's Court* (1889), a complex experiment in science fiction, reveals his growing cyni-

51. Bernard De Voto, "The Symbols of Despair," in *Mark Twain: A Collection of Critical Essays,* ed. Henry Nash Smith (Englewood Cliffs, N.J.: Prentice-Hall, 1963), 148.

52. Hoffman, *Inventing Mark Twain,* 417.

53. Ibid., 419–20

54. Mark Twain, entry for 12 August 1883 in *Mark Twain's Notebook,* ed. Albert Bigelow Paine (New York: Cooper Square Press, 1972), 170.

cism. Recklessly he lampoons the cult of chivalry, which was still heavily entrenched even in postwar southern culture. Horrifying indifference, random violence, and inequities leave most of the sixth-century king's subjects in abject thralldom. But in the course of the narrative, Hank Morgan, the Yankee hero, makes his own ruinous contribution to that world—devastation through the new technology of electricity. From our present vantage, the book appears a seemingly prophetic look at the coming era of mass military destructiveness and ethnic genocides. The stormy and forlorn closure of the novel is certainly a curious way to end what began as an almost genial satire.[55] *A Connecticut Yankee* exposes not just Twain's emotional distress but also his mordant intellectuality. Man's inhumanity, Twain protested, was at least in part God's fault—if, that is, God existed at all. It was more likely that the deity was nothing more than a creation of human imagination, Twain implied. Satan's chief failing was simply the same as that of God's natural order—a total indifference to humankind and disregard for its struggles of life and death.[56]

In old age, Twain's imagination did not find the happy ending of *Huckleberry Finn*. There was no flight into freedom and away from the irons of civilization. But was the ending of his most engaging novel really hopeful? Like his fictional Huck, Twain had always known what he wished to escape—the crabbed isolation, conventions, and hypocrisies of the rural South and the half-hidden brutalities and anti-intellectualism of small-town America. But he could not tell where he ought to go. The same was true for Huck, a Ulysses afloat on the currents without a set destination—no Ithaca, no paradise to reach. Huck might escape Aunt Sally's attempt to "sivilize" him, but what then?[57] Perhaps the question is beside the point. Twain had to stop his story somewhere.

As with any great piece of literature, the reader may choose one or more ways to apprehend the meaning of the story. In this instance, I am reminded of the last still in François Truffaut's *400 Blows*. The French film reveals the small, damaging incidents that gradually erode the innocence, the hope, and the potential of an orphan boy. Like Huck, he at the end escapes from civilization. He reaches, not fresh territory, but the mind-numbing vacancy of

55. James M. Cox, "*A Connecticut Yankee in King Arthur's Court:* The Machinery of Self-Preservation," in *Mark Twain,* ed. Smith, 126.

56. See entry for "Cave, Mark Twain's" in R. Kent Rasmussen, *Mark Twain A to Z: The Essential Reference to His Life and Writings* (New York: Oxford University Press, 1995), 63–4.

57. Twain, *Huckleberry Finn,* 363.

the sea. The last sight we have of the boy is of him staring into the vast expanse with an expression of uncomprehending grief. Despite the flippant close of Twain's novel, Huck's escape into the great unknown of the western wilderness might be read in similar fashion. That doubleness of light-heartedness and terror, cleverness and vulnerability, alienation and yet boyish innocence personified the author as well as his character.

All three of these heavy-hearted authors—Porter, Harris, and Twain— with their curious interior twinships and their descents into acute despair, helped to prepare the next generation of male writers—Faulkner and company—to delve even more deeply into their own psychological storehouses. But in the meantime, women writers were to make their amazing contribution to a southern tradition of literary penetration of pain, despair, and suffering.

IV

THE IMPACT OF FEMALE WRITERS

7

Lowering Birds at the Dawn of Modernism
Constance Fenimore Woolson and Kate Chopin

The voice of the sea is seductive, never ceasing, whispering, clamoring, murmuring, inviting the soul to wander in abysses of solitude. . . . A bird with a broken wing was beating the air above, reeling, fluttering, circling disabled down, down to the water.
> —Kate Chopin

Some people think that women are the cause of modernism, whatever that is.
> —*New York Evening Sun,* 13 February 1917

I N the late-nineteenth-century American South, women writers—not their male colleagues—were the first "moderns" of southern literature.[1] More accurately we might label them transitional romanticists or transitional modernists, for they stood halfway between the old literary ways and the new. At the start, though, a word should be said about the use of "modernism" in this text, as well as the preceding era of a sentimental character. Modernism is a slippery term, as the *New York Evening Sun* journalist suggested in 1917. The same could be said of sentimentalism. Some critics have discovered that the latter, even with its vaunted tone and soft-core sense of

1. Such fin-de-siècle American authors as Theodore Dreiser, Jack London, and Stephen Crane also belonged to this innovative coterie, but they seem to have had little influence on the southern literary scene. I owe this point to Charles Joyner.

reality, has more merit than previously thought—as in Harriet Beecher Stowe's *Uncle Tom's Cabin,* which is seen by some as not mere gush but the powerful controlling mechanism that gives great moral thrust to the anti-slavery message.[2] At the other pole, modernist fiction, fully expressed, would leave no emotion, no sexual desire, no perverse thought, no act of violence, corruption, or betrayal unwritten and unexamined. In the chaos of a war-torn, disillusioned era, modernist writers found themselves clinging to art, not for its own sake but as the sole bearable reality.[3] Even if William Faulkner, of the succeeding generation, did not push these concerns as far as my remarks might suggest, he and the other southern male writers of the 1920s and 1930s did probe deeply into the meaningless, surreal horrors of which human beings are capable. That was a mode not available to writers like Twain, Harris, and Porter.

Those to be explored in this chapter and the next—chiefly Constance Woolson, Kate Chopin, Willa Cather, and Ellen Glasgow—could not completely repudiate the Victorian culture into which they were born. Grace King of New Orleans, another forerunner of modernism, once had a novel on the Reconstruction era rejected in the 1880s. She had omitted the obligatory sweetheart theme. William Dean Howells, dean of literary conventionality, counseled the inquiring, frustrated Grace King, "Just rip the story open and insert a love story. It is the easiest thing to do in the world. Get a pretty girl and name her Jeanne, that name always takes! Make her fall in love with a Federal officer and your story will be printed at once!" Likewise, the novelist Sarah Dorsey, who belonged to the literary clan of Percys and Ellises of Louisiana and Mississippi, faced the admonitions of her publishers. Upon threat of rejection, she dutifully altered a novel's closure. Perhaps because of the change, *Athalie* (1872) was a financial success. From her plantation, Elkridge, at Lake St. Joseph, Louisiana, she wrote a friend, "The ending was made to please the Publishers who said that there was complaint made against my *endings* as being always too *sad.*" Even E. D. N. Southworth of Virginia, the most popular romantic female novelist of the era, had

2. See Jane Tompkins, *Sensational Designs: The Cultural Work of American Fiction, 1790–1860* (New York: Oxford University Press, 1985), 122–46; David Leverenz, *Manhood and the American Renaissance* (Ithaca, N.Y.: Cornell University Press, 1989), 19–20; Suzanne Clark, *Sentimental Modernism: Women Writers and the Revolution of the Word* (Bloomington: Indiana University Press, 1991), 1–4.

3. See Astradur Eysteinsson, *The Concept of Modernism* (Ithaca, N.Y.: Cornell University Press, 1990), 9.

run into similar problems. She sometimes created flagrantly dissolute female characters who set no moral example for virginal readers.[4]

Valiantly the women writers with whom we are concerned here struggled, with mixed success, to break the mold. To be sure, Freud and Marx had no place in their scheme of things. Kraft-Ebbing and Havelock Ellis did not inhabit their library shelves. Indeed, sex belonged in the domain of the unspoken. That degree of restraint could be interpreted as delicacy, not timidity. Seldom did these writers reveal their inner lives even as they explored in fiction the dark places of the mind. In this authorial troupe reticence reflected their honor-conscious sense of privacy inherited from parents and forbears. It was a most treasured aspect of genteel observance. Nonetheless, these four writers represented a significant advance toward a modernist sensibility. In creating plots, the new breed would not seek to convert the ungodly, conveniently kill off characters with otherwise unacceptable fates, punish adulteresses, and reward saintly heroines with appropriately stalwart life-partners in the manner of Sarah Dorsey or Augusta Evans. In fact, the fin-de-siècle writers in these two chapters ordinarily put aside customary male-female connections. Nor did they consider that the transcendent goal of art was morally to uplift society. Nearly all their work exhibited an almost fatalistic pessimism. Even though they retained more than a touch of romanticism in their work, their questioning of the verities far outdistanced that of their much more sentimental female predecessors.[5] The latter portrayed the downside of feelings as a temporary setback. The mood would eventually pass, or at least the story would end in some sort of unambiguous closure, even if that were death, the final inevitability. The late-nineteenth-century southern women writers mentioned already, and others too numerous to treat here, explored emotional circumstances in

4. See Susan Coultrap-McQuin, *Doing Literary Business: American Women Writers in the Nineteenth Century* (Chapel Hill: University of North Carolina Press, 1990), 50–78; Sarah A. Dorsey to Edward Lyulph Stanley of Alderley Hall, 8 April 1872, Stanley Family Collection, Ryl. Eng. MS 1094, R 84307, John Rylands University Library of Manchester. See also Bertram Wyatt-Brown, *The House of Percy: Honor, Melancholy, and Imagination in a Southern Family* (New York: Oxford University Press, 1994), 130–2. Howells quoted in Michael Kreyling, *Figures of the Hero in Southern Narrative* (Baton Rouge: Louisiana State University Press, 1987), 78.

5. See, for instance, James Woodress, who considers Willa Cather's later fiction as less affirmatively "Romantic," as he puts it, than her earlier novels. James Woodress, *Willa Cather: A Literary Life* (Lincoln: University of Nebraska Press, 1987), 483.

many shapes and varying degrees of tenure with subtlety, irony, grace, and originality.[6]

In any event, the inauguration of this literary insurgency preceded the Faulknerian flowering by a generation. The literary historian Carol Manning contends that to use the two world wars as benchmarks for the Southern Renaissance, the long-accepted paradigm, is to distort reality. Also the customary privileging of male over female writers has unjustly bounded the chronology of the southern efflorescence. Yet somehow the notion that the turn-of-the-century women novelists—as a coterie of like-minded intellectuals—were the first to adopt an almost modern sensibility still awaits full recognition in the textbooks and in the general discussion of southern literature.[7]

With regard to the formation of a large female intellectual community, what united these significant women authors? By no means are we dealing here with a select Concord-like circle of high-minded friends. Carol Manning points out that few if any meeting places existed in the South for women intellectuals. Actually, there were some gatherings of female writers in Virginia, but none achieved the eminence of the salons that Charlotte Lynch Botta and Caroline Sturgis and Maria Weston Chapman organized in antebellum New York and Boston. As early as the 1840s, however, in the slave South, Elizabeth DuPuy, later one of the first professional, highly prolific female authors, organized a work-exchanging group of plantation women

6. Given more space, I could have chosen a much larger group that would have included Grace King, Ruth McEnery Stuart, Amélie Rives, the poet Charlotte Eliot (T. S. Eliot's mother), Frances Newman, and Mary Johnston. Moreover, there was a whole set of politically minded female writers too. Sarah Barnwell Elliott (1848–1928) was an exceptionally gifted novelist. Her first and best-selling work, *The Felmeres* (1879), dealt realistically with the fall of the Confederacy and its aftermath. Influenced by Constance Woolson, Elliott's fiction treated the state of the post–Civil War South with close attention to unique detail, authentic local dialects, few resorts to sentimental stereotypes, and a muting of moral uplift. See Clara Childs MacKenzie, *Sarah Barnwell Elliott* (Boston: Twayne, 1980), 31–49.

7. Carol S. Manning, "The Real Beginning of the Southern Renaissance," in *The Female Tradition in Southern Literature*, ed. Carol S. Manning (Urbana: University of Illinois Press, 1993), 37–56. As early as 1979 Michael O'Brien had noted the achievements of the fin-de-siècle southern writers, both male and female—Chopin and Joel Chandler Harris, for instance—naming them the true founders of a regional literary efflorescence. See Michael O'Brien, *The Idea of the American South, 1920–1941* (Baltimore: Johns Hopkins University Press, 1979), 11.

in Natchez, Mississippi.[8] Southern women relied on the usefulness of rela-tionships, carefully nurtured. They held a deep respect for family and treas-ured the passing down of wisdom from mother to daughter. The southern daughter, sister, and mother were taught to enjoy experiencing many aspects of life vicariously through the dreams and actions of their fathers, brothers, and sons. Even the most venturesome were not as individualistic as perhaps these southern women writers liked to imagine themselves to be. Northern Civil War families followed a similar pattern. The historian Anne C. Rose observes of Yankee society, "The Civil War inspired a generation caught be-tween sagging faith" and opportunities for "heroic adventure," although "reliance on family" remained vibrant in northern breasts, too. Yet with a strong civil society of associations, clubs, fraternities, and church agencies promoting one noble cause or another, life in the North differed from that in the South in a lesser dependency on kinfolk loyalties.[9]

To make up for the lack of a literary community or a sympathetic social and familial environment, these post–Civil War southern female artists turned their eyes northward and even to foreign parts for inspiration. One reason for this look elsewhere was a dissatisfaction with the politically driven ideologies that the great conflict had aroused and that continued to dominate popular fiction. On the northern side were the romances of Albion Tourgée and John William De Forest. They presented the moral imperatives of abolitionist sentiment, which had little attraction for the southern group. However worthy that cause might have been, the fiction of its adherents seemed polemically designed and artistically deficient, particularly to Con-stance Woolson, a northern woman writing about the South. Though scarcely a veteran himself, Henry James thought that in the North, at least, grand causes, holy zealotry, and glorious statesmanship held no one in awe or reverence anymore. He expected that the American would become "a more critical person than his complacent and confident grandfather."[10] In any case, these different perspectives fashioned a kind of hybridity, a blur-

8. The Virginia salons were pointed out to me by Susan Donaldson, 4 July 2001. See also Susan Emiston and Linda D. Cirino, *Literary New York: A History and Guide* (Boston: Houghton Mifflin, 1976), 39, and Wyatt-Brown, *The House of Percy*, 109–10, 123–4, 155–8; Manning, "Real Beginning of the Southern Renaissance," in *The Female Tradition*, ed. Man-ning, 49.

9. Anne C. Rose, *Victorian America and the Civil War* (New York: Cambridge University Press, 1992), 184.

10. Henry James, *Hawthorne* (New York: Scribners, 1880), 139–40.

ring of the boundary between northern and southern writing. Michael Kreyling points out that in this period Henry Adams, Henry James, and John W.
De Forest among other authors composed "significant works in Southern
fiction"—James's *The Bostonians,* for instance. Kreyling argues that this
time of transition and sectional reconciliation, however costly it was for African American advance, prepared the way for a less parochial national literature.[11] That transformation from old ways of thinking and writing could
benefit the southern writers most particularly. It drew them away from the
Anglo-provincialism of the Walter Scott and Bulwer-Lytton mode.

Of course, the proponents of the ruling southern paradigm of the Lost
Cause had little use for northern abolitionist fiction writers' celebration of
racial uplift and emancipation by warfare. Yet they would have agreed with
the lament of Reconstruction novelist Albion Tourgée, champion of the
freedmen's cause, in 1888: "The man who fights and wins is only common
in human esteem. The downfall of empire is always the epoch of romance."
As if to prove his point, Alabama romancer Augusta Evans replied to a Confederate widow's complaint about the tragic effect of the war on her life,
asking did she really want her dead husband to return to her if it meant
depriving him of the "cradling arms of glory" in the battle for "our precious
cause?"[12]

Constance Woolson complained to Paul Hamilton Hayne, dean of southern letters, about the sentimental women writers, North or South: "I generally throw half across the room all the new novels of the day." The
undiscriminating reader—including her own kinfolk—Woolson grumbled,
preferred Evans's *Infelice* to George Eliot's masterpiece, *Middlemarch.* Her
New England aunt dismissed Eliot's work as "stupid!" Woolson exploded,
"What in the world *can* any cultivated reader see in that mass of words,
words, words" that constitutes Evans's *Infelice?*[13] Southern women writers,

11. Michael Kreyling, "Southern Literature: Consensus and Dissensus," *American Literature* 60 (March 1988): 88.

12. Tourgée quoted by David Blight, *Race and Reunion: The Civil War in American Mem-
ory* (Cambridge, Mass.: Harvard University Press, 2001), 220. Evans quoted in Elizabeth
Moss, *Domestic Novelists in the Old South: Defenders of Southern Culture* (Baton Rouge:
Louisiana State University Press, 1992), 193.

13. Mary R. Reichart, *A Web of Relationship: Women in the Short Fiction of Mary Wilkins Freeman* (Jackson: University Press of Mississippi, 1992), 21; Woolson quoted in Anne
Goodwyn Jones, *Tomorrow Is Another Day: The Woman Writer in the South, 1859–1936*
(Baton Rouge: Louisiana State University Press, 1981), 52. Admittedly, these aspiring women
professionals like Woolson were neglecting the quality and subtleties in the sentimentalists'
works that only lately have been appreciated. See, for further enlightenment, Susan Donaldson,
Competing Voices: The American Novel, 1865–1914 (New York: Twayne, 1998); David Shi,

she thought, "seemed to me exaggerated in style, and too full of a certain spirit, which I can best describe perhaps by saying that their heroes are always [overly] knightly—for the real life of to-day." She might have appreciated Porter's satirical portrait of Major Pendleton Talbot. Before the war, Woolson had conversed endlessly with young southern maidens at a New York City boarding school, and they spoke with simplicity, vivaciousness, and charm. But their gossip did not at all match the starchy and inauthentic dialogue found in Augusta Evans's pious *St. Elmo* (1866) or the 783-page southern gothic *The Household of Bouverie; or, The Elixir of Gold* (1860) by Catherine Ann Warfield of Kentucky.[14]

Instead of using literature as a platform for pushing political and moral ideals, the turn-of-the-century women writers sought to professionalize their craft. As a result, they found an affinity between the ideas and destinies of the South and New England. That discovery helped to bridge the time-honored fault-lines of slavery and secession. The distinctions between the literary North and South were beginning to erode. In fact, all four of the novelists with whom we are concerned in this chapter and the next—Woolson, Chopin, Cather, and Glasgow—felt themselves to be exiles from their place of birth and were therefore disinclined to march under some sectionally-inspired ideological banner. For most of her adult career, Woolson, a New Englander, sojourned in the South and Europe, calling no place home. Chopin had left a border state to spend her life in Louisiana. Cather's family moved from Virginia to the distant Great Plains. Although Glasgow lived for a time in New York, she returned to Richmond but always felt herself an alien in her homeland.

The common situation of exile or dislocation helps to explain the freeing up of these women's minds, the breaking of a stultifying provincialism and local conformity. Yet it also meant alienation from the new environment—a repulsion that sometimes brought on more than tolerable distress. Despite

---

Facing Facts: Realism in American Thought and Culture, 1850–1920 (New York: Oxford University Press, 1995); and Alfred Habegger, *Gender, Fantasy, and Realism in American Literature* (New York: Columbia University Press, 1982).

14. Constance Fenimore Woolson to Paul Hamilton Hayne, "All Saints Day" 1875[?], in "Some New Letters of Constance Fenimore Woolson," ed. Jay Hubbell, *New England Quarterly* 14 (December 1941): 725, 726, and 728. Woolson elaborated on the character of the antebellum southern belles she knew at school, noting how a Charlestonian belle, in bed reading, called a maid downstairs to shut a bedroom door that she could easily have shut herself. Slavery induced that sort of thoughtlessness, Woolson concluded in her letter to Hayne (p. 726). See also Wyatt-Brown, *The Literary Percys: Family History, Gender, and the Southern Imagination* (Athens: University of Georgia Press, 1994), 83–6.

the pain, such a reaction assisted creativity. It offered an agreeable sense of apartness, a satisfaction with the independence of mind and heart that solitude provided instead of servile dependence on the company of others. Emily Toth, Kate Chopin's biographer, for instance, perceptively observes that her novelist's heroines seem most self-possessed when by themselves. In Chopin's story "The Maid of Saint Phillippe," a motherless young woman refuses to accept a most eligible mate because "she has breathed free air and 'was not born to be the mother of slaves.' . . . In the end, she strides toward the rising sun, alone."[15]

Among the women writers, the old communal style of kinship bonding had been severed. Instead they discovered independence of spirit, and they forged new ties, largely based on gender. That process helped to draw the foursome into a kind of common and disciplined artistic detachment, and in learning self-reliance, they developed a receptivity to an unsentimental, realistic mode. Speaking of Constance Woolson, critic Fred Lewis Pattee argues, "'Realism' had come to her as it had come to Flaubert and the French pioneers, as a personal experience, not as a manner learned from imitation."[16] In the latter part of the nineteenth century, the aspiring writer found realism an almost essential outlook. With regard to sexual and maternal feelings, it should be fair to say that three of these four women yearned little for married life and child-rearing. Instead they preferred that composition should dominate their working lives. Glasgow remarked that "the maternal instinct, sacred or profane, was left out of me by nature when I was designed." Cather pointed out to a reporter, "A writer has to hide and lie and almost steal in order to get time to work in—and peace of mind to work with." At as early as twenty-two, Cather had felt herself "utterly alone upon the icy heights where other beings cannot live." Reclusive, especially at the close of her life, she customarily refused to be interviewed.[17] Only Kate

15. Emily Toth, "Kate Chopin Thinks Back Through Her Mothers: Three Stories by Kate Chopin," in *Kate Chopin Reconsidered: Beyond the Bayou,* ed. Lynda S. Boren and Sara de-Saussure Davis (Baton Rouge: Louisiana State University Press, 1992), 17.

16. Fred Lewis Pattee, "Constance Fenimore Woolson and the South," *South Atlantic Quarterly* 38 (April 1939):132.

17. Quoted in L. Brent Bohlke, "Introduction," in *Willa Cather in Person: Interviews, Speeches, and Letters,* ed. Bohlke (Lincoln: University of Nebraska Press, 1986), xxvi, and also in Terry Castle, "Pipe Down Back There!" *London Review of Books,* 14 December 2000, p. 15. See the interesting interpretation of Sharon O'Brien, *Willa Cather: The Emerging Voice* (New York: Oxford University Press, 1987), who claims that the novelist was an active lesbian. See also Katrina Irving, "Displacing Homosexuality: The Use of Ethnicity in Willa Cather's *My Ántonia,*" *Modern Fiction Studies* 36 (Spring 1990), 91–102. Cf. Ellen Glasgow, *The Woman Within: An Autobiography,* ed. Pamela R. Matthews (1954; Charlottesville: University

Chopin married and bore children. Yet, as if domesticity interfered too often in her professional pursuit, she achieved her major work after the sudden death of her husband. Like her mother, as Toth observes, Chopin did not remarry but relished the uninterrupted life of the mind that an empty household afforded—with offspring grown and gone.[18]

These women were all outsiders looking in as through a glass barrier—at their family heritage, their earlier social surroundings, and their former selves as well as at the world around them. That sort of imaginative exercise, which required a skeptical, questioning persistence, would never have occurred to their romantic female predecessors. Yet that sense of distance and isolation stimulated a search outside familiar boundaries. With a freedom that the antebellum writers, riven by sectional tensions, never enjoyed, post–Civil War northern and southern women writers began to create a new literary community. Most notably, Sarah Orne Jewett, Mary Wilkins Freeman, and Constance Fenimore Woolson, the latter of which is the only writer discussed here to venture South from the North, became personal friends with various southern sisters in the literary profession. Kate Chopin was a particular champion of "Miss Wilkins." Laughingly, she tried to forgive her friend for inspiring mediocre imitators "*ad nauseam.*" Being at least in their day more prominent than the aspiring southern writers, women like Jewett and Freeman exercised considerable influence on their protégées.

Absorbing novels and short stories of northern women authors was a means to stretch a hand of friendship across the postwar sectional divide. The southerners earnestly sought to discover grounds for reconciliation. They did so in a personal way and not by fictionally pairing off hero and heroine of the former warring sections in happy wedlock as Howells had recommended. In addition, these women writers wished to gain national, not just regional, audiences. They, of course, had little choice. The main publishing houses for fiction, female and otherwise, were located in New York, Philadelphia, and Boston, not New Orleans, Charleston, or Richmond. Nonetheless, the more contacts they had outside their region, the more realistic was their goal.

As a partial result of these associations and readings, sensitive southern artists discerned that the real drama did not lie in uncritical restoration of the antebellum ideals nor in the actualities of Yankee industrialization and

Press of Virginia, 1994), 108. Glasgow attributed her unwillingness to bear children to her growing deafness, an inheritable condition in her view.

18. Toth, "Kate Chopin Thinks Back," 15–25.

New South wealth. Rather, through fictional representation, they began to dramatize the lives of those left behind or otherwise severed from the center of things and thought they ought to be explored, celebrated, or rendered tragic. Representations of older people—some sliding toward death—appear more often in their fiction than vigorous youthful folks seeking love and recognition.[19] Such choices had only momentary vogue, however, as male authors gravitated toward themes that involved more passion than reflection, more action in war, politics, and business than contemplation of the plight of a woman ensnared in monotonous domesticity.

Just as late-nineteenth-century southerners were losing their grip on the old values of chivalric honor, high-mindedness, kinship loyalties, and Stoic resolve, so too were New Englanders abandoning a heritage of Puritan sanctity and communitarianism. In *Mind and the American Civil War: A Meditation on Lost Causes,* Lewis Simpson observes that southern loss of power as a result of the great contest spelled doom even for some of the victors. A serious erosion of status had been already underway in antebellum New England. Economic and political power was draining out of Boston and Concord and toward New York and the spacious hinterlands beyond. In a sense both sections—at least their rural backlands—shared the common fate of peripheral terrain. In her short fiction Jewett showed how New Englanders were becoming strangers to each other as a once tightly bound social and familial order unraveled. The literary historian John Seelye explains that, for Jewett and later for Edith Wharton, the northeastern section had become "a region of cellar holes and second-growth forests where farms had once stood, its former inhabitants long gone away toward the West, leaving behind elderly people only, waiting to occupy a hard-earned place in the graveyard."[20]

The subjects of northern fin-de-siècle women's fiction may have exercised an influence on similar work in the South. Take, for instance, Mary Wilkins Freeman's classic story "The Village Singer." The tale relates the displacement of the aged but vital Candace Whitcomb in a New England town. She has been the church soloist for forty years but has recently lost her post. That ostensibly trifling mark of local prestige, Freeman narrates, had "been

19. See Joyce Jensen, "Economics in Literature," *New York Times,* 4 December 2000, A2.

20. Lewis F. Simpson, *Mind and the American Civil War: A Meditation on Lost Causes* (Baton Rouge: Louisiana State University Press, 1989); Helen Fiddyment Levy, *Fiction of the Home Place: Jewett, Cather, Glasgow, Porter, Welty, and Naylor* (Jackson: University Press of Mississippi, 1992), 31–63; John Seelye, *Memory's Nation: The Place of Plymouth Rock* (Chapel Hill: University of North Carolina Press, 1998), 566.

as much to her as Italy was to Napoleon." Yet, "on her island of exile," that is, her house next to the church, "she was still showing fight." With a voice that almost drowns out the meek soloist next door during the congregational hymn-singing, Candace accompanies herself on her own organ. To the distress of the churchgoers, they cannot help but hear Candace at full volume. Though strong-willed to the end, she repents on her deathbed her conduct on Sunday morning a week before. Candace exults, however, that her replacement, the mousey, piping Alma, had "flatted a little" on the last hymn.[21] The old spirit is still aflame, but Freeman sought a larger meaning. New England life outside the urban centers, she implied, no longer had its ancient integrity. In particular, the old—largely poor and uncelebrated— were the losers. Something almost claustrophobic invades Freeman's depictions of crabbed, aging, failed lives. We find similar stories in the southern library of the same period. The novels and stories of Kate Chopin and Ellen Glasgow would deal—famously, in fact—with brave people with still greater problems: lost hopes, broken lives, and a deteriorating social order, only these tales were set in the South.

Constance Fenimore Woolson (1840–1890), James Fenimore Cooper's great-niece, has been designated by Fred Pattee as "the first Southern writer of the new period."[22] Following that classification, I treat her in greater depth than Chopin, the more familiar author. As a Yankee and only temporary resident in the South, she might be said to represent the crossing-over or merging aspect of the post–Civil War literary landscape. This was an era when southern writers traveled or at least looked hopefully northward for professional inspiration. Sometimes northern women writers discovered like-minded artists in the southern backlands. It is no exaggeration to say that, with her reclusive but highly observant nature, Woolson understood the southern white mentality better than the more sentimental southern women romancers of her time. Personal experience and a great degree of self-knowledge played a part in that understanding. Woolson was herself subject to the same inner doubts, sense of loss, and dislocation that she found in the inhabitants of the Reconstruction South.

Although quite popular in the late 1870s to the 1890s, Woolson has had only a minor revival in recent years. Her reputation benefits from the redis-

21. Mary E. Wilkins Freeman, "The Village Singer," in *Selected Stories,* ed. Marjorie Pryse (New York: Norton, 1983), 138.
22. Pattee, "Woolson and the South," 135.

covery of nineteenth-century women writers in general. In her own day, she
became almost an adopted southerner. Woolson published fifteen short stories set in the region and utilized that locale for scenes and references in
several of her novels. For instance, her most fully realized book-length
fiction, *East Angels,* published to a wide readership in 1886, was set in
"Gracias-a-Dios" or St. Augustine, Florida, her favorite spot in America.
Margaret Harold, the protagonist, is by no means the self-renouncing heroine that southern writer Augusta Evans so often portrayed. She exclaims,
"When have *I* been permitted myself to be disagreeable? When have I ever
failed to be kind? I have always repressed myself." At another point she
likens herself to a slave: "*Oh, to be somewhere . . . anywhere where I can
breathe and think as I please—as I really am! Do you want me to die without ever having been myself—my real self—even for one day!*"[23]

Nor did Woolson portray the South as a prewar paradise or a romantically decaying country. She recognized the problems of postwar mourning
and the former Rebels' sense of meaningless defeat. Sometimes she was
overly sympathetic. Her poem "At the Smithy" gives a dramatic but sentimental account of a blacksmith who has lost his sons in the conflict. Hayne
spoke of it as unusually "full of '*grit,*' vigor, and almost *manly verve.*"[24] Set
in heroic couplets, the poem does not actually deserve such enthusiasm.[25]

While her early stories, like the blacksmith poem, were overburdened
with conventional formulas, Woolson moved swiftly away from clichés to
take more a cold-eyed inspection of post–Civil War southern society. "Literature," she wrote, "must not refuse to deal with the ugly and the commonplace and even the shockingly unpleasant. It is all in life and therefore not to
be avoided."[26] In *East Angels,* Mrs. Thorne, a penurious northern woman
stranded in Florida, for instance, has to hide her disgust with southern
mean-spiritedness and suspicion in order to support herself and daughter:
"I swallowed everything. I even swallowed slavery—I, a New England girl,

23. Sybil B. Weir, "Southern Womanhood in the Novels of Constance Fenimore Woolson," *Mississippi Quarterly* 30 (Fall 1976): 566. I am much indebted to the author of this fine
article for her useful insights. Quotations are from Constance Fenimore Woolson, *East Angels*
(New York: Harper Bros., 1886), 497, 591.

24. Paul Hamilton Hayne to Margaret J. Preston, 25 October 1875, in *A Man of Letters
in the Nineteenth-Century South: Selected Letters of Paul Hamilton Hayne,* ed. Rayburn S.
Moore (Baton Rouge: Louisiana State University Press, 1982), 130.

25. Constance Fenimore Woolson, "At the Smithy. (Pickens County, South Carolina,
1874)," *Appleton's Journal* 12 (5 September 1874), 289–90.

26. Quoted in Ann Douglas Wood, "The Literature of Impoverishment: The Women Local
Colorists in America, 1865–1914," *Women's Studies* 1 (1972): 4.

abolitionist to the core! It was the most heroic thing I ever did in my life."
With a remarkable intensity, Mrs. Thorne curses "the idle, unrealizing, con-
tented life of this tiresome, idle coast!"[27] This was not the picture of the
sunny South that Henry Flagler would have wanted advertized as he built
his luxury hotels at St. Augustine.

As far as Woolson was concerned, both sections, but especially the
South, grossly underrated females' capabilities. She wrote her friend Alice,
Henry James's neurasthenic sister, that education should be taught equally
to both sexes in the same space. It was the only way "to widen the feminine
mind. Do not suppose that I think the feminine mind inferior to the masculine. For I do not. But it has been kept back, & enfeebled, & limited, by
ages of ignorance & almost servitude."[28]

Such an attitude and clarity of focus enabled Woolson to develop a
greater interest in the southern mentalité than any of the other female northern writers. Anne Rowe, an otherwise discerning critic, however, finds her
characters stereotypical. She calls Woolson's approach to southern life sentimental and even mythical about the splendor of antebellum planter culture.
Rowe laments the artist's withdrawal from the antislavery spirit of Tourgée's and De Forest's Reconstruction novels.[29] But as an artist, not ideologue, Woolson had reason to flesh out the ambiguities and reject the good-
versus-evil representations of the morally inspired writer. A different perspective led her to write of what she saw but did not necessarily admire in
her renderings of southern white defeat, descent into poverty, and nostalgia
for a past that could never be restored.

Woolson formed her perceptions of this tragic state of southern affairs
through her conversations with members of the southern planter class, once
proud and wealthy, now bitter and poor. To be sure, she was conservative
in opinions about race and other matters. Born in 1840, she was little different from the other women writers mentioned here in failing to meet twenty-
first-century standards of equity in relation to African Americans and perhaps other minorities. Nevertheless, out of necessity she had become quite
adventurous in the management of her single life. Taking care of an invalid
and gloom-tormented mother, she dwelt briefly in various parts of this

27. Woolson, *East Angels*, 219, 223.
28. Quoted in Jean Strouse, *Alice James: A Biography* (Boston: Houghton Mifflin, 1980),
260.
29. Anne Rowe, *The Enchanted Country: Northern Writers in the South, 1865–1910*
(Baton Rouge: Louisiana State University Press, 1978), 54–73.

country and abroad. Like her mother, she had a highly pronounced tendency toward depression.

No less serious a problem was the series of family losses that deeply wounded so sensitive and intellectual a soul. In Woolson's first month of life, three of her sisters died of scarlet fever, plunging the family into extended grief. When Woolson was twelve, an older sister died of tuberculosis, a disease contracted from her husband. Another sister lost her life in childbirth the next year. In 1869, when Woolson was twenty-nine, her father expired. When Alice James lost her father, Woolson commiserated, "A daughter feels [such a loss] . . . more than a son of course, because her life is so limited, so bounded by home life."[30]

Extraordinarily reserved and prudent to a fault, Woolson never married, and her relations with such men as southern writer Paul Hamilton Hayne were confined to mutual intellectual and professional interests.[31] She looked upon matrimony as a form of boredom and torturing dependence, not of mutual love. "If there is anything I dread," she once confessed, "it is a new acquaintance. I evade, and avoid, and back away from everybody." Feeling too inadequate to play the sexual game, she wrote Paul Hayne, "To enjoy society a woman must be either personally attractive, gifted with conversational powers, or else must *think* of herself as one or both, whether she is in reality or not. I do not come under any of those heads. Result, don't care for society at all." When she thought of how much southerners loved to talk and visit, she was reminded of the contrasting nature of her New Hampshire aunts: "silent, reserved, solitary, thin, and a little grim; I am as much like them as the kind of life I lead will allow."[32]

No doubt Woolson's lack of frivolity was in part owing to her chronic melancholy, a malady that affected others in the Woolson line besides her often baleful mother. She once cursed "this deadly enemy of mine [which] creeps in, and once in, he is master." These periods of deep sadness left her "overweighted with a sort of depression that comes unexpectedly, and makes everything black." She had grown up in a household where laughter seldom echoed and smiles were rare. Referring to the gloom that pervaded

30. Quoted in Strouse, *Alice James*, 202n.

31. Cheryl B. Torsney, *Constance Fenimore Woolson: The Grief of Artistry* (Athens: University of Georgia Press, 1989), 15–6; John Dwight Kern, *Constance Fenimore Woolson: Literary Pioneer* (Philadelphia: University of Pennsylvania Press, 1975), 161; Rayburn S. Moore, *Constance Fenimore Woolson* (New York: Twayne, 1963), 23–4.

32. Woolson to Hayne, 10 September 1876, in "Some New Letters of Constance Fenimore Woolson," ed. Hubbell, 732; see also Kern, *Woolson*, 51.

her family, she wrote, "My grandfather gave up to it and was a dreary useless man; my father battled it all his life."[33] Adding to her wretchedness was
an increasing deafness that shut out the sometimes comforting noises of the
world, leaving her in empty silence.

From 1873 to 1879, to overcome the succession of ordeals, Constance
and her suffering mother, who died in the latter year, moved like nomads
through the southern states, living out of trunks and portmanteaux. The
pair also traveled throughout Europe, England, and North Africa. Yet all
her life Woolson longed to settle in a cottage in Florida. For a time, she
made her experiences in the South a prime source of her fiction. Reflecting
her own feelings as a struggling female artist in a male world, she fashioned
some of her complex female characters as chiefly solitary and romantic—
but soon bitterly disillusioned—figures. Often their self-sacrifices, necessi-
tated by social convention and male demand, did not end in typical
Victorian uplift. Her many women readers found that twist against fashion
dramatic and appealing. To be sure, not all her stories express ambiguity,
indeterminacy. Some followed the usual happy post–Civil War formula of
the southern belle who proudly rejects, then succumbs to the charms of, a
handsome Union officer.[34]

"In the Cotton Country" (1876), however, represents a more serious aes-
thetic turn. In it we find a narrator who, as the intellectual historian Ann
Douglas observes, has "almost an uncontrollable need to . . . get at some
stifled part of herself, mysteriously locked in" another woman's travails.
This troubled quest makes her "capable not only of pain but of creativity."
The epigraphs opening "In the Cotton Country" consist of verses by Paul
Hamilton Hayne and Henry Timrod. They quote hymns of exaltation for
the Carolina landscape. Woolson's intention was to contrast the subsequent
story of death and wretchedness with the smiling poems. It would seem that
William Faulkner was not the first to use the decaying southern plantation
manor to symbolize the South's postwar downslide into moral decay and
impoverishment. Poe, of course, had used the image for different pur-

33. Constance Fenimore Woolson, quoted in *Women Artists, Women Exiles: "Miss Grief"
and Other Stories by Constance Fenimore Woolson*, ed. Joan Myers Weimer (New Brunswick,
N.J.: Rutgers University Press, 1988), xviii, xxiii. See Helen Taylor, *Gender, Race, and Region
in the Writings of Grace King, Ruth McEnery Stuart, and Kate Chopin* (Barton Rouge: Louisiana State University Press, 1989), 21, 39–40, 103, 105, 122–6, 163; Jones, *Tomorrow Is Another Day*, 146–7; see also Woolson to Hayne, "All Saints' Day," 1875[?], in "Some New
Letters of Constance Fenimore Woolson," ed. Hubbell, 727.

34. Torsney, *Woolson*, 20.

poses—to symbolize the dissolution of an anguished mind, for instance, in "The Fall of the House of Usher." Others, like John Pendleton Kennedy and William Gilmore Simms, exploited the decrepit mansion to underline the passing of an old aristocracy.[35] Woolson, however, depicted a very real situation—the downfall of once-prominent families in the vortex of war and violence—almost modernistic in its detail and existential depth. In the story, the South Carolina residence—a "very plain abode" rather than the grand mansion that occupies most romances—"seemed to have fallen to the hands of Giant Despair. 'Forlorn' was written over its lintels, and 'without hope' along its low roof-edge."[36] The family house had been razed by Yankee troops. The former residents were reduced to living in the overseer's lodging, a not uncommon situation in actual fact.

The story creates a desolate but not a gothic atmosphere. The mood is heightened by the unreliability of the narrator, a northern woman whose depressive nature is severe enough to seem a snake-pit of the soul. Like Woolson herself, the protagonist has been wandering through the defeated South as a "solitary pedestrian." Lacking a home of her own, the lonely narrator pursues a flock of crows, an image often adopted to symbolize the depressive condition. "The crows at home," Woolson has the speaker sigh nostalgically, "—that would be something worth seeing."[37] The southern creatures magically lead the northern visitor, a fruitless seeker of contentment in her own life, toward the ravaged house and its grieving, embittered occupant.

The use of this powerful imagery to signify the desperation of a tortured soul might be said to link the past romanticisms of Poe's "Raven" and Chapman's "War Eagle" to similar and equally compelling winged representations in the literature of Woolson's time and beyond it into modern letters. Two quick examples may serve to reveal the connection. In the closing lines of *The Awakening* (1899), Kate Chopin invokes a similar metaphor, as quoted in the epigraph opening this chapter. A bird with a broken wing falls into the sea as Edna Pontellier prepares to drown herself. In the mid-twentieth century the Virginian William Styron also made use of the feathered harbinger. Confined to walking the earth, clucking, flightless birds

35. I thank Susan Donaldson for pointing out the different uses to which the mansion in decline was put in southern literature.

36. Constance Fenimore Woolson, "In the Cotton Country," in her *Rodman the Keeper: Southern Sketches* (1880; New York: AMS Press, 1971), 181.

37. Woolson, "In the Cotton Country" in *Women Artists, Women Exiles,* ed. Weimer, 134.

appear to Peyton Loftis in her last psychotic fantasy in *Lie Down in Darkness* as she moves toward the open window of a deserted warehouse in Harlem: "I turn in the room and see them come across the tiles, dimly prancing, fluffing up their wings, I think: my poor flightless birds, have you suffered without soaring on this earth? Come then and fly." The distracted Peyton imagines the creatures miraculously taking wing as she leaps in her own doomed flight.[38]

To return to the Woolson story, the unforgiving widow, the head of her household, has good reason for anger and grief. Despite an initial reluctance, she tells her intrusive guest a tale of heartache and death. The Clayton Cotesworths, her once proud and wealthy family, lost all their men in distant battle and local skirmish. The survivors had been nearly overrun by a slave uprising late in the war. These are not presented as heroic moments. Rather, they are treated as events that might occur in any war. Gray-haired and gaunt, the widow is described as looking twice her youthful age. The foolish rush of the widow's half-mad father had earlier prompted approaching Union troops to cut him down in a fusillade. A lonely survivor with a quiet, solitary boy—her orphaned nephew—to raise, the widow mourns her fate. In the closing lines of the story, she warns the narrator, "Let us alone; we will watch the old life out with her [the South], and when her new dawning comes, we shall have joined our dead, and all of us, our errors, our sins, and our sufferings will be forgotten."[39]

In Woolson's narrative, dreams of a New South do not arise. Referring to "In the Cotton Country," she reported, "I have written stories of imagination, but this is a story of fact. It is true, every word of it, save the names given." The dull grayness of a decaying house and an unmarked grave symbolize Confederate defeat. But the narrator, who represents the triumphant North, offers no contrasting signal of happiness. She may think of herself as a "Sister of Charity" laden with "balm and wine and oil for those who suffer," but actually she has extracted from the old woman her tragic story because she compulsively seeks out others even more miserable and solitary than she is herself.[40] The literary critic Joan Weimer, who is most perceptive

38. Kate Chopin, *The Awakening: An Authoritative Text, Contexts, Criticism*, ed. Margaret Culley (1899; New York: W. W. Norton, 1976), 113; William Styron, *Lie Down in Darkness* (1951; New York: Viking, 1968), 386.

39. Woolson, "In the Cotton Country," in *Rodman the Keeper*, 196.

40. Ibid., 184; Kern, *Woolson*, 73. Kern points out that in the title story, "Rodman the Keeper," Woolson creates a female character whose bitterness and seething resentment against the victors were not at all untypical of white southerners during the post–Civil War years. At

about "In the Cotton Country," proposes that Woolson's "narrator finds only confirmation of her unstated beliefs that human connection cannot last but can only betray, and that the best protection against such loss is accepting homelessness and habitual solitude."[41] The Edwardian novelist E. M. Forster would make primary in his fiction a sense of the need for human connection. Woolson, though, saw little possibility for fulfillment of that ideal. She was always an exile, an isolate.

One reason that she found the Florida landscape so compelling a subject to write about was her recognition of its compatibility with her own solitary spirit. The swamps that she describes in *East Angels* and in the torturous story "The South Devil" are not so much gothic exaggerations as genuine descriptions of the fetid mass of tropical terrors that her characters pass through. She was gifted in natural descriptions; she wrote what she saw. William Dean Howells publicly thought otherwise, but Woolson rejoined, "Mr Howells is mistaken in thinking the situation fantastic [in *Castle Nowhere*]; the islands, the fogs, the false lights, the wreckers, the Mormons are all exactly from *real life,* true descriptions."[42] Even her positive word-paintings capture the spirit of the sight, such as her passage about the St. Johns river in Florida, "where palms stand along the shores in groups, outlined against the sky, which has a softness unknown in the North." The Florida pine barrens were not for her: "dull, desolate expanses, without beauty or use."[43]

Woolson was equally at home with the political conflicts of the day. She did not translate them into moral lessons in the manner of Tourgée but explored them with almost a scientific detachment. In "King David," another piece of short fiction about the South, she grasps the tragic degeneration in the late Reconstruction years of carpetbaggers' dreams of racial peace and African American uplift. The story involves the moral collapse of an abolitionist's grammar school for the freed people at a hamlet ironically renamed

---

a national cemetery in the South where lay the remains of fourteen thousand Union troops, the figure signs a guest book with a fiery accusation against the soldiers who "killed my father, my three brothers, my cousins." They had sown ruin and desolation "upon our neighborhood, all our State, and all our country," which would never submit its irreconcilable spirit to the blue-coated enemy. Quoted in Kern, *Woolson,* 74.

41. John Myers Weimer, "Women Artists as Exiles in the Fiction of Constance Fenimore Woolson," *Legacy* 3 (Fall 1986): 6.

42. Woolson to Hayne, 15 June 1875, in "Some New Letters of Constance Fenimore Woolson," ed. Hubbell, 720.

43. Quoted in Pattee, "Woolson and the South," 137–8.

by the former slaves as Jubilee. The community moves from idealistic promise to disillusionment on all sides. The deterioration has been engineered by
planter hostility to black independence. Yet more than so easy an explanation of failure is involved. "King David" is basically an allegory of the death
of New England ideals. It also offers an implied criticism of the new era
in which a cynically Yankee-like "New South" materialism is beginning to
flourish. The narrator explains that in their naïveté most of the field-hands
are easily fooled in that remote backwater. Yet under the guidance of the
New England teacher, they for a time have been successfully striving to create a better life.

The white abolitionist teacher at Jubilee is David King. The name under-
scores the story's allegorical character. By setting a stern but saintly example, the missionary has guarded his pupils and parents from the postwar
chaos of hard drinking and random violence. A rascally northerner, though,
brings to the sleepy community new temptations that will crush all advances
for the simple freed people. He opens a store to sell liquor to the men and
"trashy finery" to the gullible young girls. "The women of Jubilee," Woolson writes, "more faithful than the men, still sent their children to [David
King's] school; but they did it with discouraged hearts, poor things! Often
now they were seen with bandaged heads and bruised bodies, the result of
drunken blows from husband or brother."[44]

The local whites blame the freed people's dissolute behavior on the dedicated abolitionist schoolmaster, not the storekeeper and his array of consumer goods. In a confrontation between the two northern whites, the freed
people side with the owner of the store. Sadly David King realizes that "they
had taught him a great lesson, the lesson of a failure." Only one black
woman stands in the road at his departure. She hands him some flowers.
Momentarily he is touched but quickly sees that she is "unmoved" and mo-
tivated simply by curiosity at his leaving. When he returns to his Yankee
home, the villagers gossip about how he had abruptly returned and taken
up the duties of running the district school. " 'Has he now?' they say. 'Didn't
find the blacks what he expected, I guess.' " They are no more sympathetic
than the southerners, black and white, whom he had left in Jubilee.[45]

While Woolson's sympathies lay with the white missionary teacher, she
recognized that instruction of a people beset by poverty, narrow agrarian
horizons, recent bondage, and unremitting white vigilance and terrorizing

44. Woolson, "King David," in *Rodman the Keeper,* 267.
45. Ibid., 274–5.

was a daunting venture. Moreover, as the narrator makes clear, the laborers prefer a teacher of their own race. That fact David King finally has to admit to himself. The story remains a telling commentary on the clash between some age-old sectional ideals—a rigid code of chivalry and race subordination on the one hand, and a well-meaning but uncomprehending Yankee utopian principle on the other. Union victory, Woolson implied, could not overcome the tragic weight of racial traditions of inequity and oppression. The victors, she avers, brought to the South not only a reforming spirit but also a sinister consumer mentality. The tale further illustrates her capacity to render irony. Woolson recognized that "the mind dreams; life mocks the dream," in the words of an observant critic.[46] Certainly that was David King's fate.

Although Woolson admired some aspects of southern custom and life—even at times its wildness—she found the people provincial, indolent, and meanspirited.[47] Like the Cotesworth widow, too many of them were immersed in the past and unable to deal successfully with the present. Woolson compared her own New England heritage very critically to the white southerners' insistence on form and appearance over substance and reality. Perhaps she was expressing something of Yankee self-righteousness, but not without seeing through its own demise in a New England whose rural young people were heading west or to urban centers. In her novel *For the Major*, for instance, she deals effectively with the immaturity and empty-headedness of southern women, whose men like them that way. But she creates a situation more complex than that. Woolson indicates that the men are bereft, too. They are unable to revitalize their war-ravaged community and live too much on memories of happy times long vanished. An old carriage symbolizes the deterioration of Far Edgerley, the low-country settlement. The Carroll family, whose members own the broken-down vehicle, do not even have mules, much less horses, to pull it. Since the Carrolls "lived all the year round now upon one of their sea islands, whose only road through the waste of old cotton fields was most of the time overflowed, they had nothing to draw it upon."[48]

46. Joan Acocella, *Willa Cather and the Politics of Criticism* (Lincoln: University of Nebraska Press, 2000), 21.

47. Weir, "Southern Womanhood in the Novels of Constance Fenimore Woolson," 559.

48. Constance Fenimore Woolson, *For the Major and Selected Short Stories*, ed. Rayburn S. Moore (1883; New Haven: Yale University Press, 1967), 260. Anne Rowe offers an entirely different interpretation of this work. She claims that Woolson sustained from beginning to end the illusion of an "idealized presentation of a finer life" to be located in the Old South. See Anne E. Rowe, *The Enchanted Country*, 66.

Woolson captures in this and other works a mood that was very prevalent in the defeated South—despite the almost frenzied weaving of Lost Cause tapestries.[49] With subtlety and keen precision, the short-fiction writer undermined the sentimental forms and showed how inauthentic the stereotypes were. In her stories, the southern gentleman can accept only a woman who matches the youthful innocence and purity of the stylized belle. A full-fledged woman with intellect and opinions would be too much for him to handle. Yet ultimately Woolson's women submit to the demands that the world imposes on their sex—but not without recognizing and inwardly lamenting the high price paid for being unfree, never true to themselves.[50] Her own sense of displacement and loss was acute. As the critic Joan Weimer puts it, like many of her female characters, Woolson remained throughout her life a perpetual exile.[51]

Unfortunately, the native New Englander's self-esteem was insufficient to sustain her. In 1894, ill from both typhoid and influenza, she suffered from a particularly severe attack of dejection. Cold weather and lack of sun had a severe effect on her—a problem associated with chronic depression. She once wrote Samuel Mather, a Cleveland, Ohio, relation, "Let the air grow really cold," as it was in the fall, 1894, "and down I go towards the gates of death."[52] She killed herself by leaping from the balcony of her Venetian villa.[53] Shrinking from the stigma attached to suicide, Woolson's relations insisted that delirium from disease provoked her to swoon and fall. She had not merely dropped, however, but had jumped from the height. Upon hearing the news, Henry James, with whom Woolson had possibly fallen vainly in love, was horrified, mystified, and guilt-ridden. At once he wrote his friend Francis Boott, "Pitiful victim of chronic melancholy as she was (so that half one's friendship for her was always anxiety), nothing is more possible than that, in illness, this obsession should abruptly have deepened into suicidal mania."[54] Later, he wrote his brother William, "My own belief is that she had been on the very verge of suicide years ago." Had it not been

49. See Bertram Wyatt-Brown, *The Shaping of Southern Culture: Honor, Grace, and War, 1760s to 1890s* (Chapel Hill: University of North Carolina Press, 2001), chapters 11 and 12.

50. Torsney, *Woolson*, 14–21, 23.

51. See Weimer, ed., *Women Artists, Women Exiles*, 3–16.

52. Woolson to Samuel Mather, n.d., in *Constance Fenimore Woolson: Five Generations (1785–1923)*, ed. Clare Benedict, 3 vols. (London: G. White, 1923), 2:48.

53. Weimer, "Women Artists as Exiles," 3–16; Weir, "Southern Womanhood in the Novels of Constance Fenimore Woolson," 559–68.

54. Leon Edel, *Henry James: A Life* (New York: Harper, 1977), 391–2.

for a few important friendships, he guessed, she would not have lived as long as she did. But for all his speculations, he knew that his rejection of her love for him played a part.[55] Every year, Henry James visited her grave and, as an epitaph perhaps, wrote the mordant short story "The Beast in the Jungle," with its melancholy, sexless, semi-autobiographical hero John Marcher.[56]

For good reason, then, Woolson, single and unfulfilled in her own sexual longings, chose for a time the defeated South for her settings—a preference over her prospering northern homeland. Southern destiny matched her own foreboding feelings of alienation and isolation. She did not end her own life out of a loss of creative energy or worries about her place in the profession of writing. Rather she fell victim to a neurological and an emotional disease that, when under control, had stimulated her extraordinary imaginative gifts.[57]

Unlike Woolson, Kate Chopin (1850–1904) moved into the lower South not from New England but from Missouri, where North and South had fiercely clashed for dominance in the great civil conflict of her young life. That migration, as we shall also see in the case of Willa Cather, deeply affected Chopin's art even more than Woolson's sojourn in the Southeast. Yet both shared the fate of many artists—melancholia and a close acquaintance with death. Chopin's father, Thomas O'Flaherty, a prominent St. Louis, Missouri, commission merchant, died in a train accident on All Saints' Day, 1855. His daughter was only five at the time she went with the family to the Catholic cathedral for his funeral. The event drew her aristocratic and devout mother closer to the daughter who had so admired and loved her father. A Chopin biographer comments, "In the silence of deep distress in the mother's heart and strange wonder in the child's, a sympathy awoke that never ceased and never grew less while the mother lived."[58]

55. Ibid., 392.

56. Torsney, Woolson, 1, 11, 20, 14–7; Edel, Henry James, 603–11, 793; idem, Henry James: The Master: 1901–1916 (New York, Avon, 1972), 135; Henry James, "The Beast in the Jungle (1903)," in Henry James, Collected Stories, 2 vols. (New York: Knopf, 1999) 2:737–84.

57. The potential suicide cannot produce clear thought or reason toward hope: "Neuropsychologists and clinicians have found that people when depressed think more slowly, are more easily distracted, tire more quickly in cognitive tasks, and find their memory wanting." Kay Redfield Jamison, Night Falls Fast: Understanding Suicide (New York: Knopf, 1999), 92. See also Edwin S. Shneidman, ed., Essays in Self-Destruction (New York: Science House, 1967).

58. Per Seyersted, Kate Chopin: A Critical Biography (Baton Rouge: Louisiana State University Press, 1969), 17.

The understanding of others' pain is a noteworthy and poignant characteristic of Chopin's fiction. That gift for empathy may well have grown from her childhood wrestling with loss and sorrow and their reconciliation through the means of love. Further deepening the grief of the household was the death of Kate's younger sister when Kate was only five or six. The loss was bound to have a serious emotional impact (though her biographers make little of it). In addition, Kate was only twelve when her Rebel brother died of typhoid in a Yankee prison camp, a third loss that she found "crushing." For several years she refused to leave home, did not attend school, read romances voraciously in the attic, and composed poems and essays on the theme of sudden and early mortality. After Thomas O'Flaherty's death, the house was always a place of "subdued sadness."[59]

After her emergence from that period of intense grief, Chopin fell into episodes of despair only occasionally. The incidents did not seem to interrupt her work or even last very long. It seems significant, however, that her most famous work, *The Awakening,* was written after the loss of her husband. Given her artistic resilience after this blow, one might speculate that her disciplined effort of creation acted in some way as a restorative. We cannot know for certain. Professional writer as she was—but also southern in her self-restraint—she was extremely taciturn about her innermost feelings. Chopin admitted that she "would never be confidential except for the purpose of misleading."[60]

To a remarkable degree, the record of Kate Chopin's losses and sufferings had a compensatory effect. The Louisiana writer developed a sympathy for the displaced in that society—working-class Creoles and African American women. In her short stories, she treats them without sentimentality. The male characters are often handsome but also violent and abusive. Armand Aubigny, Désirée's plantation-owner husband in the grim, interracial tale "Désirée's Baby," presents a salient example. The story concerns something seldom talked about in the nineteenth century—the verbal and emotional abuse toward women of which domineering and unloving men are capable. It also treats in fresh manner the inhumanity of racial prejudice. The brief, understated story tells of how Désirée, a beautiful child-bride of unknown parentage, gives birth to a baby—a firstborn male—to the vast pleasure, initially, of Armand. By the time the infant reaches three months, however, the

---

59. Emily Toth, *Kate Chopin* (1990; Austin: University of Texas Press, 1993), 34; Seyersted, *Kate Chopin,* 16–30.

60. Quoted in Seyersted, *Kate Chopin,* 61.

child shows distinctly Negroid features. Armand, whom Désirée worships, turns viciously against mother and son. Others in the household and neighborhood follow his venomous example. Shorn of all support and distraught over Armand's smoldering hatred, Désirée walks fatally into the waters of the bayou, holding her infant in her arms.

To destroy all memory associated with the disgraced wife, the proud plantation owner has a bonfire made of the things she has loved. Then, as the flames burn fiercely, Armand discovers a hidden note, not from Désirée, but an old letter from his mother to her husband. The last lines read, "I thank the good God for having so arranged our lives that our dear Armand will never know that his mother, who adores him, belongs to the race that is cursed with the brand of slavery."[61] Fashioned in the style of Guy de Maupassant, the few pages of text became a professional success. The story opened the author to the magazines and publishing houses of the North.[62] Yet like other unconventional southern women writers of her time, Kate Chopin had to defy such editorial guardians of the genteel tradition as Richard Watson Gilder in New York. Seeking acceptance in the greater publishing world meant compromises with her own art. Intimidated, she destroyed one novel and several short stories. The texts presumably violated the code of feminine delicacy.[63]

Nevertheless, Chopin stayed the course reasonably well. While Woolson's male figures seemed at times to border on stock characters, the same could by no means be said of Chopin's. The Creoles with whom she populated her tales are on the whole a little slow in the head. Yet they may be kind—for instance, the nineteen-year-old Gilma Germain in "Dead Man's Shoes." By and large the black women in her stories are powerful Dilsey-like figures, deftly rendered. Perhaps influenced by Mary Freeman's work, she also wrote movingly about lone women. One such story, "The White Eagle," was written after she had suffered several deaths of those close to her and following the controversial reception of *The Awakening*. It is about a young girl whose only companion is a cast-iron bird with a knowing, almost human expression. Even after the protagonist has lost all her property, her youth, and her wealthy friends, the eagle inhabits a corner of her decrepit single room. After her death, the bird presides over her grave, still

61. Kate Chopin, "Désirée's Baby," in *Complete Works*, ed. Per Seyersted (Baton Rouge: Louisiana State University Press, 1969), 245.

62. Seyersted, *Kate Chopin*, 54.

63. See Taylor, *Gender, Race, and Region*, 148–9.

gazing "with an expression which in a human being would pass for wisdom."[64] This bird is not the frightening apparition of Poe's Raven or Woolson's crows but a protective companion. Yet it, too, personifies death and
sadness all the same.[65]

Regarding her most famous work, *The Awakening*, Chopin should be
remembered for what Cynthia Wolff calls her "ruthless fidelity" in portray-
ing "the disintegration" of the heroine Edna Pontellier's "character."[66] The
author helped to change fictional heroines dramatically from the earlier
mode of modesty and self-sacrifice for their men. Gustave Flaubert's Emma
Bovary had likewise striven in vain rebellion by engaging in adulterous passion. Flaubert's masterpiece closes with the agonized deaths of the lovers,
who never achieve the romantic passion they anticipated. Such figures, male
and female, demonstrated the "dissociation of the artist's imagination from
the world about, a disengagement that originated in the fiction-writer's own
psychological essence," as Michael Ignatieff observes.[67]

Despite Edna's infidelity, some critics see her as an ennobled figure, made
majestic by her death as a form of spiritual liberation. That is a misreading.
Nor is Edna, as some claim, a victim of schizophrenia. Her feelings of an
inner emptiness spring from a depressive nature, a state of mind that leaves
her no peace, no outlet. To be sure, she is more than a bundle of neurotic
symptoms. Edna Pontellier is certainly no Madame Bovary except in the
most superficial respects—both being unhappy women, resentful of the ob-
tuseness of their husbands. Unlike Emma Bovary, however, Edna Pontellier
is not engaged in self-indulgent boredom, shallow-mindedness, or simple

64. Chopin, "The White Eagle," in *Complete Works*, ed. Seyersted, 673.

65. See Heather Kirk Thomas, " 'What Are the Prospects for the Book?': Rewriting a
Woman's Life," in *Kate Chopin Reconsidered*, ed. Boren and Davis, 51–2. Thomas thinks the
view that Chopin suffered a depression after the publication of *The Awakening* is much overblown. She cites as evidence to the contrary Chopin's shrewd and meticulous real-estate deals,
declining physical as opposed to emotional health, and the production of further short stories.
These factors, Thomas says, should dispel the notion of a Chopin under special mental stress.
Indeed, that might be so, and her essay is worth serious attention. Yet the poems and stories
like "The White Eagle" (all impressive artistically), written after *The Awakening*, suggest otherwise. They concern issues of death and sadness, but why should they not? After all, she had
ample reason to feel unappreciated, and her physical declension might well have made her less
resilient emotionally.

66. Cynthia Griffin Wolff, "Thanatos and Eros: Kate Chopin's *The Awakening*," *American Quarterly* 25 (October 1973): 450.

67. B. F. Bart, ed., *Madame Bovary and the Critics: A Collection of Essays* (New York:
New York University Press, 1966); Michael Ignatieff, "Paradigm Lost," *Times Literary Supplement*, 4 September 1987, p. 939.

lust. Chopin's authorial sentiments about Edna are both positive and negative. Like William Styron was later to be, particularly in *Lie Down in Darkness* and *Sophie's Choice,* Chopin was intrigued and repelled by her main
character's condition of melancholia and suicidal inclination.[68] Flaubert was
much more outspoken than Chopin in linking his writing to his own depressive tendency. The melancholy bachelor, for instance, explained that he
found in the practice of art a kind of agonized compulsion:. "As to my
mania for work, I'll compare it to a rash. I keep scratching myself and yell-
ing as I scratch. It's pleasure and torture combined."[69] Chopin may have felt
that way but, ladylike, kept her own counsel.

There was an elusiveness in Chopin's fiction. She left it to the reader to
divine a character's inner life. The Louisiana writer offered no conveniently
unambiguous account, no indisputable portrait of the heroine in *The Awakening.* We do know, however, that Edna Pontellier has been motherless from
an early age, and that her sense of aloneness has not been assuaged by her
rather tyrannical and distant father. Like Chopin, who came from Missouri,
a state neither quite northern nor fully southern, her heroine Edna is a relative newcomer to the lower South—from Kentucky, far from the Creole society that she finds so estranging. Her Presbyterian upbringing contrasts
with the Catholicism surrounding her. Moreover, her husband, Léonce, has
no deep feeling for her or perhaps for anyone. We are given these clues
about her troubled life, and yet somehow Chopin has Edna remain mysterious. The reader has to witness Edna's seemingly triumphant wading into the
enveloping bosom of the sea, not altogether certain that the ending is justified in the narrative itself. That horrifying decision to end life makes clear
that this young wife of a prosperous, if diffident and self-absorbed, gentleman sees herself as a meaningless failure. But why? As is the case of other
transitional women writers of her generation and very much like Willa
Cather in the next, Chopin wants us to supply the meaning ourselves.

68. See Bertram Wyatt-Brown, "William Styron's *Sophie's Choice,* Poland, and Depression," Fourteenth Annual International Conference on Literature and Psychoanalysis, Bialy-
stok, Poland, 10 July 2000, published in *Southern Literary Journal* 34 (Fall 2001):56–67;
idem, "The Desperate Imagination: Writers and Melancholy in the Modern American South,"
in *Southern Writers and their Worlds,* ed. Christopher Morris and Steven G. Reinhardt (University Station: Texas A&M Press, 1996), 57–77 (also reprinted in paperback by Louisiana
State University Press, 1998).

69. Ignatieff, "Paradigm Lost," 939; Stanley W. Jackson, *Melancholia and Depression:
From Hippocratic Times to Modern Times* (New Haven: Yale University Press, 1986); Julia
Kristeva, *Black Sun: Depression and Melancholia* (New York: Columbia University Press,
1989).

In her poignant and doomed flight out of her marital cage, Edna becomes what we might now call a nearly modern woman. She tries an affair with the ambivalent Robert LeBrun that inevitably fades away. Meanwhile, she attempts an independent, artistic life under the tutelage of Mademoiselle Reisz, the imperious and dedicated professional. She finds a motherly figure in Adèle Ratignolle. Edna discovers, however, that their friendship does not fill the emptiness within.[70] Like her infatuation with Robert, all these endeavors to overcome the inner dread come to nothing.

Without career, without roots in the society into which her marriage took her, without an education that might provide a sense of intellectual discipline, and without a circle of like-minded women to give her strength, she cannot master or understand her own feelings. Emancipating death beckons instead. As Kate Chopin divined, perhaps out of her own suffering, suicides like Edna Pontellier, in making the decision to depart life, feel their irresolution, anxiety, and panic disappear. They march out of this world, not exactly with a song in their hearts, but at least with a sense that the excruciating pain of living, which girdles them, will vanish like clouds shrinking in a radiant sun. For too many would-be or actual suicides, including creative writers, death offers a remedy. As the analyst Kay Redfield Jamison reports, self-dissolution seems the "best and final response to bale and weariness."[71]

Regrettably, the ambiguity, irony, and psychological realism in *The Awakening* that we now admire made it very difficult for the Victorian reader to understand. The public was unprepared to approve wholeheartedly so radical an experiment in fiction. Although there were exceptions elsewhere, *The Awakening* was greeted in southern reviewing venues with unanimous scorn and horror. Even the perceptive Willa Cather, a fellow southern novelist, savagely denounced Chopin's greatest work. Perhaps for Cather, herself a woman beset by times of profound depression, the moods and plight of Edna Pontellier were all too familiar—dangerously so. In truculent terms, she condemned the fictional work as a sorry imitation of *Madame Bovary* with a theme both "trite and sordid." Cather interpreted the main character as a self-indulgent, spoiled young matron. Edna, she as-

70. See Virginia Ross, "Kate Chopin's Motherless Heroine," in *Southern Mothers: Fact and Fiction in Southern Women's Writing,* ed. Nagueyalti Warren and Sally Wolff (Baton Rouge: Louisiana State University Press, 1999), 51–63; Elaine Showalter, "*The Awakening*: Tradition and the Female Talent," in *Sister's Choice: Tradition and Change in American Women's Writing* (New York: Oxford University Press, 1991), 73.

71. Jamison, *Night Falls Fast,* 100.

serted, was suffocating under the weight of her own dependence on romance. Cather missed entirely Chopin's theme of how a woman, unloved, displaced, and forlorn in an indifferent world, could become a stranger to herself, alien to her own feelings.[72]

The suicidal closure of *The Awakening* utterly baffled and even infuriated its nineteenth-century pre-Freudian readers.[73] Members of the St. Louis Fine Arts Club went so far as to blackball its author. Outwardly Chopin took the rejection she received from every side with a degree of "ironic insouciance," as Edmund Wilson phrased it. "I never dreamed," she later wrote half-facetiously, "of Mrs. Pontellier making such a mess of things and working out her own damnation as she did. If I had had the slightest intimation of such a thing I would have excluded her from the company."[74] It was typical of Chopin's repressiveness to detach herself from her characters, as if someone might suspect that she was represented in her own fiction. After the barrage of criticism, however, she never attempted another major work. She wrote a friend, "I have had a severe spell of illness and am only now looking about and gathering up the scattered threads of a rather monotonous existence."[75] Chopin's masterpiece surely entitles her to be considered more than just a slight forerunner of modernism. She was a major contributor to a necessary transitional movement with its own integrity, one that Ellen Glasgow and Willa Cather carried forward to eminent effect.

72. "Kate Chopin," in Willa Cather, *Stories, Poems, and Other Writings* (New York: Library of America, 1992), 910–2. Cather's fury blinded her from recognizing that Chopin was not playing a variation on the theme of adultery in the old-fashioned style of the "scribbling" sorority. In all fairness, though, it should be pointed out that Chopin was not above similarly hostile reactions to contemporary writers. She roundly denounced Thomas Hardy's *Jude the Obscure* (1897). It was, she claimed, "immoral" and dangerous for children to read. See Taylor, *Gender, Race, and Region,* 150–1.

73. Toth, *Kate Chopin,* 336–52; Otis B. Wheeler, "The Five Awakenings of Edna Pontellier," *Southern Review* 11 (January 1975): 118–28; Kate Chopin, *The Awakening* (1899; New York: Avon, 1972), 189.

74. *Kate Chopin's Private Papers,* ed. Emily Toth and Per Seyersted (Bloomington: Indiana University Press, 1998), 296.

75. Toth, *Kate Chopin,* 87, 126, 239, 361 (quotation), 377–8.

8

A Female "Southern Renaissance"
Willa Cather and Ellen Glasgow

I did not believe that my dead father and mother were watching me from up there; they would still be looking for me at the sheep-fold down by the creek. I had left even their spirits behind me. . . . If we never arrived anywhere, it did not matter. Between that earth and that sky I felt erased, blotted out. I did not say my prayers that night: here, I felt, what would be would be.
— Willa Cather

CONSTANCE Woolson and Kate Chopin greatly contributed to a modern literary approach. Yet they did not break with the traditional ways with the same vigor that Willa Cather and Ellen Glasgow, their immediate successors among southern women writers, did. All four knew the cold grasp of despair. Woolson and Chopin had disclosed a rather quiet rebelliousness against the specter that afflicts so many writers. If, in her closing years, Chopin had felt especially beleaguered, so, too, did Willa Cather (1873–1947). Cather had all her correspondence with others burned as soon as the recipient's death permitted its return into Cather's hands. In effect, she meant not only to erase the past, a veritable suicide of memory, but also to protect her privacy by withholding the inmost self from public scrutiny, as so many southern writers did. As critic Joan Acocella explains, a crescendo of academic and high-culture criticism, from Ernest Hemingway's in the 1920s to that of Marxist polemicists in the 1930s, complained that her art was inauthentic and irrelevant. Even today, the novelist Joyce Carol

Oates appraises Cather as a "rather underrated but surely 'major' American writer." The quotation marks around "major" suggest only grudging approval. At one time, as Acocella points out, the criticism harbored more than a touch of jealousy. Despite these dismissive assessments, Cather's work was enormously popular. Negative reactions also reflected the traditional bias to which so many American male authors had been drawn since the days of Nathaniel Hawthorne's often-quoted attack on female scribblers of his era.[1]

As if anticipating future objections, Cather had developed a carapace of defiance and defensiveness from almost the beginning of her life in Nebraska. The pose helped to mask deep psychological wounds perhaps from herself but certainly from others. A photograph of her, age nine, shows a serious, dark-eyed, almost pouting countenance.[2] Born in 1873, Cather had loved the old homestead at Back Creek, in the Shenandoah Valley of Virginia. She had felt safe where "people were honest and good," as she recollected sixty years later. Cather idolized her congenial, gentle, and imaginative father. He dominated the transplanted household in Nebraska in part by reading a steady program of Thomas Nelson Page and also John Esten Cooke, the post–Civil War romancers. One of Willa Cather's brothers was even christened after Cooke. The family often—even ceaselessly— relived the war in the style that Mark Twain had described in *Life on the Mississippi.*[3]

Cather's mother, Mary Virginia Boak, though very strict, allowed all her children, including Willa, to develop along their separate paths. Oddly, the family's southern origins played a part in Cather's preferences about clothes. Jennie, as Mary Virginia was called, had kept her brother's Confederate uniform in the attic. He had lost his life at First Manassas. Young Willa loved to don the costume and always thereafter had a penchant for men's style of dress. "While paying homage to Mother's valiant brother," writes Cynthia Wolff, Willa's dressing up "also alluded to the many legends

1. Joan Acocella's *Willa Cather and the Politics of Criticism* (Lincoln: University of Nebraska Press, 2000) explores Cather's critical reception over the years; Joyce Carol Oates, "Born Female in America: Why the Lost Generation Never Recognized Willa Cather," *Times Literary Supplement*, 25 May 2001, p. 3.

2. James Woodress, *Willa Cather: A Literary Life* (Lincoln: University of Nebraska Press, 1987), after p. 27.

3. See Mary R. Ryder, "Henry Colbert, Gentleman: Bound by the Code," in *Willa Cather's Southern Connections: New Essays on Cather and the South*, ed. Ann Romines (Charlottesville: University Press of Virginia, 2000), 131.

of courageous Confederate women whose stories had recently been rekindled by the sensational novel *The Woman in Battle* (1876)."[4]

According to her friend Dorothy Canfield Fisher, Cather always appreciated her southern roots for shaping her formative years. She had come from a state that honored "continuity and stability" and from a class of the well-to-do who were "always stubbornly devoted to the old ways of doing things," Fisher recalled.[5] Then, at age nine, she accompanied the family to their new home at Red Cloud, Nebraska. They left to escape an epidemic of tuberculosis that had snuffed out the lives of so many family members living in the disease-ridden Shenandoah.

Although long identified with the Western Plains, Cather remained from first to last a Virginian and a southerner. A famous anecdote has it that a visiting judge condescended to her with customary platitudes about pretty little girls. The youngster retorted angrily, "I'se a dang'ous nigger, I is!" He must have wondered what sort of child the Cathers were bringing up.[6] The vast, strange spaciousness of the Great Plains, which always amazes easterners, was so different from the Virginian forests, hills, and valleys. The everlasting breeze, the ocean of waving grassy hillocks, the treeless landscape—all these alien features represented more than change to the little girl. In an interview with Elizabeth Sergeant she revealed just how deeply she reacted to the transplanting. Trying to explain her terrors of the great expansiveness of the West, a kind of agoraphobia, she declared, "You could not understand. You have not seen those miles of fields. There is no place to hide in Nebraska. You can't hide under a windmill." In 1913 she put her fears and anger another way: "I felt a good deal as if we had come to the end of everything—it was a kind of erasure of personality."[7] In *The Profes-*

4. Cynthia Griffin Wolff, "Dressing for the Part: [What's] The Matter with Clothes," in *Willa Cather's Southern Connections,* ed. Romines, 210.

5. Woodress, *Willa Cather,* 1–24, quotation 25.

6. Anne Goodwyn Jones, "Displacing Dixie: The Southern Subtext in *My Ántonia,*" in *New Essays on* My Ántonia, ed. Sharon O'Brien (New York: Cambridge University Press, 1999), 85–109, quotation 87; Lisa Marcus, " 'The Pull of Race and Blood and Kindred': Willa Cather's Southern Inheritance," in *Willa Cather's Southern Connections,* ed. Romines, 98.

7. Marcus, "Pull of Race," in Willa Cather's Southern Connections, ed. Romines, 36; Elizabeth Shepley Sergeant, *Willa Cather: A Memoir* (Lincoln: University of Nebraska Press, 1963), 49. I would add a personal note: In 1950, coming from the Cumberland mountains in Tennessee, I worked a summer on hay ranches in the Sand Hills of Nebraska. The relentless power of the wind, the swift accumulation of towering, racing black clouds that sucked up the air, the ominous flashes of lightning across a vast expanse of nothing but sky and waving grass is truly a revelation to anyone from mountain-and-forest country. It is not hard to understand a small child's fear of such a landscape. O'Brien offers a convincing interpretation of her alarm

sor's House we find a similar response. Godfrey St. Peter, profoundly depressed, recalls his departure at age eight from his home on the inviting
expanse of Lake Michigan and his arrival by train in featureless Kansas. "It
was like sinking a third time," the hero thinks to himself, "No later anguish,
and he had had his share, went so deep or seemed so final."[8]

In time, though, Cather became a passionate advocate for the Plains and
turned against her native land, but in a most ambivalent way. The transformation, partial though it was, owed something to the Cathers' Virginian
neighbors at Red Cloud. They, along with other Nebraskans of Anglo-
Saxon background, proved unfriendly to the so-called aliens. They felt
hemmed in by non-English-speaking French Canadians and Central Europe-
ans and Scandinavians. Yet Cather personally identified with and romanticized these "outsiders," as her family perceived them. At the same time, she
never lost her southern accent, as if unconsciously seeking to hang on to old
habits.

In light of Anne Goodwyn Jones's brilliant essay and a recent collection
of pieces on Cather's southernness, to claim Willa Cather as part of the
southern female reach toward modernity requires no stretch of the facts. As
Ann Romines, editor of the latter anthology, puts it so well, Cather "spent
her first years in a southern family surrounded by southern controversies
[between Unionism and rebellion, slavery and abolitionism], southern
speech, southern customs, southern architecture, southern food; she was im-
printed between whites and African Americans . . . many of whom had recently been enslaved."[9]

Even after the move to the West, Cather felt herself to be an exile, someone displaced. In Nebraska she was immersed in a society of newcomers
and came to revel in it. Yet she felt that something was missing. To fill the
void she looked for mentors from the early years into complete adulthood.
William Ducker, an intellectual Englishman at Red Cloud, started her on
the classics, a delight that she never lost. An alcoholic German music

---

based on the psychological approaches of Nancy Chodorov regarding the female personality.
See Sharon O'Brien, *Willa Cather: The Emerging Voice* (New York: Fawcett, 1987), 64–5. A
further complication was the preoccupation of Willa's mother with her troubled pregnancy
and loss of the fetus at the time of the move. Willa thus felt abandoned.

8. Willa Cather, *The Professor's House* (1925; New York: Random House, 1953), 21; see
also Michael Leddy, "*The Professor's House:* The Sense of an Ending," *Studies in the Novel*
23 (Winter 1991): 443–52.

9. Jones, "Displacing Dixie,"in *New Essays on* My Ántonia, ed. Sharon O'Brien; and
Romines, ed., *Willa Cather's Southern Connections,* 2 (quotation).

teacher, Herr Schindelmeisser, became a beloved companion even if her youthful piano efforts amounted to little. He appears as Herr Wunsch, a gloomy, bibulous piano teacher, in *The Song of the Lark,* Cather's romantic novel about the ambitions and loneliness of Thea Kronborg, a gifted singer.[10] Later, the novelist's five years under the roof of her married friend Isabelle McLung in Pittsburgh represented a search for a stable home, even though she seemed more often a guest than a surrogate daughter or sister.

Cather's need for significant nurturing figures had its very positive aspects. Like Chopin, she turned to outside literary sources to sustain her emotional and creative advancement. Cather was especially drawn to the author of *The Country of Pointed Firs.* (She thought it one of the best American novels ever penned, alongside *Huckleberry Finn* and *The Scarlet Letter.*) Her friendship with Sarah Orne Jewett, begun only months before Jewett died, had a major impact on the young, not-yet-published novelist from Nebraska. Jewett advised Cather in 1908 to draw upon her "Nebraska life" as well as her upbringing in "a child's Virginia." She quickly accepted the first part of the assignment, in the prairie novels *O Pioneers* and *My Ántonia* especially, but delayed converting the Virginia experience into fiction until much later in her life. In a 1925 preface to the Maine writer's collected works, Cather acknowledged her appreciation of Jewett's fiction. Jewett, she remarked, "had an individual voice; 'a sense for the finest kind of truthful rendering, the sober, tender note, the temperately touched, whether in the ironic or pathetic,' as Henry James said of her."[11] Cather followed Jewett's advice about dwelling fictionally on things she knew from personal experience. She passed along the same counsel to Eudora Welty, who became equally devoted to the immediacy of her surroundings. "Let your fiction grow out of the land beneath your feet," Cather had instructed.[12]

Despite Jewett's influence on her literary focus, Cather was not totally under the other writer's sway. There was a greater element of the fading Victorian moral code in Jewett's stories than in her young admirer's mature work. Though not totally divorced from the old romanticism, all these writ-

10. Willa Cather, *The Song of the Lark* (1915; Cambridge: Houghton Mifflin, 1963).

11. Jewett quoted in Sarah Way Sherman, *Sarah Orne Jewett: An American Persephone* (Hanover, N.H.: University Press of New England, 1989), 198; Willa Cather, "Miss Jewett," in *Not under Forty* (1936; reprint, Lincoln: University of Nebraska Press, 1988), 95 (the essay originally appeared in 1925).

12. Quoted in Michael Malone, "Arts & Letters: *Carson McCullers: A Life,* by Josyane Savigneau," *Wilson Quarterly* 25 (Spring 2001): 117.

ers would push forward a more psychologically complex agenda. "Sarah Jewett counseled sublimation," remarks Larzer Ziff. Cather, Kate Chopin, and their contemporaries, however, "pursued self-discovery and counseled not at all."[13] Cather also came to admire the romancer Emma Dorothy Eliza Nevitte Southworth, one of the most popular fiction writers of the times. While fiercely sustaining the traditional proprieties, Southworth was so dedicated a professional that she won over the skeptical Willa Cather during a lengthy interview. Indeed, Southworth recognized her own limitations—as did her more sophisticated readers later in the century. She confessed that she wrote simply to please the female readers of Robert Bonner's popular *New York Ledger* but sighed that she would have attempted greater art if financial necessity had not forbidden it. Overcoming a most unhappy childhood and a broken marriage, Southworth could well have appealed to the young Willa Cather, who also had experienced emotional deprivation. Moreover, although seeking a path toward greater realism and less sentimentality, Cather could certainly have appreciated Southworth's literary approach. While still writing in the romantic vein, the novelist, like Cather a Virginian, exposed the sins of her characters as a way to teach the moral content of fiction. Victorian readers expected a degree of sermonizing in fiction as a way to justify the indulgence in fantasy. To violate that expectation of moral uplift risked being what pure-minded Victorians thought was vulgar and unprincipled. It was closer to life than the lugubrious style of earlier feminine sentimentalists.[14]

Sharon O'Brien observes that these late-century female writers were determined to locate a woman's literary tradition and carry further the professionalism that Southworth, Harriet Beecher Stowe, and others had pursued. Some of the popular novels, like Caroline Hentz's *Rena*, were more psychologically complicated and morally ambiguous than a quick contemporary reading might reveal. But writers like Woolson, Cather, Chopin, and Glasgow felt obliged to test the moral boundaries. Cather, for instance, had always felt dismayed—even as a young child—that so much of discourse seemed pretentious, unreal, made up. If one were to succumb to the sentimental and the merely courteous, one might lose "touch with reality, with truth of experience," as critic Edith Lewis puts it. Writers like Cather found

13. Larzar Ziff, quoted in Kate Chopin, *The Awakening,* ed. Margaret Culley (New York: W. W. Norton, 1976), 174.

14. See Susan Coultrap-McQuin, *Doing Literary Business: American Women Writers in the Nineteenth Century* (Chapel Hill: University of North Carolina Press, 1990), 50–78.

in the so-called local colorists of the North a point of healthy departure away from the lingering sentimentality that Southworth and company still represented. Though scarcely feminists in today's terms, they recoiled from the gush in women's fiction of that time, as well as the harping on womanly forgivingness and submission under all manner of horrible circumstances of marital or parental abuse.[15] Removal from Virginia did not, of course, solely explain Cather's complex, elegiac temperament. But certainly her deeply traditionalist side—distaste for emotional excess, self-confession, and sexual expressiveness—had roots in her upbringing under her parents in both Virginia and Nebraska.[16]

Echoing the French poet Stéphane Mallarmé's views, Cather insisted on the indirectness of art—its withholding character for the sake of the reader's own play of imagination.[17] Perhaps that concept had some connection with her southernness and repressed nostalgia for her first home. "It is the inexplicable presence of the thing not named, of the overtone divined by the ear but not heard by it, the verbal mood, the emotional aura of the fact or the deed, that gives high quality to the novel or the drama, as well as to poetry itself," she wrote in 1936. "Can one imagine anything more terrible than the story of *Romeo and Juliet* rewritten in prose by D. H. Lawrence? How wonderful it would be if we could throw all the furniture out of the window, and along with it, all the meaningless reiterations concerning physical sensations, all the tiresome old patterns and leave the room as bare as the stage of a Greek theatre."[18]

Earlier, in her sorrowful novel *My Ántonia*, Cather's sense of loss and fond memory of Virginia found hidden expression in two respects. The first was in the characterization of Jim Burden. At the beginning of the novel, we are introduced to Burden's sense of apartness and nonexistence after his parents died. As Cather almost confesses in her introduction, Burden is her

---

15. Edith Lewis, *Willa Cather Living: A Personal Record* (New York: Knopf, 1976), 13 (quotation); "Emma Dorothy Eliza Nevitte Southworth," in *Dictionary of American Biography*, 10 vols, ed. Dumas Malone (1935; New York: Charles Scribner's Sons, 1964) 9:414–5; Woodress, *Willa Cather*, xvii, 54, 55; Mary Kelley, *Private Woman, Public Stage: Literary Domesticity in Nineteenth-Century America* (New York: Oxford University Press, 1984), 310–1; O'Brien, *Willa Cather*, 188–9; Acocella, *Cather*, 77.

16. Acocella, *Cather*, 43–65, 101, 102, re-examines the Cather-as-lesbian school of interpretation.

17. See Jones, "Displacing Dixie,"in *New Essays on* My Ántonia, ed. Sharon O'Brien, 85–7, passages that explain the female writer's indirection of "double consciousness," like that identified by W. E. B. DuBois in African American letters.

18. Willa Cather, "The Novel Deméublé," in *Not under Forty*, 50, 51.

alter ego. The boy, whose words appear in this chapter's epigraph, experiences the same sense of displacement that Willa Cather had when she left behind her Virginia homeland and confronted the flat wasteland of Nebraska. "In the face of loss," reports the analyst Roger A. Lewin, "we are propelled back sometimes to the edge of chaos."[19] That Cather was herself depressed in a clinical way is perhaps doubtful. Yet her experience of being wrenched from a beloved landscape and forced to enter a new and threatening one may help to explain the melancholic tone of her masterpiece. The other signal of Cather's remembrance of the southern past we find in a reference to the character Blind d'Arnault. Rather than recoiling from the young, horribly deformed black musician, Jim Burden responds to him with pleasure, reporting that d'Arnault has "the happiest face I had seen since I left Virginia."[20] Clearly Cather overcame at least some of the racist assumptions regarding black skills that the land of her birth impressed on her.

No less important in the novel than the nostalgia for the lost homeland are the senses of tragedy, grief, and self-destruction that inhabit the new terrain of the displaced Virginians. As discontented as Jim Burden, Mr. Shimerda, Ántonia's immigrant father, commits suicide. Jim remarks, "I knew it was homesickness that had killed Mr. Shimerda." Perhaps "his released spirit," he muses, would find its resting place in "his own country"— beyond Chicago, back in Bohemia—as if it were another Virginia.[21]

To create the name Shimerda, Cather combined the Anglo-Saxon and the French words for defecation, a curious choice for this very fastidious author. (Actually, the name is also not uncommon in Nebraska.) But strong feelings of resentment may have been behind the selection. On some level Cather's resentment of that loss fed into her fear of and near obsession with physical mutilation. The latter figures in her depiction of the black musician in *My Ántonia*, but even more so later in her fictional efforts. Shortly after the end of World War II, Cather died in the midst of writing *Hard Punishments*. The book concerns two medieval youths of Avignon, one of whom has lost the use of his hands from having been strung up by his thumbs. The other has had his tongue sliced off. The afflictions—not at all pleasant—reflected

19. Roger A. Lewin, *Compassion: The Core Value That Animates Psychotherapy* (Northvale: Jason Aronson, 1996), 83. I owe this quotation and some of the ideas herein to Daniel Ross, "The Burden of Grief in Willa Cather's *My Ántonia*," unpublished paper presented at the Fourteenth International Conference on Literature and Psychoanalysis, Las Navas, Avila, July 1997.

20. See Jones, "Displacing Dixie," in *New Essays on* My Ántonia, ed. Sharon O'Brien, 91.

21. Cather quoted ibid., 96.

her dour mood. They had their origin in an early and traumatic dread of mutilation. For Cather, being maimed represented the ultimate "power of darkness," as one literary critic has observed.[22] It seems she felt compelled to write about her deep fear. That kind of violent but creative reaction was not the style of Cather's two female predecessors, but her preoccupation with the subject is also apparent. Her earlier war novel, *One of Ours*, deals with violent death and maiming. The book was awarded a Pulitzer Prize in 1922. As often appears in literature, reckless bravery in battle can be an escape from deep melancholia (one recalls Harry Hotspur, whom Shakespeare portrays as a victim of the malady). Perhaps it is this link that drew Cather to the subject of combat—something she could not have personally experienced but felt a need to conquer with pen and paper. Through art and the sense of mastery and control it provides, the blasting of hope becomes bearable, even triumphant.

The literary critic Anne Wyatt-Brown points out how Cather in *One of Ours* intermixes the romantic tendencies derived from her southern upbringing with psychological realism. For instance, the writer introduces a German-American farm boy who dies on shipboard from starving himself out of homesickness and from contracting a viral disease. Cather portrays him as expiring just as he should—"like a brave boy giving back what was not his to keep." Throughout the novel, Wyatt-Brown observes, the author "shows the unconscious pain of abandoning . . . a belief in the nobility of battle and the possibility of male honor. These were the ideals she had absorbed in childhood from her mother's stories of her Confederate brother, who died in the Civil War."[23]

In *One of Ours*, Lieutenant Claude Wheeler, the protagonist from Kansas, fights with no desire to live. He has been unable to shake off his lifelong chronic depression, made worse by his over-attachment to a pious and constricting mother. He is estranged from his sexually frustrating wife, who left him to pursue missionary work in China. Instead of seeking ways simply to survive the horrors of war, he finds exhilaration in sharing danger with brave comrades. Cather ends the novel with Claude's death. His mother

22. See Woodress, *Willa Cather*, 27; Merrill Maguire Skaggs, *After the World Broke in Two: The Later Novels of Willa Cather* (Charlottesville: University Press of Virginia, 1990), 7 (quotation).

23. Anne Wyatt-Brown, "Therapy and War in Cather's *One of Ours* and Barker's *Regeneration*," in *Literature and Psychology: Proceedings of the Tenth International Conference on Literature and Psychology,* ed. Frederico Pereira (Lisbon, Port.: Instituto Superior de Pscicologia Aplicada, 1993), 54, 56.

muses that those valorous men who had served with her son too often returned only to "quietly die by their own hand." God had saved her boy
from that disillusionment, for he had "died believing his own country better
than it is."[24] The distance from this sentiment back to the war poetry of
Timrod and Theodore O'Hara is enormous. Yet one can detect beneath the
postwar skepticism that the novel reflected a yearning for the old platitudes
of honor and glory in warfare that Faulkner both celebrated and condemned in his work. Quite clearly Cather had found highly imaginative
ways to handle her deep sense of displacement and skepticism. Her clear,
unadorned prose and deep penetration of human nature thus reveal the
common issue with which we are concerned in all these pages: the development of art through despair and alienation in southern letters.

Of course, the indirect, introspective approach to art that Cather employed was by no means purely an outgrowth of a southern background.
Cather's devotion to the nineteenth-century French poets, Mallarmé among
them, was a factor. The aesthetic issue was also generational, a matter of a
deeply-rooted Victorianism, which played into the wrestlings of faith versus
science, tradition versus change. Many artists found themselves straddling
a divide. At once a writer like Henry James—complex, introspective, and
yet conventional in social attitudes—springs to mind. Nonetheless, we do
find that ineffable sense of the unspoken in the work of later southern artists—say, of the intensely southern Tennessee Williams—along with a powerfully understated spirit of solitariness, longing, and intense mourning. The
Virginia that Cather had lost meant much to her. In that 1913 interview,
she remarked, "I would not know how much a child's life is bound up in
the woods and hills around it, if I had not been jerked away from all these
and thrown out into a country as bare as a piece of iron."[25]

In light of how those early years had affected Cather's psychological and,
later, artistic development, it seems entirely fitting that her last novel was
prompted by an incident that had occurred to her in 1879. Nursing a cold,
the little girl was bedded down in her mother's room when word came that
Nancy Till had arrived downstairs for a visit from Montreal. Nancy was
formerly a slave in the household of Rachel Boak, Cather's antislavery
grandmother. In 1863 Boak had accompanied Nancy to the far bank of the
Potomac river and into the care of operatives who ran the nearest Under-

24. Willa Cather, *One of Ours* (1922; New York, Random House, 1991), 370.
25. Bernice Slote, ed., *The Kingdom of Art: Willa Cather's First Principles and Other Writings* (Lincoln: University of Nebraska Press, 1996), 448.

ground Railroad. Sixteen years later, there in her mother's chamber, Cather watched a scene specifically designed for her to witness—the reunion of the beautiful "gold-skinned" former fugitive and her wizened mother, who still worked for the family. Wordlessly, they fell into each other's arms. "There was something Scriptural in that meeting, like the pictures in our old Bible," Cather later commented. She remembered how her mother used to rock her to sleep singing, "Down by de cane brake, close by de mill / Dar lived a yaller gal, her name was Nancy Till."

Thanks to Toni Morrison's advocacy and a change in academic literary tastes, *Sapphira and the Slave Girl* has entered the canon after years of neglect and dismissal. Its composition represented at last Cather's appreciation of her southern heritage, to which she added her own inventive contribution. Literary critic Janis Stout calls the book "an imaginative return home, a return to the mother-place."[26] It was written after a series of deaths had reduced the author's circle of friends and kinfolk and weighed down her spirits. Especially traumatic were the deaths in 1938 of her brother Douglass, a favorite, and her longtime friend Isabelle McClung, with whom she may have been in love. (McClung's marriage many years before had flung Cather into despair for a time.) Yet the setting of Virginia had been on her mind for nearly a decade. Her use of characters out of her own family helped to revive her long-dormant thoughts about those first nine years in Virginia. The story was based upon that dramatic incident in 1863, as Cather's autobiographical epilogue explains. In this rendition of the plantation legend, Cather tells a much more complex, darker tale than its contemporary and much more popular romance, Margaret Mitchell's *Gone With the Wind*. As Merrill Skaggs notes, Cather did not strive to meet readers' conventional expectations but rather "saw the dark side of every positive fact, as well as vice versa."[27]

In her melancholy, reticence, and extraordinary power of imagination,

26. Janis P. Stout, "Playing in the Mother Country: Cather, Morrison, and the Return to Virginia," in *Willa Cather's Southern Connections*, ed. Romines, 189–95, quotation 190. The account is rendered in Woodress, *Willa Cather*, 26, from which the quotations are drawn as well as the facts.

27. Skaggs, *After the World Broke in Two*, 172; *Willa Cather: Later Novels: Sapphira and the Slave Girl*, ed Sharon O'Brien (New York: Library of America, 1990), 927–39. The story, Cather admits, contained much autobiographical material. Yet many of the characters in it bore names that she could not identify as individuals in her home county. Whenever her mother and father returned from trips elsewhere in the state, they talked about such people as "Mr. Bywaters, Mr. Householder, Mr. Tidball, Miss Snap" and others with memorable names. She found especially delicious the name of a "Mr. Pertball" (p. 939).

she helped to lead a southern literary tradition toward a modern sensibility. Although criticized for her conservative politics and rather Victorian social habits and values, Cather in the last thirty years has gained greater stature. Doubtless the rise of the feminist movement and the consequent attention given to women writers, especially the exceptional ones, account for that well-deserved turn of critical opinion. Cather's future reputation might rest on what Joyce Carol Oates calls "her dark vision of the contemporary, debased world." Yet, Oates continues, her rich lyricism is often overwhelmed by a deliberate, tightly held reticence. Such constraint arose out of Cather's southern roots and the rigid codes of behavior that those entailed.[28]

Although even more reserved than Cather, Glasgow, too, found that the source of her literary inspiration lay in her sometimes morbid temperament. By surrendering herself to the unexpected pathways of the imagination, she may have found that a down-turned mood set free powers of fancy that a less troubled, less gifted spirit could never attain.

From the feminist perspective, Ellen Glasgow, no less than Chopin and Cather, advanced immeasurably the new, realistic, and unsentimental approach in southern letters. The Virginia novelist (1873–1945) enjoyed as long and prosperous artistic career as her contemporary Willa Cather. Her progenitors belonged to the Richmond aristocracy. Yet, like the other women writers discussed here, she grew alienated from southern culture— its intellectual triviality and its consignment of educated women to parlor, bedroom, and kitchen. Glasgow once declared that "the Protestant Episcopal Church," to which her mother was devoted, "was charitable toward almost every weakness except the dangerous practice of thinking." Certainly more than Cather, she protested the "inarticulateness" of southerners. In the constricted upper-class society in which she was reared, self-imposed restraint grew from of fear of saying something that really mattered. To utter forbidden thoughts might demolish the fragile appearance of things. Glasgow rebelled against that false constraint. Moreover, she questioned whether the chief artistic purpose of post–Civil War novelists should be a defense of the everlasting Lost Cause, which was simply "a sentimental infirmity." Her first best-selling novel, *The Battle-Ground* (1902), broke courageously with the Page, Cooke, and Dixon school that had for so long

28. See Phyllis Frus and Stanley Corkin, "Cather Criticism and the American Canon," *College English* 59 (February 1997): 206–17; Skaggs, *After the World Broke in Two*, 17–8; Oates, "Born Female," 3.

romanticized the old regime and the Confederacy. The novelist painted a picture of the wartime South that included not just the derrings-do of heroic officers and the adoration of their belles, but women of all classes, blacks, and people from the lower orders. To be sure, the novel ends with smiles through the tears over the tragic losses. "We will begin again," declares the well-born, charming Betty Ambler to her war-maimed hero Dan Montjoy, "and this time, my dear, we will begin together." The close might be conventional, but in the course of the narrative Glasgow had moved the Civil War genre from romance to something approaching realism.[29]

Like so many in this study (though not Willa Cather), Glasgow feared and at times hated her father. He was, she observed, too "Roman," too Calvinistic. "He never committed a pleasure," she wrote. In his Bible, Francis Glasgow "never read of love or mercy, for, I imagine, he regarded these virtues as belonging by right to the weaker gender, amid an unassorted collection of feminine graces." When her father took pets away to be destroyed without offering an explanation or reason that a child could grasp, she resented him to the depths of her soul. One is reminded that little Willa Cather was no less heartsick when, on leaving Virginia, her sheepdog companion, Old Vic, broke his tether and vainly raced across the meadow to catch the departing carriage.[30] Although head of the Tredegar Iron Works, the largest industrial firm in the city, and prominent in Presbyterians' affairs, Francis Glasgow was for his daughter not a tower of moral strength and provider of good things. To her he was a sanctimonious bigot, philanderer, and hypocrite. She claimed that her mother caught him in bed with one of the black maids and never forgave him his adultery.[31]

Glasgow's anger and frustration, though, were not entirely a result of cruel paternal whim and alleged deceptiveness. The family may well have had some genetic problems with depression. Her mother's life was punctuated by a fearful unhappiness, an illness that might well have had an effect on her sexual disengagement from her husband. She was often drawn

29. Anne Goodwyn Jones, *Tomorrow Is Another Day: The Woman Writer in the South, 1859–1936* (Baton Rouge: Louisiana State University Press, 1981), 228–31 (Glasgow quoted, 229); second quotation, Ellen Glasgow, *The Battle-Ground* (1902; Tuscaloosa: University of Alabama Press, 2000), 512.

30. Ellen Glasgow, *The Woman Within: An Autobiography,* ed. Pamela R. Matthews (1954; Charlottesville: University Press of Virginia, 1994),16, 68–73, 85 (quotation); Woodress, *Willa Cather,* 31.

31. Susan Goodman, *Ellen Glasgow: A Biography* (Baltimore: Johns Hopkins University Press, 1998), 19–20.

toward the well of emotional blackness. As a child, Glasgow recalled, "I would wonder all the way home whether I should find my mother cheerful or sad. Usually, she sent us off brightly; but the brightness would fade as soon as we turned the corner, and the deep despondency would creep over her."[32] Bearing eleven children during the upheavals of war and Reconstruction was another burden for Ellen's mother to endure.

Anne Glasgow died from typhoid fever. At the time her daughter was in her twenties. The loss left her feeling as if "some other self . . . buried yet alive" still "stands in the center of that desolate room."[33] When Glasgow herself died in 1945, her bedroom was found to be arranged identically to that of her mother's so long before. Daniel Singal observes that the novelist "was afflicted with a debilitating neurosis most of her life, lapsed into frequent depressions, and continuously sought psychiatric care."[34]

Some of the Glasgow's siblings were also touched with psychological difficulties. Like his mother, brother Frank followed a spiritless course in life. Always delicate and intellectual, he had been inappropriately sent to the Virginia Military Institute to "harden" him, as his strong-willed father liked to say. Frank's four years there, however, "merely increased his unconquerable remoteness," his sister remembered. Unable to rebel against the difficult father, he eventually gave up on life itself. A Glasgow biographer speculates that homosexual tendencies added to his distress.[35] On 7 April 1909, at the age of thirty-nine, he shot himself in his office at the Tredegar mill. The fate of Ellen's brother-in-law George Walter McCormack also moved her greatly. He had been instrumental in her intellectual development. During a business trip to New York, McCormack killed himself on 18 June 1894 in his hotel room.[36]

Thus, as in Woolson's case, death was a frequent visitor in Glasgow's life. As early as 1875, diphtheria had carried away Anne Glasgow's newborn son, Samuel, and within days, the sixteen-year-old Joseph, similarly stricken, followed him to the grave. Ellen's mother was devastated by the losses. Her grief acutely affected her young daughter. Two sisters of whom Ellen had been especially fond grew to adulthood but also died young. One

32. Glasgow, *Woman Within*, 69.

33. Ibid., 84.

34. Daniel Joseph Singal, *The War Within: From Victorian to Modernist Thought in the South, 1919–1945* (Chapel Hill: University of North Carolina Press, 1982), 95. Singal's insights about Glasgow are especially acute.

35. Glasgow, *Woman Within*, 65; Goodman, *Ellen Glasgow*, 30.

36. Glasgow, *Woman Within*, 100; Goodman, *Ellen Glasgow*, 44–7.

was Cary, Walter McCormack's widow, a victim of cancer.[37] Ellen Glasgow spoke feelingly of tumbling into an "icy vacuum, which, if nothingness has a superlative, grows deeper and deeper." She tried to maintain an "artificial brightness" as "the safest defense against life," but her success was problematic.[38]

Indeed, the feelings and experiences related in Glasgow's poignant autobiography, *The Woman Within,* suggest how different the book is from other Victorian women writers' self-histories. The work stresses the author's loneliness, which parallels that of the death-haunted aurelian William Alexander Percy of the Mississippi Delta, as revealed in *Lanterns on the Levee.*[39] Feminist critics have noted how women writers usually place their lives in the context of others'; this connectedness, however, is not to be found in Glasgow's account. In the words of Pamela Matthews, the "disrupted chronology, use of ellipsis, and lack of smooth transitions" of *The Woman Within* are partially attributable to "Glasgow's persona as an exile." Matthews argues that the novelist's reticence stemmed solely from a difficulty in writing about selfhood "in other than expected ways."[40]

The issue was surely cultural, as Matthews implies, but we should not dismiss the suppressive power of cultural expectations. Inhibitions about revealing things that were thought to belong to inmost circles of family, and the concomitant fear of raising speculation, very much applied in Glasgow's case. In her autobiography, she gives almost no details or even clear indications that Walter McCormack, her brother-in-law, or her brother Frank, killed themselves. Suicide was a tragic disgrace to be kept well hidden. In Richmond's upper-class circles, all too much conjecture, it seems, was focused on her father's infidelities. Needless to say, she alludes to no such scandal in the autobiography.[41]

By the standards of disclosure that we have so far encountered, however, Ellen Glasgow's account of her life is actually dominated by candor. She

37. Goodman, *Glasgow,* 13,15; Glasgow, *Woman Within,* 100–1, 185–94.
38. Jones, *Tomorrow Is Another Day,* 228, 231, 269 (quotation); Glasgow, *Woman Within,* 67, 99–100.
39. See "Prodigal Daughters: The Journeys of Ellen Glasgow, Zora Neale Hurston, and Eudora Welty," in Lucinda H. McKethan, *Daughters of Time: Creating Woman's Voice in Southern Story* (Athens: University of Georgia Press, 1990), 37–63, for an insightful reading of Glasgow, *Woman Within.* William Alexander Percy, *Lanterns on the Levee: Recollections of a Planter's Son* (1941: Baton Rouge: Louisiana State University Press, 1973).
40. Pamela R. Matthews, "Introduction," in Glasgow, *Woman Within,* xviii–xix.
41. Goodman, *Glasgow,* 19–22.

wrote about her own desperate attempt at either death or a deathlike sleep. A "bold mortal sickness of the spirit," she acknowledged, struck her in 1918, in the midst of the Great War. She had felt deserted after her lover, Henry Anderson, had set out to direct the Red Cross effort in the Balkans. As her most recent biographer notes, she often had "violent love affairs that never went anywhere," partly because of unsubstantiated jealousy and fear of abandonment. Such ill thoughts as these could have been part of the burden that a depressive like Glasgow had to bear.[42] That evening in 1918, she recalled, "ghosts" became "my only companions. I was shut in, alone, with the past. . . . I stood there in that empty house . . . and felt, literally, that I was attacked by fear, as by some unseen malevolent power." She took an overdose of sleeping tablets, but fortunately awoke the next morning merely feeling nauseated.[43] The memoirist had lived to tell her own story.

Glasgow's account, as critic Nancy A. Walker proposes, has elements of concealment *and* revelation. But that tension figures in the writing of any memoir, even today. To portray oneself as simply pure hero or heroine would be quite unconvincing, but to indulge solely in victimization would seem just an indulgent whine. *The Woman Within* does neither; it is instead a remarkable document, even if we must question the author's accuracy about her much-resented father and her over-identification with the mother whose emotional problems Glasgow herself had partially inherited.[44] She was more "modern" in her openness in relating her feelings to her art, her work more psychologically sophisticated than either Woolson's or Chopin's. Sometimes Glasgow is even permitted to join the latter-day "sacred circle" of Faulknerian modernists. Certainly her novels of Virginians' travails, delusions, and fragmented personalities, which have been so well and critically explored, make such a placement plausible.

Finally, we address the role that foreign writers played in helping to shape the ideas and themes of all these women writers. As in any field of intellectual life, knowledge of what has been done, what is fresh and original, and what experiments have been tried on other soil help the aspiring professional to fashion a unique path for herself. Woolson was the least venture-

---

42. Ibid., 151; see, for instance, Stuart Sutherland, *Breakdown: A Personal Crisis and a Medical Dilemma* (New York: Oxford University Press, 1998), 4–9.

43. Goodman, *Ellen Glasgow,* 151; Glasgow, *Woman Within,* 237.

44. Nancy A. Walker, "The Romance of Self-Representation: Glasgow and *The Woman Within,*" in *Ellen Glasgow: New Perspectives,* ed. Dorothy M. Scura (Knoxville: University of Tennessee Press, 1995), 33–41.

some of the women discussed here. The works of George Eliot and those of her good friends Henry James and Sarah Orne Jewett most influenced her writing.[45] Yet northern writers, including Jewett herself, had begun to look abroad for new ideas about fiction. Jewett was especially influenced by Jane Austen and Ivan Turgenev, so much so that William Dean Howells claimed for her a very heavy indebtedness.[46]

Rather than take as models the English and New England writers, Willa Cather, Kate Chopin, Ellen Glasgow, and others gradually found the more introspective and melancholy spirit of continental writers especially useful in their own work. The French sensibility, so different from the constricted Anglo-American style, seemed especially helpful. The moody Gustave Flaubert, Guy de Maupassant—who died of syphilis in a French insane asylum, 1893—and the half-suicidal poet Charles Baudelaire were most especially esteemed. In the 1890s Chopin read, admired, and translated a number of the bitter and passionate short stories of Maupassant, some of which were too strange and sexually graphic to meet American publishers' tastes. One of them, "Suicide," bears a very striking resemblance to *The Awakening.* Also, the Norwegian playwright Henrik Ibsen became prominent in Chopin's reading. Inspired by *Ghosts,* and perhaps by Maupassant's fate, she wrote "The Evil Men Do" (1891), which deals with the taboo subject of venereal disease. That narrative accumulated more rejection slips from magazine editors than did any other she ever wrote.[47]

With a temperament and personal history that matched the kind of bleak novels she most appreciated, Ellen Glasgow, not Chopin, was foremost in the reading of foreign literature. The discovery of the full range of Russians—Glasgow being among the earliest to appreciate them—would have a most important but seldom fully appreciated effect upon southern letters in the twentieth century. Although at first much drawn to Honoré de Balzac and Flaubert, Glasgow later immersed herself in the works of Tolstoy, Dostoevsky, Gogol, Chekhov, and Turgenev. What the Virginia novelist found so impressive, as she put it, was that "the illumination" of the human soul came not from "without but from within. For the radiance streams from some central glow of the spirit." By no means did Glasgow sentimentalize the Russians' perspective. Rather, she noted that they "have the courage to

45. Cheryl B. Torsney, *Constance Fenimore Woolson: The Grief of Artistry* (Athens: University of Georgia Press, 1989), 6, 28–33, 151–4;

46. See Elizabeth Silverthorne, *Sarah Orne Jewett: A Writer's Life* (New York: Overlook Press, 1993), 201.

47. O'Brien, *Willa Cather,* 135, 248, 384; Toth, *Kate Chopin,* 198, 199, 244, 272–3.

confront pain and evil and ugliness; and they have also that rare courage which faces beauty and tenderness and truth even when it is not ugly." She singled out Dostoevsky for his willingness to seek inspiration in "the desperation of pity. His vision of life is spun, not like ours, of the thin negations of reason, but of the quivering radiance of dreams and the power of tragic conviction."[48]

This willingness to entertain new ideas, whether from home or overseas, had no doubt helped Glasgow to see with some detachment "The Problem of the South." An essay of hers bears that title. Unlike Woolson and Chopin, she felt free enough from old biases to be horrified by the racial violence and brutal proscription of black rights in Virginia as well as in the rest of the former Confederacy. In the 1920s Glasgow spoke out for African American enfranchisement. She declared her opposition to the South's "insidious sentimental tradition," which hid its cruelty and "inhumanity" beneath a layer of what she called "evasive idealism."[49] By no means were these home-grown ideas.

According to a recent biographer, her advanced positions showed her intention to "follow in the footsteps of Zola, Ibsen, and Taels." No matter it was an all-male trio; what other women shared her feelings of indignation and wrote about it memorably in fiction? To be sure, female members of the next generation—Evelyn Scott, Edith Kelly, and Katherine Anne Porter—would, but Glasgow was surely among the earliest.[50] What mattered to Glasgow, though, was not the gender of the authors but a willingness to look at the horrors of world events and the emotional depths of the human condition with ruthless exactitude. The expansive spirit, whether politically tinged or guided solely by artistic considerations, posed a troubling problem to other southerners. Conservative intellectuals wailed over the fall of southern civilization, as they had romantically imagined it. Referring to one of Glasgow's close friends, a fellow novelist, Donald Davidson in *I'll Take My Stand* grumbled, "Why does Mr. [James Branch] Cabell seem so much nearer to Paris than Richmond, to Anatole France than to Lee and Jefferson? Why does Miss Glasgow, self-styled 'social historian' of Virginia, prop-

48. Ellen Glasgow, "Impressions of the Novel," in *Ellen Glasgow's Reasonable Doubts: A Collection of Her Writings,* ed. Julius Rowan Raper (Baton Rouge: Louisiana State University Press, 1988), 144–5, 149.

49. Glasgow, *Woman Within,* 104; Goodman, *Ellen Glasgow,* 154–6.

50. I thank Susan Donaldson for her pointing out these other female southern artists with similar (but later) views.

agate ideas that would be more quickly approved by Oswald Garrison Villard than by the descendants of the first families?"[51]

Glasgow's initial interest in Maupassant and Flaubert (the latter of which has often been called the first modern novelist in Western society) waned when she discovered they were more interested in art than in how people actually lived.[52] In her disillusionment with the French school, she concluded that these authors offered only an artificial rendering of everyday realities. "Life isn't like this. Things don't happen that way," she remarked to herself. Glasgow observed, "Life is a stream, it is even a torrent; but it is not modeled in clay; it is not even dough, to be twisted and pinched into an artificial perfection." Then she read Tolstoy's *War and Peace* and reacted as if it were "as [much] a revelation from heaven, as the trumpet of the Judgment." Later, she found Chekhov, in whose work the "missing" element from Maupassant was revealed. Summing up her assessments, she returned to Tolstoy's *Anna Karenina* and *War and Peace,* resolved "to write of the South not in elegy, as a conquered province, but, vitally, as a part of the larger world." The great Russian author made her "see clearly what I had realized dimly, that the ordinary is simply the universal observed from the surface, that the direct approach to reality is not without, but within. Touch life anywhere, I felt after reading *War and Peace,* and you will touch universality wherever you touch the earth." *Barren Ground,* one of her masterpieces, was so inspired.[53]

Willa Cather was also an early admirer of nineteenth-century Russian literature. Like Glasgow, she found Tolstoy especially intriguing. Cather told an audience of undergraduates at Bowdoin College in 1926 that "Tolstoi's majestic tale," *Anna Karenina,* converted a common love story into one in which the amorous instincts flamed "up as volcanic fires through the crust."[54] The American author praised the Russian's facility in giving emotional meaning to material objects. Yet from her college years until her last years, she was most influenced by the French—Flaubert, George Sand, Alphonse Daudet, and Théophile Gautier. Flaubert, though, was her favorite.

51. Goodman, *Ellen Glasgow,* 50; Davidson quoted in Fred Hobson, *Tell about the South: The Southern Rage to Explain* (Baton Rouge: Louisiana State University Press, 1983), 214.

52. Herbert Lottman, *Flaubert: A Biography* (New York: Little, Brown & Co., 1989).

53. Glasgow, *Woman Within,* 123–8; Glasgow quoted also in Will Brantley, *Feminine Sense in Southern Memoir: Smith, Glasgow, Welty, Hellman, Porter, and Hurston* (Jackson: University Press of Mississippi, 1993), 100.

54. Bohlke, ed., *Willa Cather in Person: Interviews, Speeches, and Letters* (Lincoln: University of Nebraska Press, 1986), 164–5.

She took the special trouble to visit his house in Normandy on a trip to the continent. Cather wrote that she had come to Rouen, "where Gustave Flaubert was born and worked and which he so sharply satirized and bitterly cursed in his letters to his friends in Paris. In France it seems that a town will forgive the man who curses it if only he is great enough." She also made a pilgrimage to the graveside of Honoré de Balzac[55] These influences from abroad, though briefly treated here, would deeply enrich the fiction of the southern women professionals.

Their example would be followed assiduously by later women writers in the South, most notably Georgia-born Carson McCullers. In 1941, the author of *The Ballad of the Sad Café* wrote the first essay ever published on the affinities between modern southern and nineteenth-century Russian literary figures. Tolstoy, Dostoevsky, and company greatly influenced Faulkner, Flannery O'Connor, and others, she explained, with their melancholic tendencies and their "outwardly callous juxtaposition of the tragic with the humorous, the immense with the trivial, the sacred with the bawdy, the whole soul of a man with a materialistic detail." One might add the late Eudora Welty to the list of Russian enthusiasts. With an admiration for Chekhov, she and Stark Young were among the few southern intellectuals to treat the influence of Russian letters upon southern writers. Welty found Chekhov more of a "kindred" soul than Jane Austen could ever be. The Russian playwright was "so close to today's world, to my mind, and very close to the South" because he "had the sense of fate overtaking a way of life."[56]

We should look upon the evolution of southern literary alienation and inner heartbreak as something to acclaim rather than deplore. My purpose has not been to condemn these writers' dark preoccupations, but to marvel that by a creative probing of death, ruin, and inner turmoil they could disclose so much about the human condition. The emergence of a melancholy sensibility with each generation—from Poe to Glasgow and then to Faulkner,

55. O'Brien, *Willa Cather*, 135–6, 319; Cather quoted in Mildred R. Bennett, *The World of Willa Cather* (1951; reprint, Lincoln: University of Nebraska Press, 1961), 129.

56. Carson McCullers, "The Russian Realists and Southern Literature," in *The Mortgaged Heart,* ed. Margarita G. Smith (Boston: Houghton Mifflin, 1971), 252–3; Linda Kuehl, "The Art of Fiction LVII: Eudora Welty," in *Conversations with Eudora Welty,* ed. Peggy Whitman Prenshaw (Jackson: University Press of Mississippi, 1984), 74–5. See also Eudora Welty, "Reality in Chekhov's Stories," in *The Eye of the Story: Selected Essays and Reviews* (New York: Random House, 1977), 61–81. In her essay, Welty does not, however, identify Chekhov's Russian culture with that of the South, although in *Conversations* she does so.

McCullers, and O'Connor—furnished the American literary landscape with works of extraordinary and distinctive forcefulness. A throng of twentieth-century white and African American writers from the South—both male and female—would follow in the paths laid out by their predecessors, some of whom I have discussed in this study. Although never admitting any debt to the women writers of the Victorian era, Faulkner and company, knowingly or unknowingly, built upon the foundations of those who had long been groping toward a modern sensibility. Even the amateur but sadly driven southern poets of the sentimental period had helped to set the tone of a culture from which the most estranged and ingenious of the modern fiction writers freed themselves, though not always entirely. But all of the writers, mostly melancholiac, whether they were gifted or unskilled, voiced long-repressed emotions of anger and grief. Their work was to them a worthy compensation for the pain and mental affliction that most of them in their separate ways had experienced. Their efforts opened the way to the mid- and late-twentieth-century cluster of creative southern artists.

That outcome scarcely meant, however, mutual appreciation between the predecessors and their heirs. Faulkner and his male compatriots seldom acknowledged any of the women writers of the previous generation. On the other hand, Ellen Glasgow had no kind words for William Faulkner and his devotees either. After reading Faulkner's *Absalom, Absalom!* in 1936, she complained, "All I ask him to do is to deal as honestly with living tissues as he now does with decay, to remind himself that the colors of putrescence have no greater validity to our age, or to any age, than have—let us say to be very daring—the cardinal virtues."[57] Her revulsion with the new age reflects just how powerful among the aging was the hold of the old romantic ideals. No doubt, had she lived as long, Kate Chopin, by no means a radical feminist, might have heartily agreed with Glasgow's haughty dismissal.

The reactions of the early-twentieth-century southern artists to their literary forbears involved a degree of gendered irony. They owed much to their predecessors, no less anguished than they were themselves. Faulkner very explicitly acknowledged an indebtedness to the Russians, and so, too, did other southern writers. Yet they ignored such splendid artists as Glasgow and Chopin. These women's themes may have been tamer than Faulkner's as they had written largely about an impoverished gentility, the poor underclasses, the single woman, the aged. By and large Faulkner's characters were larger than life, and although ancients and women appear in his

57. Quoted in Goodman, *Ellen Glasgow,* 204.

work in vivid portraitures, the stories center around the travails of the young in dealing with their futures and their troubles with flawed and tragic progenitors. To be sure, failure to recognize old literary debts to women writers is scarcely peculiar to the Mississippian's generation. Nevertheless, the entrenched modes of honor, reticence, and stoic resolve that Simms, Timrod, and, in many ways, Cather and Glasgow represented, exercised more influence in the next century than the Faulknerians ever recognized.

The customs of a distant past offered the new breed of southern novelists a tense drama of conflict between the old that would not wholly die and the new that could not fully be born. Is that not a theme in much of William Faulkner's work? The achievements of the southern modernist literary group are prodigious: the works of male novelists Faulkner and Richard Wright; poets Robert Penn Warren and James Dickey; female fiction writers Evelyn Scott, Katherine Anne Porter, Gail Godwin—to name only a handful. These and other major artists, sorely tried in heart and soul, established the South as a cultural promontory in both prose and poetry. Their achievements have rivaled in height the pinnacle of Emerson, Hawthorne, and Henry James's literary New England in the earlier American Renaissance. In the course of mastering their creative impulses, like the Victorian thinkers before them, the modern southern men and women of mind wrestled desperately against moods of hopelessness and dread. Yet to paraphrase Melville's opening epigraph, truth, beauty, and self-understanding may only be realized when the "utter darkness" of the soul is transformed by the miracle of imagination into the light of art.

A veritable host of complications were to beset the resourceful Faulknerian successors to the romantic era. The consequences, both tragic and inspiring, are too tangled, however, to be explained here. That story should be a separate quest.

Index